CRIME, JUSTICE AND THE MEDIA

Crime, Justice and the Media examines and analyses the relationship between the media and crime, criminals and the criminal justice system. This expanded and fully updated second edition considers how crime and criminals have been portrayed by the media throughout history, applying different theoretical perspectives to the way crime, criminals and justice are reported.

The second edition of *Crime, Justice and the Media* focuses on the media representation of a range of different areas of crime and criminal justice, including:

- new media technology, e.g. social network sites;
- moral panics over specific crimes and criminals, e.g. youth crime, cybercrime, paedophilia;
- media portrayal of victims of crime and criminals;
- how the media represent criminal justice agencies, e.g. the police and prison service.

This book offers a clear, accessible and comprehensive analysis of theoretical thinking on the relationship between the media, crime and criminal justice and a detailed examination of how crime, criminals and others involved in the criminal justice process are portrayed by the media. With exercises, questions and further reading in every chapter, this book encourages students to engage with and respond to the material presented, thereby developing a deeper understanding of the links between the media and criminality.

Ian Marsh is Principal Lecturer in Criminology at Liverpool Hope University. His recent publications include *Crime and Criminal Justice* (with Gaynor Melville, Keith Morgan, Gareth Norris and John Cochrane – Routledge 2011) and *Sociology: Making Sense of Society* (fifth edition, Pearson 2013).

Gaynor Melville is Lecturer in Criminology at Liverpool Hope University. Her publications include *Crime and Criminal Justice* (with Ian Marsh, Keith Morgan, Gareth Norris and John Cochrane – Routledge 2011) and *Criminal Justice: An Introduction to Philosophies, Theories and Practice* (with Ian Marsh and John Cochrane – Routledge 2004).

CRIME, JUSTICE AND THE MEDIA

Second edition

Ian Marsh and
Gaynor Melville

Routledge
Taylor & Francis Group

LONDON AND NEW YORK

First published 2009
by Routledge

Second edition published 2014
by Routledge
2 Park Square, Milton Park, Abingdon, Oxon OX14 4RN

and by Routledge
711 Third Avenue, New York, NY 10017

Routledge is an imprint of the Taylor & Francis Group, an informa business

British Library Cataloguing in Publication Data
A catalogue record for this book is available from the British Library

Library of Congress Cataloging in Publication Data
Marsh, Ian
Crime, Justice and the Media / Ian Marsh and Gaynor Melville. — Second edition.
pages cm
Includes bibliographical references and index.
1. Crime in mass media.   2. Mass media and criminal justice.   I. Melville, Gaynor.
II. Title.
P96.C74M37 2014
364.2'54—dc23
2013037620

ISBN: 978-0-415-81389-1 (hbk)
ISBN: 978-0-415-81390-7 (pbk)
ISBN: 978-0-203-51911-0 (ebk)

Typeset in Garamond 3
by RefineCatch Limited, Bungay, Suffolk

Printed and bound by CPI Group (UK) Ltd, Croydon, CR0 4YY

CONTENTS

PREFACE

The intention of this book is to provide students (and tutors) with an analysis of the relationship between the media and crime, criminals and the criminal justice system. It considers how crime and criminals have been portrayed by the media over time, and examines a number of specific areas of crime and criminal justice in terms of media representation.

CONTENTS

Crime, Justice and the Media, second edition, starts with a consideration of the media portrayal of crime and criminals over time. Chapter 2 looks at the major theoretical perspectives on the media and their effects, from the early hypodermic syringe model to the postmodern influence and culture criminology, and applies these to the representation of crime. A separate chapter (Chapter 3) focuses on moral panics and the media's role in establishing and perpetuating such panics – it considers historic and recent examples, including the panics over hoodies and paedophiles. The next three chapters move the focus from media representations of crime to an examination of how the media portray criminals (Chapter 4), victims (Chapter 5), and criminal justice agencies (Chapter 6). In Chapter 4 we look at how the class background and environment, the age, the gender and the ethnicity of offenders influence the way they are shown and reported by the media, and how these categories can and do overlap. The ways in which the media socially construct images of victims, as deserving and undeserving for example, are discussed in Chapter 5. Chapter 6 turns to the media portrayal of the police, the courts and legal system and prisons – in both documentaries and 'real life' commentaries as well as in fictional contexts. Cybercrime has become one of the most prolific crimes in recent years, especially as the Internet has become an integral part of social activity and businesses. Chapter 7 explores the difficulty of locating, reporting on and policing such crime and the problems of finding laws and regulations that achieve a balance between freedom and control. The final chapter (Chapter 8) offers a brief discussion of how the media can play a major role in influencing public opinion toward crime and punishment, and can thereby exert a strong influence on the style and form of punishment that particular societies use.

FEATURES

Crime, Justice and the Media adopts an interactive approach which encourages students to respond to the text and think for themselves. The active engagement of students with the material is something that will distinguish this from other texts in the area and will enable it to be a real teaching resource for tutors. There are reflective question breaks throughout the book which encourage students to consider perhaps a particular case study or the previous discussion and respond to questions on it. And at the end of the chapter there are suggestions for further reading.

This book, along with the recently published texts *Criminal Justice* (2004), *Theories of Crime* (2006) and *Crime and Criminal Justice* (2011), has been a collaborative venture and the authors would like to thank Gerhard Boomgarden, Emily Briggs and the rest of the production team at Routledge for their help and support with the development of the text.

CHAPTER 1

Introduction – A Brief History of the Media Portrayal of Crime and Criminals

A glance at the television schedules for tonight, or the film listings for your local cinema, or the headlines in today's national or local newspapers, will quickly indicate both the vast and seemingly insatiable interest the general population has in crime and criminals, and the key role the media play in portraying and describing all aspects of criminal behaviour. Some of this crime will be fictional, others, 'real life', and our appetite for reading and watching about both appears to be enormous – popular television programmes such as soap operas invariably include criminality in their storylines; television documentaries, news programmes and our newspapers highlight and discuss crime and criminal justice issues on a daily basis. And the knowledge and understanding the public have about crime and criminals is largely based on what they have seen or heard through the various media forms. More generally, it is impossible for us to know through direct experience everything about our society. In a study looking at crime news in the USA, Dorfman (2001) found that over three-quarters (76%) of the public said they formed their opinions about crime from what they see or read in the news, more than three times the number of those who said they got their primary information on crime from personal experience (22%).

Given the popular media and general populist interest in this area, it is not surprising that the academic interest in crime and criminal justice is growing – and that there are more and more criminology courses available for students to study, with the consequent increase in the number and range of criminology textbooks such as this one.

QUESTION BREAK

Look at TV listings for tonight. How many programmes are clearly focused on crime and criminals? How many other programmes are likely to include criminal incidents in them (e.g. in plays, soap operas, etc.)?

Do a similar exercise with the films at a local cinema.

Look at a couple of newspapers on one particular day (ideally a 'quality' paper, such as *The Guardian*, *The Independent* or *The Times*, and a popular one). How many crime stories are there and roughly what proportion of the paper do they account for?

Consider how the different newspapers report those crime stories.

When we look back through history it is apparent that this massive interest in crime and criminals is not just a recent phenomenon; and although the forms of media have changed over time they have always reflected and reported on this interest. In the rest of this chapter we will provide an overview of the media reporting and depicting of crime over the last two hundred or so years, and in doing so, will look at how specific criminal cases have been presented by the different media of the day.

While the history of crime goes back way beyond two hundred years ago, this account will focus on the period from the late 1700s/early 1800s – the period of the industrial revolution in the Western world and the democratic revolutions in France and the USA. This was a period that led to the development of the social sciences (see Nisbet 1970) and the 'birth of the prison' (Foucault 1977) and, in general terms, the development of what was seen by social theorists of the nineteenth century as the emergence of 'modern society'. In terms of the media, it was a time when the press was expanding and becoming a major source of information – as Sharpe (1999) puts it,

By the 1760s, another literary form was making its contribution. By that decade it was possible, even in a provincial town, to witness that most modern of phenomena, the significance of a crime wave being amplified by newspaper reporting. In 1765, public fear, engendered by a series of robberies in Colchester, was considerably heightened by the hyperbolic reporting of these offences in *The Chelmsford Chronicle*.

So our focus in this introductory history of the media reporting of crime will be on the period from the late eighteenth century, through the Victorian period and then the twentieth century. In his writings on the history of the press, Curran (1977) examines how the emerging national and local press in Britain developed its independence in the nineteenth century. He quotes Chaney's (1972) view that 'the British press is generally agreed to have attained its freedom around the middle of the nineteenth century' and argues that this has been reiterated in other histories of the

British press. Curran suggests that this 'watershed in British history' came as a consequence of a struggle against state control of the press – while concessions in terms of press reporting were gained in the eighteenth century it was only in the Victorian era that 'the forces of progress finally triumphed' and an independent press emerged free from the legal and financial control which governments had previously exercised. It should be pointed out that Curran does question this view of a sort of triumphant rise of a free press in Britain – while the emerging press may have performed a 'democratizing function for society' it is important to bear in mind the arguments that the press also served the interest of the powerful groups or classes in society and could be seen as an instrument of social control. We will look at different theoretical perspectives on the media in Chapter 2, and here it is enough to highlight the point that there are different interpretations of the emergence of the media in Britain.

In contemporary society, the media come in a massive and ever growing range of forms and formats. However, in looking at the early part of our historical period our focus will be on the press, which was very much the key media form in the nineteenth and well into the twentieth century. Broadcasting, first radio and then television, developed its mass market in the mid-twentieth century. In his account of broadcasting history, Seaton (1981) points out that broadcasting is a social rather than technical invention and that the capacity for transmitting programmes for a mass audience existed long before it was utilized. Indeed, for some time after popular broadcasting started in the 1920s, the radio was seen as 'little more than an experimental toy'. However, once radio manufacturers became aware of the potentially huge market, applications for setting up broadcasting stations expanded. This new development needed to be controlled, and the BBC emerged. This is not the place to go into the academic debates concerning the development of mass broadcasting, but merely to note the emergence of the BBC as the starting point for this form of mass media in Britain and elsewhere.

We will start our review by looking at some examples of early press reporting of particular and well-known crimes. Probably the most (in)famous of all Victorian crimes were the murders attributed to the serial killer Jack the Ripper. These crimes excited a mass interest at the time and still continue to intrigue, even though there have been many more prolific and brutal serial killers since – indeed doing a Google search on 'Jack the Ripper' shows over two million online results. As Creaton (2003) puts it, 'why does one Victorian murderer still exert such world-wide fascination in an age hardly short of its own violent crime?' While a good deal of the interest in this case has been over the supposed identity of Jack the Ripper, we will refer briefly to how the crimes were reported. In 1888, five (or maybe six) prostitutes were killed and mutilated in the East End of London by an unknown murderer who was never caught. The public panic, fuelled by a 'media frenzy', according to Creaton, spread well beyond London. After four months the attacks ended. In his study *Jack the Ripper and the London Press*, Curtis (2001) examined the role of newspaper reporting during the police search for the Ripper, focusing on 15 London-based papers. They were seen as playing a key role in heightening the public's alarm by portraying the East End as inherently dangerous. The press coverage emphasized and exaggerated the stereotypical view of the East End of London as being a 'crime and disease ridden, uncivilized "jungle" full of semi-barbarians' – with the press adopting the name Jack the Ripper (taken from a letter sent to the Central News Agency, almost certainly by a hoaxer after the fourth murder). And they turned the murders into a media event, assuming all the murders in that area were committed by the Ripper – only five of the nine murders in the Whitechapel area between 1887 and 1888 were eventually attributed to the Ripper, the others being just part of the routine brutality of the area. A great deal of newspaper column space was devoted to these crimes, with the newspapers varying in the amount of graphic detail they printed, with the emphasis being on the violent nature of the murders rather than the sexual aspects. The papers varied in their style of coverage according to their political allegiances, the Liberal and more radical press focusing on the police's incompetence to protect working-class Londoners and the Tory leaning press seeing the crimes as evidence of a growing semi-criminal underclass. Curtis also highlights the speed with which the newspapers managed to get their stories to the public – for instance, the Sunday paper *Lloyds Weekly* gained information about the murder of Catherine Eddowes at 2.10 a.m. on 30 September, 20 minutes after her body was found; and by 4.00 a.m. was able to print a special edition so the news could reach people's homes by breakfast that morning (impressive even by today's high-tech standards).

As mentioned above, there was a good deal of media speculation as to the identity of Jack the Ripper – speculation which has never been resolved. Some of this speculation was evidenced in the publicity surrounding other murder trials of the time. The trial of Florence Maybrick in Liverpool in 1889 for the murder of her husband James, as well as exciting a massive media interest around the marriage and affairs of the Maybricks and James Maybrick's use of arsenic, also led to suggestions that James Maybrick himself was Jack the Ripper. Although there has never been conclusive evidence for this suggestion, Maybrick was a Liverpool businessman who made regular overnight trips to London at the time of the Ripper killings which stopped after 1889, when James Maybrick was killed. There was an enormous public outcry at the conviction of Florence Maybrick which led to her death penalty being commuted to life imprisonment (she was eventually released from prison in 1904).

The almost mythical status attributed to Jack the Ripper is evidenced in contemporary reporting of murders of prostitutes where the name Ripper is typically given to the murderer – especially when the killings are unfolding and the killer has not been found. So the series of murders in Yorkshire in the late 1970s led to the hunt for the 'Yorkshire Ripper' leading to the arrest and subsequent demonization of Peter Sutcliffe. Indeed the widespread fascination with these serial killings is evidenced in the massive media coverage that was given to the Yorkshire Ripper case and that is still generated by anything to do with Peter Sutcliffe over 30 years after his life sentence in May 1981. For instance, Sutcliffe's relationship with ex-TV personality and DJ Jimmy Savile was widely reported during the investigations into the alleged paedophilia of Savile, with headlines including, 'Jimmy Savile was suspected of being the Yorkshire Ripper' (*The Daily Telegraph*, 5 December 2012) and 'Ripper: Savile is Innocent. Yorkshire Ripper Peter Sutcliffe insists his old mate Jimmy Savile is innocent' (*The Sun*, 6 November 2012). More generally, as well as a Yorkshire Ripper website (www.yorkshireripper.co.uk) there have been numerous books and television programmes about Peter Sutcliffe (including *Wicked Beyond Belief* (Bilton 2003) and *Somebody's Husband, Somebody's Son* (Burn 1984)).

The more recent killings of five women in Suffolk within a short period of time in 2006 were accompanied by headlines displaying the same (lack of) originality, such as 'Suffolk Ripper's Rampage' and 'Suffolk Ripper Body Count' (*The Sun*, 13 December 2006). In similar manner the arrest of Stephen Griffiths in 2010 for the murder of three prostitutes in Bradford (and as part of an investigation into several other murders) led to further use of the 'ripper' tag – for example 'Stephen Griffiths: Loner with a Ripper Obsession' (*The Daily Telegraph*, 27 May 2010). The reporting of this Bradford case made great play of the fact that Griffiths was studying for a PhD in Criminology and of his obsession with the history of serial killers and his macabre collection of books and videos on killers such as Fred and Rose West and Ian Brady as well as the 'original' Jack the Ripper and the 'Yorkshire Ripper', Peter Sutcliffe.

QUESTION BREAK

Find two web sources of information on Jack the Ripper and his crimes. To what extent does their description focus on (a) the crime, (b) the criminal and (c) the victims?

Find two similar sources on the more recent cases of the 'Yorkshire Ripper' (1970s), the 'Suffolk Ripper' (2006) and the 'Bradford Ripper' (2010). Compare the coverage of these cases with the earlier one in terms of the crime, the offenders and the victims.

Of course, reporting of brutal and sensational crime was commonplace well before these late nineteenth-century murders; however, the development of a national daily press allowed for the unfolding of a crime story to be developed – and the activities of a serial killer certainly fitted into that category of crime reporting. Other crimes got massive press coverage, both in Britain and elsewhere. Cohen (1998) cites the brutal murder of New York prostitute Helen Jewett in 1836 as being the event that 'inaugurated a sex-and-death sensationalism in news reporting' – a style of reporting very typical of contemporary media accounts. Helen Jewett was an intriguing and mysterious figure who had a number of aliases that encouraged the press to try and outdo each other in trying to establish her identity. It turned out that Jewett was herself the source of the various different stories about her, fabricating versions of her life and circumstances to build up her clientele. Unlike many prostitutes of her time (and indeed of other times) Jewett had gained a good education and used this to establish working relationships with only selected, 'suitable' clients. However, this changed in April 1836 when one of her 'suitors' violently slashed her to death and set her brothel room on fire. The case became a classic who-done-it and encouraged the new style of reporting referred to above. As Cohen (1998) suggested:

Up until the 1830s, most standard newspapers were very low key about crime reporting, considering it to be beneath newsworthiness or else too local to put into print. But a new kind of newspaper had emerged by mid-decade, the penny press, a humorous, irreverent, and cheap daily paper that claimed crime as news. There were three or four such papers in competition with each other in New York City in 1836, and they latched onto the Jewett murder, taking different views of it as a way to pump up circulation figures.

Another popular form of nineteenth-century media reporting of crime was printed transcripts of court cases. Publishers of these transcripts chose trials that had particular appeal – those exposing the more bizarre, mysterious or humorous cases. Nowadays these trial pamphlets look rather quaint, but they certainly captured the public interest in their day. The one detailing the trial of Albert Tirrell in 1846 sold in large numbers. Tirrell was a young man from a respectable family who murdered a prostitute in Boston and set her brothel on fire; however, his ingenious lawyer convinced the jury that Tirrell had been sleepwalking. The Tirrell pamphlet went through a number of reprintings, selling over 80,000 copies in less than a month (Crain 2002).

Trial pamphlets included those dealing with divorce cases (divorce still being a relatively rare occurrence) as well as criminal trials. Trials that involved particularly gory murders and those involving celebrities were typically popular. Another example of a trial transcript cited by Crain was *The Trial of Hon. Daniel E. Sickles*. Sickles shot his wife's lover Philip Barton Key, who was the son of the author of 'The Star Spangled Banner', giving the case a 'celebrity angle' as well. In addition to their entertainment value, the trial pamphlets were also used as evidence in court and cited as precedent in some cases.

So the penny press and trial pamphlets provided popular coverage of crime and criminal justice in the nineteenth century. Reporters were sent to court every day to write daily instalments, which were collected and issued as pamphlets at the end of the trial.

The interest generated by real life crimes in these early days of newspaper reporting was reflected in the popularity of fictional crime representations. The most famous of these was the fictional detective Sherlock Holmes, created by Sir Arthur Conan Doyle. Holmes first appeared in popular magazines in the late 1800s, with the short stories of his crime detecting attracting a tremendous following. Between 1887 and 1927 Holmes featured in four novels and 56 short stories; and his popularity has continued unabated since then and since Conan Doyle's death in 1930. There have been 47 feature films (most recently *Sherlock Holmes: A Game of Shadows* in 2011) plus hundreds of television series and spin offs centred around this fictional crime fighter. The overlap between fact and fiction in the reporting of nineteenth-century crime is indicated by the linking of real-life detectives with the fictional character of Holmes and for the role Holmes (through Conan Doyle's writing) played in the early developments in the forensic investigation of crime. One example of this was in the famous murder trial in 1915 which became known as the 'brides in the bath case'. This involved the trial of George Joseph Smith who, under a variety of aliases, married and then murdered his three wives by drowning them in baths. The case was solved by a young forensic pathologist, Bernard Spilsbury (later Sir Bernard Spilsbury) who was likened to Holmes for his application of the scientific mind to solving crime. Conan Doyle based the character of Holmes on Dr Joseph Bell who worked at the Edinburgh Royal Infirmary and was acknowledged for his ability to draw correct conclusions from the smallest observations.

Another aspect of the general interest in crime and punishment evidenced in the media was the reporting of public executions (see the question break box below).

QUESTION BREAK

Read the extract below adapted from Walliss (2013) and consider the questions that follow it.

The press reporting of public executions

On the 26th of May 1867, Michael Barrett, a member of the Fenians, was executed outside Newgate Prison, for his part in the attempt to free fellow Fenians from the Middlesex House of Correction, Clerkenwell by planting a bomb against the walls of the prison in order to bring down its walls, thus releasing the prisoners. The bombing, however, failed; although it brought down an eighteen-metre section of the wall, no prisoners escaped and the blast destroyed several houses opposite to the prison, killing twelve persons and injuring many more.

Barrett's execution was the last to take place in public. Following decades of parliamentary and public debate about capital punishment, executions were removed from public view in 1868 to inside prison walls, where they would continue until the abolition of capital punishment in 1965.

Public executions were great affairs that were greatly attended and widely reported in both the national and provincial presses, with provincial newspapers syndicating reports from the capital and other counties. The authorities intended executions to be highly ritualised, hoping that those who witnessed the 'lesson on the scaffold' would then avoid a life of crime. Central to this was the penitent behaviour of the condemned on the scaffold, and any confession or last words they uttered – this being reported, as verbatim as possible in the press:

> Much of the night previous to their execution was passed in prayer and devotional reading . . . Fortis [a prisoner who was to be executed], with much natural and impassioned eloquence, addressed his fellow prisoners in a long and well-adapted exhortation, which he thus concluded: 'In a few minutes I shall be no more: remember my dear fellow prisoners the dying words of poor George Fortis; and may God bless you, and have mercy on you all!' They then took an affecting leave of their companions in confinement, and thanked the Governor for his kindness and humanity. Upon reaching the scaffold . . . Fortis, with a loud voice, repeated part of his exhortation at chapel.
>
> ('Execution', *Norfolk Chronicle*, 20 April 1822, p. 2)

The reality, however, was often different. Crowds were often raucous, their behaviour more akin to a fair or a modern music festival than the air of solemnity intended by authorities. Newspapers would regularly bemoan how crowds would sing, chant bawdy phrases, or throw someone's hat in the air and laugh as it was thrown around the crowd. In other cases, members of the crowd would be lifted onto the heads of the packed mass, and would then be passed forward like a modern 'crowd surfer'. Bored crowds would also amuse themselves by throwing clods of earth at each other, or start fights with each other, and there was always the constant danger of pickpockets. Indeed, even the call for 'hats off!' when the condemned came out on the scaffold was motivated more by the desire to not have one's view blocked, than any sense of solemnity.

In other cases, the condemned would reject the ritual of the execution, and attempt to die 'game', either by denying their guilt to the last or, through their behaviour, undermining the theatre of execution. A particular notable example of this phenomenon was James Taylor, executed in Salisbury in March 1841 for the execution of his wife. The Berkshire Chronicle reported how 'during the interim between the unhappy man's sentence and execution, he has conducted himself in a manner most extra ordinary':

> His conversation was blasphemous, lewd, and insulting to the authorities – justification of his own conduct, and determination not to repent. Even on his last day, his first words were imprecations, alleging that the workmen were lazy fellows for not coming and putting up his drop (the scaffold) at an earlier hour . . . Finding that it was his determination to display this conduct to the last, the under-sheriff and other officers were resolved to allow him no time to corrupt the public morals on the scaffold, and a few minutes before twelve o'clock the prison bell announced the approaching time of his dissolution . . . He arrived on the fatal spot without betraying any very evident symptoms of intimidation, and went readily and placed himself under the fearful beam, saying in a hurried manner – 'Ladies and gentleman, I am very glad to see so many of you present – such a grand assemblage of people to see me hanged! And mind, if you ever any of you go a robbing, be sure and take a double-barrelled gun with you to murder all you can! – and mind and do it as it should be . . . I am glad I killed my wife, and I don't mind being hanged' – (here the executioner drew the cap over his eyes, and the unhappy man resumed) – 'I don't care for that, I can keep on talking. Oh! What a pleasant view – what a grand sight. I likes this sort of fun!' At this moment the bolt was withdrawn, and he was launched into eternity.
>
> ('Public Execution of James Taylor, for the Murder of His Wife', *Berkshire Chronicle*, 20 March 1841, p. 4)

Newspapers, however, did not only report executions, but they debated them through editorials and by publishing letters from members of the public.

Perhaps the most famous such letter was that published by Charles Dickens in *The Times*, describing the execution of Frederick and Marie Manning in November 1849:

> Sir – I was a witness of the execution at Horsemonger-lane this morning. I went there with the intention of observing the crowd gathered to behold it, and I had excellent opportunities of doing so, at intervals all through the night, and continuously from daybreak until after the spectacle was over.
>
> I believe that a sight so inconceivably awful as the wickedness and levity of the immense crowd collected at that execution this morning could be imagined by no man, and could be presented in no heathen land under the sun. The horrors of the gibbet and of the crime which brought the wretched murderers to it, faded in my mind before the atrocious bearing, looks and language, of the assembled spectators . . . When the day dawned, thieves, low prostitutes, ruffians and vagabonds of every kind, flocked on to the ground, with every variety of offensive and foul behaviour . . . When the two miserable creatures who attracted all this ghastly sight about them were turned quivering into the air, there was no more emotion, no more pity, no more thought that two immortal souls had gone to judgment, no more restraint in any of the previous obscenities, than if the name of Christ had never been heard in this world, and there were no belief among men but that they perished like the beasts.
>
> I am solemnly convinced that nothing that ingenuity could devise to be done in this city, in the same compass of time, could work such ruin as one public execution, and I stand astounded and appalled by the wickedness it exhibits. I do not believe that any community can prosper where such a scene of horror and demoralization as was enacted this morning outside Horsemonger-lane Gaol is presented at the very doors of good citizens, and is passed by, unknown or forgotten.
>
> (Charles Dickens, 'To the Editor of *The Times*', *The Times*, 14 November 1849, p. 4.)

QUESTIONS

- Why do you think newspapers published reports of executions? Do you think that there are any parallels with our own contemporary media?
- Newspapers often related their life of the criminal and their last words in their execution reportage. Why do you think they did this?
- What do you think execution reports can tell us about attitudes to crime and the criminal justice process in the past?

Moving away from the specifics of the nineteenth-century reporting of crime, in a renowned and widely cited study of the history of street crime in Britain, Geoffrey

Pearson (1983) examined the way the popular media had described and reported crime and criminals over the last two hundred or so years. He argued that popular accounts of crime showed how important it was not to view criminality in modern society as a new or unique problem. In a journey back through the history of crime and delinquency and of the popular responses to it, Pearson shows that for generations, Britain has been plagued by the same problems and fears. As his historical account made extensive use of contemporary journalistic reporting of crime, it is worth considering Pearson's study in a little detail. His history of street crime starts by looking at current accounts of youth crime – and as the book was published in 1983, this period was the late 1970s and early 1980s. Pearson argues that as each generation tends to look back with nostalgia and fondness to the recent past, it is sensible to start with present day society and compare it with the situation a generation previously, and to compare that generation with its predecessor and so on. While there are bound to be methodological difficulties in comparing different periods of time – given the changing definitions of crime and the lack of adequate records of crime in previous times – an impression of the extent and form of street crime and, particularly, of the popular concerns about it, can be gained by looking at contemporary media accounts.

QUESTION BREAK

Before the summary of Pearson's study below, think about the images of youth at different periods of history.

How are youths typically portrayed in the media today? (Consider newspaper and television representations.)

Going back a generation, how would you describe the youth of the 1970s? What media images can you recall of 1970s youth?

Do the same for youth of the 1960s and 1950s.

As mentioned, Pearson starts his history by looking at the 'fears' of crime, and how they were reported, in the early 1980s – indeed the subtitle of his study is 'a history of respectable fears'. Here we will just provide a few newspaper headlines and comments from some of the periods Pearson considered. His study, then, commences with concerns over the inner-city riots or disorders of 1980 and 1981 and the popular media interpretation of these events as demonstrating a new and previously unknown violence in Britain. As the *Daily Express* put it in July 1981, 'there has been a revulsion of authority and discipline . . . there has been a permissive revolution . . . and now we all reap the whirlwind' and 'People are bound to ask what is happening to our country . . . having been one of the most law-abiding countries in the world – a byword for stability, order and decency – are we changing into somewhere else?' In similar vein, in March 1982, *The Daily Telegraph* was suggesting that 'we need to consider why the peaceful people of England are changing . . . over the 200 years up to 1945, Britain became so settled in internal peace'. Indeed, Pearson points to the consistently expressed view that Britain's history has been based on stability and decency and that the moderate 'British way of life' is being undermined by an upsurge in delinquency.

However, 20 years or so previously, we find remarkably similar comments and press accounts. Youth subcultures such as the Teddy Boys in the 1950s and Mods and Rockers in the early 1960s were arousing similarly apocalyptic warnings of the end of 'civilized' British society. The reaction to the Teddy Boys was one of outrage and panic, with the press printing sensational reports of violence at cinemas and concerts featuring rock and roll films and music. An article in the London *Evening News* of 1954 suggested that 'Teddy Boys . . . are all of unsound mind in the sense that they are all suffering from a form of psychosis. Apart from the birch or the rope, depending on the gravity of their crimes, what they need is rehabilitation in a psychopathic institution'. And this sort of reaction was widespread; Teddy Boys were viewed by the rest of society as 'folk devils', to use Stan Cohen's phrase (see p. 47), and off-duty soldiers were banned from wearing Teddy Boy suits. Nowadays, when we look back at old photographs and films of these youth subcultures, it is difficult to imagine what all the fuss was about and groups such as the Teddy Boys are remembered with a degree of nostalgia – however, the hostile reaction and panic at the time was real and is illustrated by the media of the day.

The Mods and Rockers of the early 1960s excited similar media reaction. In a now famous comment, made during a press conference scene shown in the Beatles' movie *A Hard Day's Night*, Ringo Starr responded that he was a 'Mocker' in response to being asked whether he was a Mod or a Rocker. This was at a time when those youth groups were beginning to be news and the media of the day played a big part in creating this (and other) divisions within British youth culture. At a time when the Hell's Angels were gaining publicity and notoriety in the USA, the British press were looking for an equivalent. The phenomenon of scooter gangs – the Mods – versus motorbike gangs – the Rockers – was developed (if not caused) by the press reports of two days of comparatively mild violence in Clacton, Essex, over the Easter Bank Holiday weekend of 1964. Headlines such as 'Wild Ones Invade Seaside' and 'Day of Terror by Scooter Groups' were followed up by TV and newspaper reporting of clashes between youth groups and the police at Margate over the May Bank Holiday – with the *Daily Mirror*, May 1964 front-page headline, 'Wild Ones "Beat Up" Margate', illustrating the tone of this reporting. The media response to and reporting of these post-war youth subcultures is discussed in more detail in relation to Stan Cohen's work on moral panics later (see pp. 48–52).

Returning to Pearson's historical overview, his study then looks back to the 1920s and 1930s to see if Britain before the Second World War was a more stable and law-abiding society, given that the War has sometimes been seen as a kind of watershed with the post-war period viewed as morally inferior to the 'life and culture of pre-war England'. However, when we look more closely at this period, familiar allegations and concerns appear, with the media homing in on similar targets of criticism such as football hooliganism and increasing crime and disorder. As *The Times* put it in

1937, 'There has been a tendency of late to paint a rather alarming picture of the depravity of the youth of the nation . . . Headlines scream the menace of "boy gangsters".' It is clear that crime was rife in the inter-war years and was characterized by razor gangs, feuds between armed gangsters, vice rackets and so on.

Moving back to the late 1800s and early 1900s there is little evidence of the traditional British way of life based on a 'healthy respect for law and order' and as ever the youth of the day were compared unfavourably with previous generations. Indeed, Pearson describes the founding of the Boy Scout movement by Baden-Powell as a response to the widely held feeling that British youth were a major problem. In 'Scouting for Boys', published in 1908, Baden-Powell comments that:

> We have at the present time in Great Britain 2 million boys of whom a quarter to a half a million are under good influence outside their school walls . . . The remainder are drifting towards 'hooliganism' or bad citizenship.

It was in the late 1890s that the words 'hooligan' and 'hooliganism' were first used to describe delinquent youth and there were regular newspaper reports of hooligan gangs smashing up coffee stalls and public houses, robbing and assaulting old ladies, foreigners and the police. As with many later youth subcultures and gangs, the hooligans had a distinct look and style of dress and were no doubt over-reacted to – although, again, at the time the media and public reaction was one of alarm and panic.

Earlier in the Victorian period, in the 1860s, a major panic swept through respectable London over a new type of crime called 'garotting', a type of violent robbery that involved choking the victim. The press of the time reacted in familiar style, with *The Times* observing that it was 'becoming unsafe for a man to traverse certain parts of London at night'.

Similarly, it does not seem to be the case that it was industrialization that destroyed a stable and peaceful pre-industrial Britain – from the late seventeenth century there were complaints of increasing crime and disorder, while the streets of London were extremely dangerous, with no effective system of street lighting nor a police force.

Time and again, then, a permissive present is contrasted with the not too distant past and if such accusations were accepted uncritically, we would be forced to conclude that with each generation crime and disorder have increased dramatically. Looking back over Pearson's historical review it is difficult to believe that Britain's cities are any more perilous nowadays than those of pre-industrial Britain or when they were frequented by garotters and hooligans. What Pearson shows is that a preoccupation with violence and lawlessness is part of a long tradition, rather than a uniquely modern phenomenon, and that media commentaries have taken a similarly outraged and moralistic stance over many years.

In a more recent analysis of press reporting of crime, Reiner *et al.* (2003) looked at the media reporting of crime from the end of the Second World War in 1945 to the 1990s. In particular, they analysed samples of stories from *The Times* and the *Daily Mirror*, in order to compare a 'quality/broadsheet' paper with a 'popular/tabloid' one. They considered a random 10 per cent of all home news stories between 1945 and 1991 as the basis for their analysis. Their study was set in the context of a review of previous work on media representations of crime, whereby they highlighted certain distinctive characteristics of the media reporting of crime stories. Reiner and colleagues aimed to consider whether their content analysis supported these general findings.

These key characteristics of the media reporting of crime stories are summarized below:

- Both news (factual) and entertainment (fictional) crime stories are prominent in all media.
- These stories overwhelmingly focus on serious violent crime, especially murder.
- Offenders and victims in these stories are of higher status and older than actual offenders and victims (as processed by the criminal justice system).
- The risks of crime are portrayed as more serious than the actual figures on victimization would indicate.
- The effectiveness of the police and the wider criminal justice system tends to be shown in a positive light.
- Stories focus on specific cases and events rather than on general trends or policy issues.

(adapted from Reiner *et al.* 2003, pp. 15–16)

Without going into great detail on their study, Reiner and colleagues found that the reporting of violent crime was as great in *The Times* as in the *Daily Mirror*, although the reporting of sex offences was slightly lower. Over the period of their study, they found that the reporting of property crime declined markedly and was only rarely reported at the end of the period unless such crime related to celebrities or had some particularly unusual features. This is in contrast to the fact that over 90 per cent of officially reported crime is property crime. Fraud stories were reported more frequently in *The Times* than the *Daily Mirror*, as were drug offences. In relation to the list of general characteristics highlighted above, the majority of offenders in the crime reports were older than the official figures would suggest and of a higher social status. Overall, they found that 'the pattern of crime news found in previous studies holds for most of the half-century we studied – but even more so . . . Crime in the news is overwhelmingly violent . . . Perpetrators and victims are typically older and higher in social status than their counterparts in the official statistics. The police are presented as honest and effective guardians of the public against crime' (Reiner *et al.* 2003, p. 24).

QUESTION BREAK

Look at two current newspapers from the same day (possibly use the ones suggested for the question break on page 2 – a 'popular' and a 'quality' newspaper).

Compare their reporting of crime stories to the findings of Reiner *et al.* (2003) and consider the extent to which they support the differences between quality and popular newspapers referred to above.

One aspect of this study, the reporting of victims of crime, did indicate a significant change in approach over the period of the study. They referred to a case of serious child abuse reported in the *Daily Mirror* in 1945 – after detailing the injuries to a two-year-old girl the majority of the story focused on the offender, who was sentenced to six months hard labour and whose behaviour was explained by the suffering he endured in the war. Reiner and colleagues point out the absence of any demonization of the offender and the concern with understanding his point of view. Recent cases of child abuse are reported in a very different manner, with much more emotional language to emphasize the offender's evilness (see Chapter 3, pp. 69–74).

Greer and Reiner (2012) refer to a study that analysed the reporting of homicides in three British newspapers (Peelo *et al.* 2004). It found that sexual homicides were most likely to be reported in all three newspapers with the least likely reported being the most common homicides, those arising from an argument or rage. The characteristics of the victims were also linked to the likelihood of reporting, with children, female or 'higher status' victims more likely to be reported.

Another aspect of the role of the media in relation to crime is the way in which the media can be used to appeal to the public for help in solving crimes. This aspect of the media's role is discussed later when we look at the relationship between the media and the police (see pp. 151–152). It can, however, lead to bizarre situations where those appealing for help with solving crime turn out to be the perpetrators of that crime. This was evidenced most recently in the tearful appeal of Mairead and Mick Philpott after a house fire killed six of their children in Derby in 2012; and which was followed shortly afterwards by their being arrested and subsequently charged with murder.

In the following chapters, we will be referring to the reporting of particular crimes to illustrate wider arguments and to comment on, for example, moral panics, media portrayal of criminals and victims and of criminal justice agencies. It is clear that certain crimes become massive media stories and capture the interest and mood of a particular time. Studying the manner of the reporting of these crimes is essential for an understanding of the relationship between the media and crime and here we will refer briefly to such 'signal crimes' (Innes 2003).

Recent such crimes in Britain include the killings of Rhys Jones (2007), Anthony Walker (2005), Holly Wells and Jessica Chapman in Soham (2002), Damilola Taylor (2000), Sarah Payne (2000), Stephen Lawrence (1993) and James Bulger (1993). In all these cases, the victims were children/youths and the detailed and extensive media reporting led to a social reaction that seemed to go well beyond the cases themselves. They lead to, as Innes puts it, 'widespread popular concern that it signals that something is wrong with British society and its criminal justice process, which requires some sort of corrective response' (2003, p. 51). Innes defines signal crimes as 'events that, in addition to affecting the immediate participants (i.e. victims, witnesses, offenders) and those known to them, impact in some way upon a wider audience'. Such crimes are responded to with decisions to do something about preventing such crimes in future through more policing, better risk-avoidance techniques, situational crime-prevention measures, and so on.

The response to such crimes overlaps with the notion of moral panics (Cohen 1972 and see Chapter 3) and the way in which the media present key factors as representing a symbolically loaded 'crime problem' which then leads to the wider population, egged on by the media, demanding that something be done, typically through widening the 'social control net' (Cohen 1985). In concluding his discussion, Innes argues that, in order to understand such signal crimes, it is necessary to examine the role of journalists and broadcasters in relation to the activities of the police and criminal justice system, with the police, for instance, often actively encouraging media publicity for a case so as to assist them in their detection work. Indeed, it is often in the interests of both detectives and journalists to work together to, on the one hand, get help in 'cracking' the case and, on the other hand, to get a 'newsworthy' story. However, such collaboration will, according to Innes, amplify the signal value of a crime and 'either intentionally or unintentionally transform it into a focal point for public concerns about crime and crime control'.

These signal crimes, though, do not just relate to child or youthful victims, who are perceived as innocent and/or defenceless, and we will finish by considering the coverage of the recent murders of prostitutes in and around Ipswich, Suffolk, in 2006 and in Bradford in 2010.

QUESTION BREAK

The Suffolk and Bradford Ripper murders – 2006 and 2010

As mentioned, it is conventional and sensible to compare the coverage of a particular event or crime provided in different media representations – in this case from the BBC and in quality newspapers and popular newspapers – in old terminology to compare a broadsheet with a tabloid (although the quality newspapers in Britain have now abandoned the broadsheet format).

Below, we include extracts from *The Sun*, the *Daily Mail*, the *BBC News* and *The Guardian*. Read them and consider the questions at the end.

Suffolk Ripper Body Count Rises
The bodies of two more victims of the Suffolk Ripper were found yesterday – taking the monster's grim tally to FIVE.

The dead girls are thought to be missing Ipswich hookers Annette Nicholls, 29, and Paula Clennell, 24.

Shaken cops described the shocking speed at which the fiend is claiming his victims as 'unprecedented'. He has murdered the five prostitutes – all were Heroin addicts and three were mothers – in less than six weeks.

By comparison, it took Yorkshire Ripper Peter Sutcliffe SIX YEARS to kill the first five of his 13 victims. And his reign of terror in the 1970s and 1980s spanned a total of 11 years . . .

The spree has already equalled the toll of the original Ripper – Jack, who strangled prostitutes in London in 1888 . . .

It is thought the Suffolk monster murders girls, then STORES their bodies before disposing of them at the dead of night from his car or van . . .

Experts offered a series of theories about the Ripper's motives and actions. Psychologist Dr Wilson, 63, said: 'The killer seems to have embarked on a rampage – a kind of pre-Christmas spree . . . He seems to be racing against time to kill as many times as possible before he is caught. And he is certainly not going to stop until he is caught. He is killing at a much faster rate than Peter Sutcliffe did, possibly because he fears he could get caught at any moment and wants to pack in as much excitement as possible'.

(Troop J. and Sullivan M., *The Sun*, 13 December 2006)

Snatched, Killed and Discarded

The man walking along Old Felixstowe Road, near the village of Levington, could not be sure at first. In the failing light he stepped off the road and approached the darkened form. Only then was he sure. She was naked, lying in the wet scrubland where she had been dumped. It was 3.05 pm. Forty minutes later a police helicopter hovered over the open ground south of Ipswich as detectives sealed off the area and covered the body with tarpaulin . . .

Within a few minutes the worst suspicions of police officers in Suffolk were confirmed. Any lingering hope that this was not a serial killer disappeared in the late afternoon with the discovery of the suspected fourth and fifth victims of a predator on an apparent mission to murder young women who work in the red light area of the East Anglian town.

What they were witnessing, Detective Chief Superintendent Stewart Gill said, was what he called a 'crime in action' . . .

'This is an unprecedented inquiry', said the chief constable of Suffolk police, Alistair McWhirter. 'When you look back to the Yorkshire Ripper, you are talking about murders carried out over months and years'.

Last night Suffolk police were faced with the task of investigating five murders. Already overstretched, the small force called in a senior Metropolitan police commander, Dave Johnston, an experienced homicide detective . . .

As detectives worked through the night, they could not disguise their shock at the sudden increase in the speed of the killings, fearing that as they spoke another woman could be attacked.

(Laville S., *The Guardian*, 13 December 2006)

Man Held Over Suffolk Murders

Police today arrested a man on suspicion of murdering five women working as prostitutes in the Ipswich area. The 37-year-old man, named in a series of reports as Tom Stephens, a supermarket worker, was arrested at his home near Felixstowe, Suffolk, early this morning. Detective Chief Superintendent Stewart Gull told a news conference. 'Detectives investigating the murder of five women in the Ipswich area have today, Monday 18 December 2006, arrested a man', he said in a brief statement read out to reporters . . .

Police sealed off Jubilee Close, a small street of semidetached suburban houses in Trimley, where Mr Stephens lives. Officers later erected a protective screen around the front of the building as forensic examinations began inside. Yesterday's Sunday Mirror *carried a lengthy interview with Mr Stephens in which he admitted having used the services of the murdered women and said he was a suspect, though he strongly maintained his innocence . . . 'I am a friend of all the girls', said Mr Stephens, who told the paper he had begun seeing prostitutes 18 months ago, after his eight-year marriage ended. He added: I don't have alibis for some of the times. 'From the police profiling it does look like me – white, male between 25 and 40, knows the area, works strange hours. The bodies have got close to my house', he told the paper, adding that police had already questioned him four times. The first interview had taken place days after Miss Nicol was reported missing on 30 October, he said . . .*

Asked in the interview why he thought he could be arrested, Stephens said: 'I would have complete opportunity, the girls would have trusted me so much . . . I know I am innocent and I am completely confident it won't go as far as me being charged', he added.

(*The Guardian*, 18 December 2006)

'Horrific' flat of Bradford killer Stephen Griffiths

Stephen Griffiths had been seeing Zeta Pinder for almost two years before he let her step inside his home for the first time. What she found there horrified her so much that she immediately wanted to end their relationship. Shelves carrying hundreds of horror films, books about serial killers and the sight of a crossbow and samurai swords in the living room made her feel 'really scared' and desperate to leave. She ended the relationship over the telephone as soon as she arrived home and did not see Griffiths again. Ten years on, Mrs Pinder was watching the news when she saw her ex-boyfriend had been arrested on suspicion of murdering three women in Bradford . . .

Mrs Pinder met Griffiths through a lonely hearts column in a newspaper and they had their first date in a local pub. She said: '{He was} very charming. He brought a photograph of himself which he gave me straight away, said he'd had them done professionally . . . I was laughing and called him a poser'. Mrs Pinder said the couple enjoyed a 'normal, typical relationship', but she did find some of Griffith's behaviour disturbing. She said: 'He had a thing about horror films. But he'd think they were really funny, the really horrible slasher horror films . . . and when somebody got murdered he'd just laugh his head off and go: "Great look at that"'.

(BBC News, 21 December 2010, www.bbc.co.uk/news/
uk-england-bradford-west-yorkshire-11985080)

Bizarre double life or murder suspect: Privately educated loner studying PhD is charged with murder of three prostitutes

The man charged with the Bradford prostitute murders attended one of the leading private schools, it has emerged. Stephen Griffiths . . . benefited from a high quality education at a £9,000-a-year day school and went on to a top university. Despite a fine start in life, the criminology student soon became obsessed with the history of serial killers and descended into a seedy, internet-addicted existence . . . In addition his parents split up when he was young . . . Griffiths was arrested on Monday after police were handed graphic CCTV footage showing a prostitute being killed. Body parts of missing prostitute Suzanne Blamires, 36, were later found dumped in bags in a river.

(*Daily Mail*, 29 May 2010)

QUESTIONS

- How would you describe the style of reporting of these murders by each newspaper?
- What similarities are there? What differences?

FURTHER READING

Pearson G. (1983) *Hooligan: A History of Respectable Fears*, London: MacMillan. This excellent history of crime and responses to it is based around contemporary media accounts of crime, and particularly newspaper reporting, at different periods of time.

Reiner R., Livingstone S. and Allen J. (2003) 'From Law and Order to Lynch Mobs: Crime News since the Second World War', in Mason P. (ed.), *Criminal Visions*, Cullompton, UK: Willan Publishing. This article provides a comprehensive analysis of crime news reporting since 1945 based on a sample of stories from *The Times* and the *Daily Mirror*.

Sharpe J. A. (1999) *Crime in Early Modern England 1550–1750*, 2nd edn, Harlow, UK: Longman. A detailed analysis of crime and punishment and how it was represented in the period specified.

CHAPTER 2

- Media effects – hypodermic syringe model and developments from that

- Sociological theorizing

- Postmodern/cultural criminology

Applying Theoretical Perspectives on the Media to Crime

Breaking the rules and laws of society has occurred throughout history, so much so that what we know as criminal behaviour can be seen as part and parcel of social life. And throughout history, behaviour that breaks the rules has been described and discussed – in contemporary historical records, including the media of the day, that describe 'actual' criminal and rule-breaking behaviour and in fictional writings of different historical periods. Given the everyday nature of crime and criminality, it is no surprise that the contemporary media, in all its forms, is saturated with crime news and stories. As we suggested in Chapter 1 (p. 1), a glance at the news headlines in today's press, on the television or on Internet news programmes, or a review of popular films or literature, will demonstrate the massive media coverage given to crime and criminals.

In general terms, it is clear that the media, and particularly the visual media, play an ever larger part in the lives of more and more people. Reiner (2007) starts his chapter on the representation of crime in the mass media in the *Oxford Handbook of Criminology* by quoting Lord Winston's comment that 'in contemporary Britain, the average three- or four-year-old now watches a screen for around five hours each day and more than 50 per cent of three-year-olds have a TV set in their bedrooms' (Reiner 2007, p. 302).

More generally, British TV viewers watched an average of 225 minutes of TV every day in 2010, although this was behind the US figure of 280 minutes a day. This includes the finding from Ofcom that just under a quarter of UK consumers also watch the TV over the Internet (www.digitalspy.co.uk). With the spread of new media, and particularly social media, it becomes even more difficult to track the extent of media usage. However, with around 2 billion people connected to the Internet worldwide, with YouTube generating 92 billion page views per month and with Wikipedia hosting 17 million articles, the influence and extent of the media is clearly enormous. Bearing these sorts of statistics in mind, and given the amount of crime and violence on the media, it is likely that more and more people see more and more criminal and violent behaviour on the screen than ever. Although fraught with difficulties of definition and measurement, it has been widely commented and accepted as a fact that by the time the average American child finishes elementary school he or she will have seen 8,000 murders and 100,000 acts of violence on television (this figure has been quoted in a number of sources, including the *New Scientist* 2007, cited on www.cybercollege.com).

This media coverage raises a number of issues for the study of crime and the media. Why is crime such a popular form of entertainment and news – after all, although most people might have broken laws or rules from time to time, few plan to become full-time criminals? Is the media coverage of crime helpful or harmful? Does it increase people's worries about crime? These questions highlight the importance of studying the relationship between the mass media and crime and in this chapter we will try to provide a general overview of the main research and theoretical positions that have focused on this relationship. In attempting such an overview in one chapter we can only provide a broad picture, and in following essentially a chronological review it is important to bear in mind that there were rarely obvious and specific times when each theoretical perspective started and finished – indeed, most of the differing theoretical approaches developed concurrently. Our review will look at this theorizing under three broad headings: media effects theory, based largely on psychological research; sociological theorizing from Marxist and pluralist perspectives; and more recent work from postmodern and cultural criminological perspectives.

MEDIA EFFECTS – HYPODERMIC SYRINGE MODEL AND DEVELOPMENTS FROM THAT

The early attempts to theorize about the impact and effect of the mass media were mainly developed from a psychological perspective. This psychologically based research, from the turn of the twentieth century up until the 1930s, argued that the mass media had a direct effect on behaviour – an immediate and often dramatic effect. The thrust of this line of argument is shown in the name given to this approach – the hypodermic syringe model. The effect of the mass media was seen as comparable to that of the injection of a drug into a vein. This underlying notion that the media had a direct effect on those who received it – the audience – encouraged the development of laboratory-based experiments to try and measure this effect. Such an approach assumed that the laboratory and 'real life' were interchangeable. The questioning of this assumption has been central to the wider criticism of the laboratory method as a means of studying people and their behaviour. And implicit in this type of approach is a belief that the mass of the population can be manipulated and controlled by the mass media they receive.

QUESTION BREAK

Before considering in more detail research into media effects, consider how your opinions and behaviour might have been influenced by the media.

How has the media influenced your views about different towns or cities and different areas of the world? What negative opinions have you received about different parts of Britain or different countries?

Relate these media portrayals of different areas to crime – which cities or countries are shown as particularly prone to crime? And what sorts of crime?

In terms of crime and criminal justice, what has influenced your views of the police? How has media portrayal of the police (in both fictional and factual accounts) affected or determined your views?

Can you think of any types of crime that tend to be glorified by the media?

There are some obvious weaknesses in the hypodermic syringe model – in particular the implication mentioned above that it ignores the fact that people are individuals who live in social networks of families, friends and colleagues and do have a degree of choice and free will. In response to this line of criticism, Katz and Lazarsfeld (1955) developed what became known as the 'two-step flow model' which highlighted the key role of social relationships in determining how people responded to the media. They stressed that opinions are formed in a social context and that within this context certain individuals are especially influential in shaping the views of others. These individuals, opinion leaders as Katz and Lazarsfeld called them, transmit and filter media messages to others who have a less active or powerful role. However, the notions of opinion leaders and active or passive members of society are not really developed and tend to present a rather simplistic approach to influence and power. Katz and Lazarsfeld's work is associated with the pluralist perspective on the media that we consider later (see pp. 39–42).

In spite of the criticisms of the hypodermic model, this approach has been very influential in the history of theorizing about the media. Indeed, it laid the groundwork for the development of a range of research and theorizing under the broad banner of 'media effects' – with the academic study in this area known as 'effects research'.

Early research into the direct effects of the media, in the first decades of the twentieth century and before the spread of television, focused on the impact and effects of the cinema. For instance, the studies financed by the Payne Fund, set up in New York in 1928, examined the effects of film-watching on the attitudes, emotions and behaviour of young people and, specifically, the relationship to juvenile crime. As with many later studies the findings were inconclusive with no consistent relationship found between cinema attendance and criminal behaviour. However, this early research illustrates perhaps the key debate in academic and lay circles concerning the media – the extent to which the media cause criminal or antisocial behaviour (Jewkes 2004). With the massive technological developments in the mass media in the first half of the twentieth century, there was a widely held belief that the media had a tremendous influence on people and that it could exert a powerful hold on society.

Perhaps the most famous example of the powerful effects of the media, and an example which seems to support the hypodermic syringe model, was the American radio broadcast of H. G. Wells' novel *The War of the Worlds* on 30 October 1938.

The radio programme was simply the weekly broadcast of Orson Welles and the Mercury Theatre, but on this particular night, because it was Halloween, they delivered a dramatized and updated version of H. G. Wells' classic story. Although the broadcast was fictitious, many listeners believed they were listening to a real invasion from Mars and while the programme was on air a panic broke out across the country. The question break below considers this widely reported and commented-on event in a little more detail.

QUESTION BREAK

Invasion from Mars

Below we will provide a bit more detail about the broadcast followed by an extract from the front page of *The New York Times* of 31 October 1938.

During a CBS radio broadcast of live music from the Park Plaza in New York, there was an interruption with an important announcement that astronomers had detected blue flames shooting up from the surface of Mars. The music was interrupted a bit later with more news about a meteor landing in New Jersey and the broadcast shifted to a continuous coverage of this landing. The audience was told that the meteor was not a meteor but a spaceship from which a creature (presumably a Martian) had emerged and blasted onlookers with a deadly heat-ray. This Martian started marching across the landscape joined by others who proceeded to blast people and communication lines at random. At this point listeners began to panic, some loading blankets into cars and preparing to flee the Martian invaders, others hiding in cellars hoping the poisonous gas being fired by the Martians would blow over them.

By the end of the night most people had learned the broadcast was fictitious. However, it had reached a huge audience of almost 6 million and it was estimated up to 1 million people were taken in enough to panic.

In considering why many people did panic (even if the figure of 1 million might have been exaggerated) there are a couple of points to note. Many people missed the very start of the broadcast when it was announced this was a dramatization. Furthermore, the late 1930s was a time of depression and a period when tensions in Europe were rising (leading eventually to the Second World War) and many believed an attack by a foreign power was possible; indeed, around this time it was relatively common for radio programmes to be interrupted with important news announcements.

Radio Listeners in Panic, Taking War Drama as Fact
Many Flee Homes to Escape 'Gas Raid from Mars' – Phone Calls Swamp Police at Broadcast of Wells Fantasy

A wave of mass hysteria seized thousands of radio listeners between 8:15 and 9:30 o'clock last night when a broadcast of a dramatization of H. G. Wells' fantasy, 'War of the Worlds', led thousands to believe that interplanetary conflict had started with invading Martians spreading wide death and destruction in New Jersey and New York.

The broadcast, which disrupted households, interrupted religious services, created traffic jams and clogged up communications systems, was made by Orson Welles, who as the radio character, 'The Shadow', used 'to give the creeps' to countless child listeners. This time at least a score of adults required medical treatment for shock and hysteria.

In Newark . . . more than twenty families rushed out of their houses with wet handkerchiefs and towels over their faces to flee from what they believed was to be a gas raid. Some began to move household furniture.

[. . .]

The radio play, as presented, was to simulate a regular radio program with a 'break in' for the material of the play. The radio listeners, apparently, missed or did not listen to the introduction, which was: 'The Columbian Broadcasting System and its affiliated stations present Orson Welles and the Mercury Theatre on the Air in "The War of the Worlds" by H. G. Wells'.

[. . .]

Despite the fantastic nature of the reported 'occurrences', the program, coming after the recent war scare in Europe and a period in which the radio frequently had interrupted regularly scheduled programs to report developments in the Czechoslovak situation, caused fright and panic throughout the area of the broadcast.

Telephone lines were tied up with calls from listeners or persons who had heard of the broadcasts. Many sought just to verify the reports. But large numbers, obviously in a state of terror, asked how they could follow the broadcast's advice and flee from the city, whether they would be safer in the 'gas raid' in the cellar or on the roof . . .

So many calls came to newspapers and so many newspapers found it advisable to check on the reports despite their fantastic content that The Associated Press agency sent out the following at 8:48 p.m.:

'Note to editors: Queries to newspapers from radio listeners throughout the United States tonight, regarding a reported meteor fall which killed a number of New Jerseyites, are the result of a studio dramatization'.

Similarly police teletype systems carried notices to all stationhouses, and police short-wave radio stations notified police radio cars that the event was imaginary.

(Adapted from *The New York Times*, 31 October 1938)

QUESTIONS

- List the reasons why this broadcast had such an impact on the American population.
- Suggest why the media was able to deceive the public.
- To what extent do you question the news coverage that you read about and see in the media?

With the continuing developments in media technology through the latter half of the twentieth century, psychologists, in particular, conducted research and experiments in attempting to find a direct link between exposure to the media and changes in behaviour and attitude. Many of these experiments considered the relationship between media exposure and violent, antisocial behaviour. One of the most famous and well documented of these experiments was Albert Bandura's 'bobo doll study' (1963) which set out to examine and measure the impact of watching aggressive film images on young children. This involved children being shown one out of three film sequences. Each sequence showed an inflatable doll being violently attacked – in one film, the person attacking the doll was rewarded, in another punished and in the third neither rewarded nor punished. After viewing one or other of the film clips, the children were allowed to play with the inflatable doll. Bandura found that those children who had seen the attacker punished were less likely to copy the film sequence whereas those who had seen one of the other two clips tended to imitate the violence they had seen. The aggressive behaviour of these two groups of children was taken as evidence that a direct relationship existed between violence on film and aggressive behaviour in juveniles. Bandura and his research team argued that this demonstrated the clear social learning impact of television in relation to violent and aggressive behaviour. Another experiment in similar vein was conducted by Liebert and Baron (1972). It involved 136 children aged from five to nine, half of whom watched a violent television clip and half an exciting sports sequence. The children were then taken to a room where they were given a box with buttons marked 'help' and 'hurt' on it. They were told that a child in another room was playing a game that involved turning a wheel and that they could either help that child by pressing the help button or hinder them by pressing the hurt button (which made the wheel hot). In fact, the button had no effect but the children pressing them did not know that. The experiment results showed that children who had watched the violent film clip were significantly more likely to hurt another child than were those who had watched the sports film. While other experiments have produced similar results, they have been criticized for being too artificial to generalize to real-life contexts.

There is no doubt that a considerable amount and range of violence is shown in the media – we will witness many thousands of murders in film and on television as well as reading about them on a regular basis. In a detailed review of the research evidence on the effects of violence in the media on individuals, Eysenck and Nias (1978) claim that television violence can directly cause violence amongst juveniles. However, while this argument has general popular support, there is no clear evidence for such a claim from academic research into the effect that viewing violence has on behaviour. The research evidence is far from conclusive: it does not show a direct link between violence in the media and violent behaviour. Indeed, one argument is that being exposed to so much violence will lead to a blasé attitude whereby little shocks us anymore. There are, of course, other possible arguments over the potential influence of the media in relation to violent and criminal behaviour – some of which will be explored later in this book. Questions such as:

- do media amplify crime?
- do they glamorize violent offending?
- can violent images increase sexual and violent arousal in some viewers?
- can media portrayal create 'moral panics'?

The media effects model explored: Mass society and social behaviourism

Nonetheless, these ideas about the powerful and often harmful effects of the mass media on the general population have gelled with the broad theoretical assumptions about the changing nature of society, away from rural-based, pre-industrial, personal social groupings, towards a modern, mass, urban industrial society. This analysis of social change as a consequence of the development of industrial, urbanized society is an argument found in the work of many of the early, classic social theorists, including Durkheim, with his notion of 'anomie' characteristic of modern industrial society and Tönnies' depiction of a change from intimate, communal social relationships to the impersonal and anonymous nature of modern society. Although there is a lack of evidence that criminal and violent behaviour is more serious and widespread in contemporary societies compared to pre-industrial ones, the disruption of previously stable, small-scale societies, where people were socialized in tight-knit community groups, and their replacement by the anonymous, impersonal, industrialized and urban societies, is assumed by many commentators to have inevitably led to a breakdown of respect for law and order.

In terms of looking into the whole idea of media effects in relation to criminal and antisocial behaviour, Jewkes (2004) points to the two main sources of academic study in the area as mass society theory and behaviourism. Although the former is essentially sociologically based, and the latter derives from psychology, they both support the generally pessimistic view of modern society that underlies the work of earlier social theorists, such as Durkheim and Tönnies, referred to above. Before considering these two approaches, it is useful to remind ourselves that although it is a widely held view, and one that has become seen as 'common sense', that society has become more violent as the mass media has expanded, historical study of crime and violence exposes such notions as myths. For example, Pearson's (1983) study, looked at in Chapter 1 (pp. 9–12), described crime waves and public outrage at crime going back throughout history and well before the almost universal ownership of and access to television and the Internet. Indeed, each major development and advance in media technology has been accompanied by particular concerns and led to varying degrees of moral panic (see Chapter 3) – from the early comics and 'penny dreadfuls', through the expansion of film and cinema attendance in the early to mid-nineteenth century, to television, videos and the Internet. This point was made by Tim Newburn at the time of the trial of the child-killers of Jamie Bulger on Merseyside in 1993 (which is also looked at later in this chapter, p. 28):

> At the turn of the [twentieth] century, there was great concern about violent images in Penny Dreadful comics. In the 1950s, panic that horror comics would lead to children copying the things they saw, led to the Children and Young Persons (Harmful Publications) Act 1959. Ten years ago, there was the huge panic about films such as *Drillerkiller*, which also led to a new law. There's been a recurrent moral panic about violent images which looks back to a mythical golden age of tranquil behaviour.
>
> (Newburn, quoted in *The Guardian*, 26 November 1993)

The concerns about the impact of mass society as a result of industrialization and urbanization were reflected in the negative view of the 'mass' or 'crowd' that characterized social theory in the middle half of the twentieth century. The mass were seen as lacking individuality, being easily influenced and essentially apathetic, with a taste for 'low' culture. In such a context, where society was viewed as essentially a mass of individuals cut off from previous close knit community life, crime and anti-social behaviour were seen as bound to increase. And in relation to the media, mass society theory suggested that the media could be used as a powerful way of controlling people's behaviour and manipulating their thoughts.

In a modern mass society, where traditional forms of social control appeared to be losing their influence, the mass media were felt to be a potentially powerful force for controlling behaviour. These sorts of views were particularly prevalent in the period around the First and Second World Wars – propaganda from both the British government and the German government nurtured the idea that political elites could manipulate the mass of the population through the media. This sort of elitist view of the mass of the population as being easy to influence through the media still persists of course – witnessed in the concerns over the influence of film, TV, magazines, video games or whatever media genre is in vogue at the time.

The hypodermic model or theory is also linked with the behaviourist approach in psychology. This approach, developed and popularized in the 1920s by the work of John B. Watson, focused on the relationship between people's behaviour and their environment. Rather than focus on the mind and how it determined an individual's behaviour, behavioural psychologists viewed behaviour, and how people learned, in terms of stimulus and response and so seemed to suggest that social action was strongly influenced by outside factors and forces – and that the mass media would be likely to be one of the most powerful of these stimuli in modern society. The messages put over via the media would have a strong effect on individuals' emotions and feelings and cause them to respond in a determined way, even to the extent of changing their beliefs and actions.

Alongside the development of a behaviourist approach in psychology, the scientific study of crime was becoming a field in its own right – early 'positivist' approaches argued that a cause for criminal behaviour could be found through biological, psychological or social influences over which the individual would have little control. The most famous of the early criminologists was Cesara Lombroso, who argued that criminals were 'born so' and claimed his research proved that the criminal could be recognized by their biological make-up and physical characteristics. And while criminology was looking for scientific explanations for crime, media theorists were also developing scientific methods and approaches. These methods were exemplified in the experiments mentioned above into the relationship between media images of violence and violent behaviour (pp. 24–25) – trying to measure the extent to which an individual's actions were determined by responses to stimuli in the social environment (including the media).

The copycat syndrome

One of the key issues that the early research into media effects focused on was the extent to which the media directly impacts on the population who receive it – people who are, essentially, passive recipients. In terms of the media and crime, the focus of this interest and research has been on whether and to what degree there is a direct causal link, which demonstrates that the media portrayal of violence does influence people to behave in a violent manner. There are great difficulties with proving the media acts as a causal factor – for instance, with regard to 'copycat' crimes and the problems in proving or not (in a legal context, for example) that a particular media portrayal (in a film, game, website, etc.) caused a particular criminal act.

QUESTION BREAK

Copycat crime

The following extract is adapted from the study by Eysenck and Nias, *Sex, Violence and the Media*. Read it and consider the questions below.

There are difficulties in dealing judicially with the 'copycat' syndrome, i.e. the acting out in real life of a crime seen on stage or screen. An example is Ronnie Zamorra, a 15-year-old TV addict whose parents are suing all three major US networks for $12,500,000. Ronnie, who is serving a life sentence for shooting and killing a neighbour, is claimed by his lawyer to be unable to tell real life from the TV programmes to which he is devoted . . . The difficulty is, of course, in proving that a particular film or TV show produced a particular effect in a particular person. It is not enough to show that there is general evidence for a causal connection between TV violence and acting-out of violence in viewers.

(Eysenck and Nias 1978, p. 36)

QUESTIONS

- To what extent do you think the boy's parents were justified in suing the TV companies?
- What arguments might TV companies use in their defence?
- What other examples of copycat crimes can you find?

Although this brief introduction has highlighted a number of problems with and criticisms of the early work on media effects, the assumptions about the media's power to influence criminal behaviour are still prevalent. Indeed, it is often the media themselves who are aware of their power to influence people and to bring pressure on governments and other forms of authority. It is hardly likely that so many media sources would be able to finance themselves from advertising revenue if those paying to advertise did not believe in the power of the media. The case is made by Jewkes (2004) when she points out that the classifying of videos and films in terms of their suitability for viewing and the introduction of software to help parents monitor their children's use of the Internet are further illustrations of the assumption that the media are a major influence on human behaviour.

Concern about the relationship between media violence and criminal behaviour hits the headlines when serious and high-profile crimes suggest such a link. This was most graphically illustrated by the horrific murder of two-year-old James Bulger in 1993. In November of that year, two 11-year-old boys from Merseyside, who had been captured on CCTV walking away from a shopping centre with James, were found guilty of murder. The 'horror' video *Child's Play 3* had been rented by the father of one of the boys shortly before the murder and there were similarities between scenes in the video and the killing of James. There was no evidence that the two killers ever saw the video; however, the judge still stated at the trial that, 'I suspect that exposure to violent video film may in part be an explanation'. This view was echoed in newspaper editorials at the time:

The uncanny resemblance between the film *Child's Play 3* and the murder must be of concern. A link between the film and the crime would not prove that the former caused the latter. Yet it seems quite possible that exposure to images of brutality could turn an already disturbed child towards violence.

(*The Independent*, 26 November 1993)

Before moving away from media effects and psychologically based theorizing, a brief comment on some other examples of the copycat crime phenomenon would be worth considering. In 2004, a BBC documentary reconstructed a crime which they argued left an indelible mark on the nation – the Hungerford massacre of 1987 – and which raised the issue of copycat killings.

On 19 August 1987, in Hungerford, Berkshire a 27-year-old unemployed labourer, Michael Ryan, armed with a Kalashnikov, an automatic rifle and a Beretta pistol, took to the streets, firing at anyone in his path. He shot and killed 16 people, including his mother, and wounded 15 others before fatally shooting himself. In the days after the massacre, the British media was full of stories about Michael Ryan's life – and about the elaborately constructed fantasy world he lived in. He was obsessed with firearms and owned magazines about survival kills and firearms, such as *Soldier of Fortune*. He was also said to be a fan of the film *First Blood*, which some of the press claimed had sequences similar to the events that occurred in Hungerford. Indeed, there was a claim that these killings were an example of the hypodermic syringe model of media effects. However, it is doubtful Ryan had ever seen the film *First Blood*, even though he did own a number of violent films (Webster 1989).

Another example relates to the accusations of copycat crimes and other violent acts following the release of the horror film *Scream* in 1996. CBS News in the USA reported on the killing in January 1998 of Gino Castillo by her 16-year-old son Mario and his cousin Samuel Ramirez (aged 14). This murder became known as the 'Scream murder' after the two killers claimed they were inspired by *Scream* and *Scream 2*. However, the trial judge ordered that no evidence pertaining to *Scream* be allowed and that the case should not be referred to as the 'Scream murder'. Another '*Scream*-related' case is mentioned in the question break below.

More recently, in reporting on the mass shooting at the screening of the new Batman film, *The Dark Knight Rises*, in a cinema in Colorado in July 2012, *The Guardian* headlined an article, 'Will The Dark Knight Rises shootings revive the debate on "copycat" crimes?' (*The Guardian*, 21 July 2012). In that case 24-year-old James Holmes walked into a showing of the Batman film and opened fire with a selection of weapons, killing 12 people and wounding many others.

QUESTION BREAK

Many violent films and television programmes have grabbed the headlines and been 'blamed' for violent and criminal behaviour. *The Matrix* has been related to several 'copycat killings', including the massacre of children at

Columbine High School in 1999. *Scream* has been associated with violent murders in Europe and America, including a case in Belgium where the killer, a lorry driver, put on a *Scream* costume before killing a 15-year-old girl with two kitchen knives.

(Adapted from *The Observer*, 9 July 2002)

What other films or programmes have been linked with 'copycat' violence?

Suggest the arguments for and against there being a causal link between film violence and real-life violence.

Further examples of the copycat effect are cited in Coleman's study (2004) which details a number of mass killings, including a series of school shootings in the United States, that are related to this. While providing a catalogue of patterns and connections between different events, as with the examples of Hungerford and the Bulger murder given above, the evidence generally seems to be circumstantial at best. Certainly, some studies conducted under experimental conditions (such as Bandura 1963; see p. 24) suggest that violence on the screen leads to aggressive attitudes and violent behaviour, but whether this is the trigger or cause of that behaviour is another matter. It is hardly surprising that young offenders are interested in films that sensationalize crime and violence, or that sex offenders show an interest in pornography. However, this does not prove an original cause; rather it suggests an attraction to the behaviour that has got them into trouble in the first place and that this attraction is fuelled by the media.

In a study that examined the extent of self-reported copycat crime amongst a sample of serious and violent juvenile offenders, Surette (2002) summarized the somewhat limited previous research in the area and suggested that there was a growing amount of anecdotal evidence which indicated that criminal events that are quite rare in real life are sometimes committed soon after similar events are shown in either the news or entertainment media. However, he found most of those individuals who did copy media crimes already had criminal records or histories and that it was more likely that the media influence how people commit crimes rather than why they commit them in the first place. In his own study of 81 youths he found that about one in three reported having considered a copycat crime with one in four having attempted one. Bearing in mind the limitations of quite a small-scale survey, Surette suggests that a significant number of juvenile offenders who identified themselves as engaging in copycat behaviour do seem to see the media as a significant influence.

This discussion of the copycat syndrome highlights the more general debate about the effects of violence in films and the media more generally. Indeed the various mass killings referred to above, plus the recent (December 2012) school killings in Colorado, inevitably lead to discussion about the role of the media and, in the US particularly, about gun control. However, violence is part of life and so it is not surprising that films and the media more generally reflect this (nor is it unreasonable for society to regulate such media).

Cultural effects theory

The early examples of research and theorizing into the effects of the media has been developed in a number of different directions; and, while there might have been flaws in the research undertaken in earlier studies, the basic notions behind effects theorizing are still widely held. Comments on the power of the media to influence the young, for instance, indicate a popular belief (that is reflected in the media) in the direct effects of the media that are similar to the ideas behind the hypodermic syringe model. Cultural effects theory assumes the media does have important effects on its audience. However, while insignificant, these effects are not as immediate or dramatic as those suggested by earlier research. Rather, it is argued that the regular broadcast of images and ideas over a period of time will affect how the audience see and understand the world. So, if the various forms of the media present particular groups of people, for instance, women or ethnic minority groups, in a certain way on a regular basis, then this image will gradually filter into the public consciousness. The influence of the media is also seen as depending on the social situation of the audience and it is assumed that different groups or categories of people (old, young, ethnic minority and so on) will interpret the content of the broadcast in terms of their social situations and experiences. Of course, taking this more contextualized view does not make it easier to actually measure the effects of the media on attitudes or behaviour – and raises the problem of how media effects can be separated from the range of other factors influencing people's attitudes and behaviour.

Jewkes (2004) highlights another version of this approach based on the mass society theory, which emphasizes the globalization of culture and in particular the 'Americanization' of popular culture, with the implication that there has been a 'dumbing down' of 'high' culture by 'low' popular cultural forms (this issue of the globalization of culture will be returned to when we look at postmodernism and the media, see p. 42).

A critique of the media effects model(s)

In the reviewing and discussing research into the effects of the mass media, it is clear that, in spite of many years of work, the attempts to find a direct, measurable connection between people's behaviour and their use and consumption of the media have not yielded any firm or conclusive evidence. In a critique of the media effects theorizing, Gauntlett (2007) highlights a number of major flaws with this body of work and the section below is based on this critique. He starts by suggesting that two basic conclusions can be drawn from a review of effects research. First, no direct effects of the media on behaviour have been found because there are simply none to be found. Second, media effects research has adopted the wrong approach to studying the mass media. He then raises and discusses some major problems with the media effects approach.

Gauntlett begins by arguing that, rather than start examining a social problem, such as violent and criminal behaviour, by focusing on those who engage in it, the media effects approach starts by looking at the media and then trying to connect the media with other social factors, like the background and lifestyle of criminals. As he puts it, 'it comes at the problem backwards' by focusing initially on individuals, rather than society, in relation to the mass media. In contrast, criminologists will try and explain crime through social factors such as poverty, pressure and so on, rather than start by turning to the role of the media. Gauntlett refers to a study of young offenders by Hagell and Newburn (1994), which found that young offenders watched less television than their non-offending peers and they showed no particular interest in specifically violent programmes.

The effects model has been dominated by psychologically based research, which has tended to take an individualistic approach. This can be seen in the studies into the impact of the media on children, with young users of the media viewed as inept victims of the media; the media has managed to trick them (but has not had the same influence on adults) into behaving in particular, often antisocial, ways.

As regards violence and the media, the focus of research tends to be on the amount of violence available in the media rather than the context and meaning of the violence; and it cannot be assumed that violence is shown for 'bad' reasons. Linked with this point, media effects studies seem to take for granted that some media material is 'antisocial', while other material may be 'prosocial', and do not properly consider that such definitions involve ideological value judgements.

As well as these definitional and contextual criticisms, Gauntlett also raises some important methodological issues to consider when reviewing effects research. The research that has been done in this area is characterized by artificiality, in that much of the psychologically based work has taken place in laboratories or in a context where the researcher is very conspicuous, rather than in a typical environment where people, especially children, would use the media. For instance, the subjects of a particular research study may be shown specially selected clips of television or film, which lack the meaning and context inherent in the usual way people watch television. Or, more obviously, they may be observed simulating real-life situations (as in Bandura's 'bobo doll' research referred to earlier, see p. 24).

Gauntlett makes the point that the conclusions of some 'correlation' studies (between the consumption of violence on media and violent behaviour) are blatantly self-evident. Studies that show violent people like to watch violent films, for example, cannot clearly demonstrate that media-viewing has actually produced that behaviour. It is to be expected that children whose behaviour is antisocial and disruptive will show greater interest in noisy, more violent television programmes.

We have mentioned the point that effects research often assumes that some people, especially children, are more prone to being influenced than other people, such as 'sensible' adults like ourselves. And this view can be seen by the fact that researchers, who presumably spend many hours in regular contact with corrupting and violent media material, seem unconcerned that they may be affected and would seem to implicitly assume that any media effects will only be on others rather than themselves. This seems to assume that those who are subject to media effects are somehow inferior to the rest of society!

In summarizing, Gauntlett suggests that the media effects model is based on a set of questionable assumptions, including that the media, rather than individual people, are the starting point for research; that categories such as 'violence' and 'antisocial behaviour' are unequivocal and self-evident; that the connections looked at by the effects model can be proved by scientific research; and that researchers have a special ability to observe and classify social behaviour and its meanings. However, the 'failure' of this model does not mean that the impact of the media should be ignored; indeed, the influence of the media on our perceptions of and behaviour in the world can and should be explored through asking and considering other questions. The media effects model chimes with common-sense views and is often given credence in the popular press and from politicians; this does not mean academic study and research has to encourage and support these views.

SOCIOLOGICAL THEORIZING

Critical/Marxist perspectives

From the mid-twentieth century, and particularly the 1960s, a more critical atmosphere was apparent in the Western world, with political and social protests disrupting the stability of post-war society. This was reflected in and maybe fuelled by a growing radicalism in the academic world with growing interest in and support for Marxist-based interpretations of society. And the media was one area which was subject to a more critical scrutiny.

In the previous sections, we have referred to the influence of the media; Marxist approaches emphasize a difference between influence and control and highlight the way the media can and do exert control. While other perspectives or models (such as pluralist approaches, see pp. 39–42) acknowledge that the media has influence, the Marxist approach stresses the power of the media to control people in society. This approach is based on the classic 'base-superstructure' model in Marxist thought. For Marx, there were two essential components of a society; first, the economic base or infrastructure that provides the material needs of life; and, second, the superstructure, basically the rest of society, including the family and education system and also the mass media. The base, or material world, comes first and determines the non-material world, the superstructure – indeed all aspects of the superstructure depend on the economic base. So, in terms of the media, the Marxist argument would emphasize the power of the economy (through, for instance, owners and advertisers) to determine the content of the media and, thereby, to influence public agendas. This power has been enhanced by the increasing concentration of ownership of different forms of media and the deregulation of the media and, as part of these developments, the increasing globalization of the media. Marxists argue that most of the media is privately owned and that it is big business and that, naturally, those who own and control it are people who are going to be supportive of the social system as it is – and in particular the capitalist system.

QUESTION BREAK

Concentration of media ownership

Consider the items in the table below on media ownership and Rupert Murdoch's media empire and then answer the questions at the end.

National newspaper ownership

Table 2.1 National newspaper ownership

Group name and executive control	Titles	Market share (%)
News International/ Rupert Murdoch	The Sun, The Times, The Sunday Times, News of the World	34.5
Trinity Mirror/ Victor Blank Daily	Mirror, Sunday Mirror, The Sunday People	19
Daily Mail and General Trust/ Lord Rothermere	Daily Mail, The Mail on Sunday	19
Northern and Shell/ Richard Desmond	Daily Express, The Daily Star, Sunday Express	12
Hollinger/Conrad Black	The Daily Telegraph, The Sunday Telegraph	7.5
Guardian Media Group/ The Scott Trust	The Guardian, The Observer	3.5
Pearson/The Pearson Board	Financial Times	3
Independent Newspapers/ Tony O'Reilly	The Independent, The Independent on Sunday	1.5

Source: Adapted from Peak (2003) (Figures are from May 2001).

It has been the tradition in Britain for newspapers to be privately owned. In the last fifty or so years, the number of private owners has diminished and newspaper ownership has been concentrated into large, multinational conglomerates, with extensive holdings, across the whole media and beyond.

For instance, Rupert Murdoch has built up a massive media empire under his corporation, News International. This empire included, in Britain, the *News of the World, The Sun, The Times* and *The Sunday Times,* as well as the Sky Television network that merged with British Satellite Broadcasting to form BSkyB. In the US, he owns Fox Networks and the *New York Post* as well as a large share (34%) of the operator of the largest American satellite TV system, DirecTV.

To elaborate on the situation in Britain and Ireland, Rupert Murdoch owns the best-selling tabloids *The Sun* and *The Sun on Sunday* as well as the broadsheets *The Times* and *The Sunday Times* and 39 per cent of the satellite broadcasting network BSkyB. BskyB, in turn, owns a significant part of ITV plc and 5 per cent of Shine Limited. In March 2011, the United Kingdom provisionally approved Murdoch to buy the remaining 61 per cent of BSkyB; however, subsequent events (the *News of the World* hacking scandal and that paper's closure in July 2011) leading to the Leveson Inquiry have halted this takeover.

Daily Mail and General Trust (DMGT) owns the *Daily Mail* and *The Mail on Sunday*, *Ireland on Sunday* and the free London daily, the *Metro*, and controls a large proportion of regional media, through the subsidiary Northcliffe Media, in addition to large shares in ITN and GCap Media. Richard Desmond owns *OK!* magazine, Channel 5, the *Daily Express* and *The Daily Star*.

Hacking: Miliband and Clegg seek media ownership limits

Labour leader Ed Miliband has called for new media ownership rules to limit Rupert Murdoch's 'dangerous' and 'unhealthy' concentration of power. He told the Observer Mr Murdoch's large market share led to 'abuses of power'.

Deputy Prime Minister Nick Clegg backed new ownership rules to foster more press diversity but said an independent inquiry should be completed first. The call follows last week's closure of the News of the World, which Mr Murdoch owned, amid claims of phone hacking.

With that closure, the Sun, the Times, the Sunday Times and 39 per cent of digital broadcaster BSkyB remain in the News Corporation stable. Under pressure from the entire British political establishment, Mr Murdoch dropped plans to buy out the rest of British Sky Broadcasting.

Calling for new ownership rules, Mr Miliband said: 'I think that we've got to look at the situation whereby one person can own more than 20 per cent of the newspaper market, the Sky platform and Sky News . . . If you want to minimize the abuses of power then that kind of concentration of power is frankly quite dangerous.'

(BBC News Online, 17 July 2011,
www.bbc.co.uk/news/uk-14175552)

All Eyes on Murdoch Empire

The scale and reach of Rupert Murdoch's UK media empire will come under unprecedented scrutiny following the government's decision to refer BSkyB's acquisition of a 17.9 per cent stake in ITV to the Competition Commission. Mr Murdoch's newspaper assets – the Sun, the News of the World, the Times and the Sunday Times – were central to trade secretary Alistair Darling's concerns about Sky's £940m swoop last November.

'The Secretary of State has decided that, as a result of the merger situation, there may not be a sufficient plurality of persons with control of the media enterprises serving the UK cross-media audience for national news and the UK TV audience for national news', the DTI (Department of Trade and Industry) said in its decision published today.

Mr Murdoch's titles have a 36 per cent share of the national newspaper market, while between them ITV and Sky – in which Mr Murdoch's News Corporation is the largest shareholder, with a 39 per cent stake – have more than 30 per cent of the audiences for national TV news, according to the DTI.

(*The Guardian,* 24 May 2007)

QUESTIONS

- What effects might the sort of concentration of ownership illustrated above have on the content of newspaper and news broadcasts on TV?
- What factors will limit the influence that owners such as Rupert Murdoch can have on the content of newspaper and programmes?

Of course, power and control go beyond physical coercion and Marxists regard the media – along with other capitalist institutions – as having a key role in establishing ideological domination. Here, the focus is on the way in which the media transmit a conservative, conformist view and promote established attitudes and values – the media are seen as working against change and, in doing so, working against the interests of the majority. Put simply, the media support the interests of the rich and powerful who control the media and have a vested interest in portraying capitalist society in a positive light. The media, then, promote a 'false consciousness', preventing people from seeing the reality of their situation. Marx's ideas on the media were developed by Gramsci, with his discussion of hegemony, a concept which has been very influential in theorizing on the relationship between the media and crime (Jewkes 2004). Gramsci's writings and arguments from prison (1971) had an important influence on media research, with his argument that the media had a key role to play in ensuring the compliance of the mass of society, so that the ruling groups dominated not merely by force but, more importantly, by gaining the consent of the majority. Hegemony refers to the process by which powerful groups maintain and extend their power through winning the consent of the masses, rather than relying on coercion. It combines the notions of force and consent and suggests that ideologies become most powerful when accepted by the mass as common sense. Gramsci understands that ideological domination is never absolute and fixed, there is always a struggle to influence the thinking of the wider public; and in this struggle for hegemony the media has a crucial role.

Although mainly known for his innovative work on language and not a mainstream Marxist theorist, Noam Chomsky adopted a broadly Marxist approach to considering the role of the media (1989). He developed a 'propaganda' model that saw the media as an instrument of class domination, due to the concentration of ownership in media and other conglomerates, which was reflected in the content of the commercial broadcasting, press and other media outlets that they controlled. Chomsky believed the media controlled and limited debate in a way that protected the dominant conglomerate and state interests; reflecting the more liberal, pluralist view that the media enable the public to have some influence and control over the political process through providing a variety of ideas, opinions and information.

As mentioned above, Marxist, critical views came to the fore in the 1960s and 1970s and informed a wide range of research and theorizing in the social sciences. Here we will look at two examples of Marxist-influenced theorizing – Miliband's study *The State in Capitalist Society* (1973) and the work of the Glasgow University Media Group. Miliband's work is an example that applies the Marxist argument to the media. He argued that the state (including the government, the police and the judiciary) exercise power in the interests of the ruling classes and that it is able to do this through controlling ideology – the most effective means of social control. This is the mechanism that persuades people to accept the system as it is, with all the inequities in it. How, for example, are people persuaded to accept as fair a system that pays one person massively more than another for more or less the same effort? Miliband argues that it is through the power of the dominant groups to control the knowledge and ideas available to the wider population – and that the media is one of the key institutions enabling them to exert this control. Although there is a wide range of media sources (and far more than when Miliband's study was published over three decades ago) providing for different audiences and viewpoints; the notion that there is real diversity is seen by Miliband as a misleading and superficial view. The mass media may provide a degree of impartiality through presenting different opinions and views, but this impartiality is only within the boundaries of what is deemed as 'acceptable'.

Alternative ideas and opinions which fall outside of the general consensus are given little support or credibility. Miliband argues that the content of the media reflects the views of the dominant groups in society – and, specifically, the white, middle-class viewpoint – and it is not just news-based content, but also the content of entertainment programmes that are seen as supporting the present social system through portraying it in a basically favourable light. Indeed, popular soap operas and dramas provide enjoyment and even a sense of well-being for millions and help to divert attention from and distort our view of the social system through giving the impression that nothing is drastically wrong with the world in which we live. Using language reflecting the Marxist thrust of his argument, Miliband describes the media as an 'agency of conservative indoctrination' that conditions people against dissent. The media are seen as the new 'opium of the people', paraphrasing Marx's famous comment that 'religion is the opium of the people'. The media act like a drug, keeping the working population quiet and supportive of a system that, in reality, works against their interest. It cannot foster complete compliance but does, according to Miliband, 'foster a climate of conformity' by presenting any views that fall outside of a general consensus as 'curious heresies, or, even more effectively, by treating them as irrelevant eccentricities, which serious and reasonable people may dismiss as of no consequence' (1973, p. 213).

So the media are seen as one part of a system of ideological domination, which supports the position of the powerful; it helps to socialize the mass of the population to a life of subordination and to accept things as they are.

Although not presenting a classic Marxist approach, the work of the Glasgow University Media Group over the last thirty or so years has provided an important critical examination of media and, in particular, news reportage. Their work has taken issue with the common-sense view that news reporting merely reflects what is going on in society and that news reporters are professional journalists who know their jobs and work under pressure in a fast-moving world. However, these journalists will have their own beliefs and values and their own prejudices and if these are expressed in and through their news reporting then there may well be cause for concern. In a series of studies that were based on detailed content analyses of television news, including *Bad News* (1976), *More Bad News* (1980), *Really Bad News* (1982), *War and Peace News* (1985) and *Getting the Message: News, Truth and Power* (1993), the Glasgow University Media Group criticized broadcasters' claims that they presented the news impartially.

The major finding of their studies was that television news reproduces the dominant ideology and does not present the diversity of opinions available in any given situation. They considered the issue of agenda-setting in the news and the assumption held by journalists that the news is an objective, 'real' phenomenon and that certain items have 'news value'. However, journalists have to organize the news they present from a whole mass of information and opinion – they have to select, interpret and edit and, in doing so, the Glasgow Group argue, certain viewpoints are emphasized to the exclusion of others. In one of the early studies, they quote from a BBC pamphlet on the news that makes the point, 'the news value of a story is something immediately recognizable, intuitively sensed by a journalist . . . [who] learns to spot the significant news point . . . which distinguishes a newsworthy story' (1980, p. 113). This highlights the questions as to just what is 'the significant news point' and seems to suggest that what is presented as news is based on the inherited 'wisdom' of journalistic assumptions about the world and the audience to which they are reporting. As the Glasgow Group put it:

> The assertion of impartiality as a regular professional achievement is little more than the unsupported claim to a unique understanding of events. This serves only to obfuscate what is in fact the reproduction of the dominant assumptions about society – the assumptions of the powerful about what is important, necessary and possible within it.
>
> (Glasgow University Media Group 1980, p. 115)

The early research of the Glasgow University Media Group involved studying the media portrayal of industrial disputes – a portrayal, they argued, which demonstrated that what the media presents as news is a reflection of the interests and assumptions of the powerful. They found that in reporting strikes, for example, management were presented in a far better light than striking workers. For instance, management were usually shown in an office context and were allowed to make their points quietly, while trade unionists often had to shout over the noise around them or were interrupted by reporters. Furthermore, in reporting strikes, little time was devoted to detailing the background to the particular dispute and the emphasis was invariably on the effects on the wider public.

In summary, the Glasgow Group's work rejects the pluralist perspective (considered below) that the media is essentially neutral and impartial. Rather the news is seen as leading rather than reflecting opinion, it 'sets the agenda' and structures people's attitudes.

Consensus perspectives – pluralism and functionalism

The main focus in this brief overview is on pluralism; however, this approach does overlap with the functionalist perspective, one of the major theoretical positions in sociology. Based on the work of the social theorist, Émile Durkheim, functionalist social theory emphasizes consensus, rather than conflict, and how social order is maintained within society. Functionalists stress the importance of ensuring that people conform to generally held social values and norms of behaviour. They consider the major ways in which order is created and then maintained; and in doing so highlight the ways in which people are socialized into conformity. Socialization can and does occur through the family and kinship systems but also from cultural subsystems, including the mass media. So the media are examined in terms of how they function to maintain the social order as it is. In this context, the roles of the media include spreading knowledge and information across society as a whole and performing a social control function by presenting to the population a set of values that reflect the requirements of the society. In other words, a primary function of the media is seen as promoting an ideology that broadly supports the wider society, and the institutions within it.

In terms of ownership and control of the media, the functionalist perspective focuses on the need for there to be a range of views on offer through different media forms. The stability of a society is promoted when there is a reasonable range of different media for people to choose from; so that very popular publications and programmes sit alongside more specialist media offerings. The media, then, are seen as largely driven by the market and consumer demand. These ideas about the role of the market are similar to the pluralist perspective considered next. First, however, it is worth considering a couple of problems with this consensus-based, functionalist position.

What are deemed to be generally held social values may be the values of one particular class, rather than those of 'society as a whole'. It is pretty clear that the media do not, and maybe cannot, reflect equally all points of view – some views are inevitably down-graded, perhaps because of the political perspective of newspaper owners, broadcasters and others in control of different media forms.

The pluralist perspective has a similar theoretical position to functionalism but focuses more on the role of the state. Pluralists believe that societies are made up of a range of different but complementary sections, each of which has access to resources and influence; and these different sections and groups are overseen by an essentially neutral state which works to ensure that the general public interest is served. Applying this to the media, the conflict-based theoretical approaches looked at earlier see the media as having a good deal of power to influence their audiences; and tend to suggest that the less powerful groups and sections of society are more vulnerable to media influence. In contrast, pluralist theories adopt a much more positive approach to explaining the role of the media; arguing that they provide a massive and increasingly wide range of material to a diverse audience. Different aspects of the media cater for the different sections within society; so that overall the media come to reflect society. Just as there is diversity of tastes and opinions in a society so there is diversity within the media.

The title 'pluralist' is one used to categorize and encompass other approaches to theorizing about the media. These theories are sometimes called 'market' or 'liberal' theories of the media. The basic thrust of this general range of research and theorizing on the media is that the media reflects what the mass of the public want – the mass media basically respond to the market demand. Even if the media may reflect certain viewpoints more than others, and even be biased in some ways, they still reinforce the most popular and generally held attitudes and beliefs, and the views they give most coverage to are those that most people support and sympathize with. The less mainstream opinions and attitudes are still catered for, but by more specific media outlets – such as minority magazines and specialist radio and television channels and programmes. Those who own and control the media will argue that they are serving the market; their particular media forms have to remain viable and so have to provide what the public wants.

Pluralist theories of the media are based on the wider pluralist theory of power in society, which argues that power is shared by a range of interest groups and that no one group or elite dominates the rest of society. Ideally, pluralists see the involvement of groups representing as wide a range of interest as possible in a society as being essential to decision-making in that society (and the role of a government is to arbitrate between the different groups that seek to influence decision-making processes). Of course, it is accepted that certain groups have greater access to decision- and policy-makers and that some interests are under-represented (for instance, the interests of less powerful groups, such as unemployed or migrant workers, perhaps). However, governments have to consult and take into account the views of a range of interest groups so as to minimize conflict and because even less powerful and poorly represented groups can still have a significant impact in terms of voting at elections. The nineteenth-century French political thinker and historian, Alexis de Tocqueville, is generally regarded as the founder of pluralism. In his seminal work, *Democracy in America* (1835), he argued that in a democracy it was normal and necessary that individuals would have a large number of specific interests; and that a democracy would not work if any one division or group in society came to dominate all of the others.

From the pluralist perspective, the mass media is seen as reflecting this variety of interests; and as a consequence of this choice, pluralists argue that the media have little direct media influence on people's attitudes and viewpoints and that what influence they do have tends to reinforce already held attitudes and views. So, unlike the conflict, Marxist-based approaches, the influence of the media is not seen as a particular cause for concern. Indeed, advocates of this theoretical approach see the increased diversity in the media as part of a new era of freedom. More and more media outlets, including television and radio channels, magazines and computer-based media, provide a choice that was almost unimaginable a few decades ago. Media proliferation has ensured that an ever wider range of views and ideas are accessible to far greater numbers of people. Texts and writing on the mass media have often been from a basically pluralist position, particularly those that have been written by media professionals. Katz and Lazarsfeld's early theoretical work (1955), which developed and critiqued the hypodermic syringe model, offered a fairly positive and pluralist take on the role and effect of the media. In one study of news reporting, a BBC radio broadcaster, Nicholas Jones, argued that the news presentation on radio was neutral, fair and balanced, reporting a range of relevant views and not favouring one opinion over others (cited in Haralambos and Holborn 2004).

The pluralist perspective on to the role and effect of the media developed as a criticism of the more negative approaches looked at earlier in this chapter. Some of the early pluralist writers and theorists, such as Robert Dahl and Herbert Gans, celebrated the spread of democracy and the variety of popular culture within such societies. The media were seen as playing an important role in the democratic process by providing access to information, widening debate and giving all groups and sections in society an opportunity to promote and share their views and tastes with others. This is essentially a liberal, market-driven approach, whereby the obvious way of providing genuine freedom of choice for a widely diverse public is seen as being through a deregulated mass media – where the demand for different media offerings is met by a range of media outlets.

However, it is idealistic and unrealistic to suggest that all minority interests are now served by this explosion in the number and the range of the mass media. As Jewkes (2004) argues, there are still many vested interests in media ownership and control and, 'for all the proliferation of new channels, media industries are still owned and controlled by a small handful of white, wealthy, middle-class men (or corporations started by such men)' (p. 22).

As mentioned earlier, the thrust of the pluralist approach is indicated by another title it is sometimes considered under – 'market theory'. And market-based approaches, for all their supposed democratic intent, lead to an increasing emphasis on commercialization, which results in media institutions sticking to what they know sells – which tends to be entertainment aimed at a 'lowest common denominator' audience. This has led to the trend commonly called 'dumbing down', with audience ratings the be all and end all; and this occurs at the expense of in-depth political commentary and analysis. This can be seen in media coverage of crime, whereby programmes and news coverage tend to focus on unusual and spectacular crimes – such as cases involving serial killers and child abusers. While computer-based media and, in particular, the Internet would seem to offer a wide variety of ideas and views, they are not equally available to all sections and groups in society.

QUESTION BREAK

TV schedules from a Saturday night

Saturday 12 January 2013

BBC 1

6.00 Richard Hammond's Secret Service
6.50 Britain's Brightest
8.00 The National Lottery
8.50 Casualty
9.30 Mrs Brown's Boys

ITV 1

6.00 New You've Been Framed
7.00 Splash
8.30 Take Me Out
9.30 Take Me Out

You might also look at the schedules for the massive variety of satellite channels and at the press headlines from a particular day in a popular newspaper such as *The Sun* or *The Daily Star*.

Suggest any evidence that might be used to support the view that there has been a 'dumbing down' of the media in Britain.

What points could be made to counter that argument?

So, while the ideas and philosophy behind the pluralist approaches are fine in theory – the notion of a wide and free choice for everyone – the reality suggests a less-positive and optimistic picture. As Jewkes (2004) puts it, 'pluralism, then, might best be viewed as an expression of how things could be, rather than how things are' (p. 24).

POSTMODERN/CULTURAL CRIMINOLOGY

Societies have always been subject to change and it is probably commonplace for people to view the changes they are currently facing as being particularly momentous and rapid in comparison to earlier periods of time. Certainly, there have been rapid transformations in the social, political, cultural and economic arenas of life in the later years of the twentieth century and into the current century. Indeed, the extent and rapidity of these changes have led theorists to suggest that modern Western societies had reached a condition of 'postmodernity'. This new theoretical paradigm has been seen as a response to the major transformations in global cultural, political and economic life; transformations that have replaced the social structures associated with 'modern' societies, such as class divisions, capitalism and the nation state. The role and influence of the mass media in postmodern society has been an important aspect of the writing and theorizing from this theoretical position. It is generally accepted that we live in a media-dominated society, so much so that the media does not merely reflect social reality but rather that media images are realities in themselves. Postmodern society is also characterized by the importance given to image and style; and the media play a key role in promoting image and style, through adverts as well as films and television programmes.

QUESTION BREAK

Considering adverts and also other aspects of media coverage such as films or television programmes, what images are used by the media to promote:

1. men's clothing
2. women's clothing
3. alcoholic drinks
4. cars
5. holidays?

Give examples of each of the above categories.

Strinati (1992), in his discussion of postmodernism and the media, describes how the media encourage us to cross and criss-cross time and space, with film and television, in particular, providing collages of images from different times and places. Increasingly, then, the mass media come to dominate our definition and sense of reality, with images from television, computer games, the Internet, DVDs and personal music players depicting our everyday world. This is seen by many as a worrying development with, according to Strinati, media images encouraging 'superficiality rather than substance, cynicism rather than belief, the thirst for constant change rather than the security of stable traditions, the desires of the moment rather than the truths of history' (1992, p. 7).

The mass media has contributed to producing a cultural context centred on immediate consumption and sensationalized impact, with a consequent lack of depth and context – the stress and pressure is on entertainment and audience gratification. The focus on entertainment rather than information can be seen as undermining meaningful debate. Entertainment and sensationalization, and the media emphasis on them, can be used by different political and other groups for both positive and negative ends. Jewkes (2004) uses the example of terrorists who have taken and utilized the sensational impact the media can have for their own ends, and with devastating effect. The most obvious and appalling example of this 'postmodern media performance', as Jewkes puts it, was the terrorist attack on the World Trade Center on 11 September 2001. The attack was watched on television by millions in America and elsewhere as it unfolded – and this event had such a massively overwhelming impact because of the immediacy and dramatic impact of the images on television and film. Terrorist attacks bring home to everyone the idea that anyone and everyone is a potential victim of crime; presenting us with a picture of random criminality and violence that governments are apparently unable to prevent or do anything about.

In considering the different representations of crime, both factual and fictional, that is presented by the media, it is clear that it is those crimes that are very rare, or that have some unusual features, which are given by far the most media time and coverage. Serial killings and child abductions, for instance, although very untypical crimes, are given widespread coverage. This, Jewkes (2004) suggests, increases the anxiety of the public and deflects the focus from more commonplace crimes, including corporate crime and abuse within families.

Postmodernism has been presented as a major, decisive break with previous structures and theoretical stances. However, whether the postmodern society is fundamentally different and unique, or whether there has just been a more rapid development of modernity in recent years, is open to debate. Nonetheless, there have been a range of new freedoms and associated new uncertainties that are seen as characteristic of contemporary society. The features typically seen as characteristic of postmodernism include a rejection of all-encompassing theoretical perspectives (meta-narratives) and of the notion that there are absolute truths and, in their place, an extolling of variety and differences, particularly within the media, but also in other cultural areas such as architecture, art and literature. Modernity (seen by postmodern theorists as the predecessor of postmodern society) has been seen as associated with the development of industrial society and the classic theoretical explanations that proliferated at the turn of the twentieth century – it is seen as characterized by a certain degree of moral certainty and a belief that theoretical thinking would be able to explain the problems facing humanity. In contrast, postmodernity emphasizes moral ambiguity and the belief that there are a range of truths and discourses that can all have value and be acceptable at different times and for different people. The emphasis is on diversity – of theoretical explanations as well as of cultural forms, notably the media, and this has had an impact on criminological theorizing.

Indeed, a particular influence of postmodernism that can be related to theorizing about crime concerns the spread of the media, including the scope this offers for new forms of criminal behaviour and the role it has played in the development of 'cultural criminology'. Particularly associated with the theorizing of American criminologist Jeff Ferrell, cultural criminology emphasizes the importance of image, style and representations and the way these have encouraged a mediated construction of crime and criminal justice. It takes on the postmodern position that 'style is substance' and the meaning of something is based on its representation to suggest that crime can be best understood as part of an 'image-driven media loop' (Ferrell 2001). Ferrell points to a number of areas in which this new theoretical approach has developed. First, crime is seen as a subcultural phenomenon organized around symbolic communication. Cultural criminology also examines the mediated construction of crime and the control of crime; considering the interconnections between the criminal justice system and the mass media – it looks at how certain activities come to be constructed as crimes and others do not. It also considers the everyday consumption of crime as drama and entertainment:

> The notion of cultural criminology references the increasing analytic attention that many criminologists now give to popular culture constructions, and especially mass media constructions, of crime and crime control.
>
> (Ferrell 1999, p. 395)

A good deal of research in cultural criminology has looked at 'subcultural style', seeing this style as defining the way deviants and criminals characterize their activity and also the way such activities are viewed and constructed from outside. It has also introduced the idea of 'culture as crime', whereby aspects of popular culture become criminalized:

> performers, producers, distributors, and retailers of rap and 'gangsta rap' music have likewise faced arrest and conviction on obscenity charges, legal confiscation of albums, highly publicized protests, boycotts, hearings organized by political figures and police officials, ongoing media campaigns and legal proceedings against them of promoting – indeed, directly causing – crime and delinquency.
>
> (Ferrell 1999, p. 405)

In addition to framing how crime and criminal activities are viewed, the media also frame and determine our perceptions of crime control. With regards to the police, 'reality' policing programmes determine public perceptions of the police and will play a part in recruitment to the police. Policing is interpreted as a set of practices situated, like criminal practices, within subcultural conventions of meaning, symbolism and style (Ferrell 1999 and see Chapter 6).

Indeed, the postmodern analysis of the relationship between the media and crime can be applied to all areas where the two intersect.

FURTHER READING

Greer C. and Reiner R. (2012) 'Mediated Mayhem: Media, Crime, Criminal Justice', in Maguire M., Morgan R. and Reiner R. (eds), *The Oxford Handbook of Criminology*, 5th edn, Oxford: Oxford University Press. This article considers the content, consequences and causes of media images of crime and criminal justice.

Jewkes Y. (2011) *Media and Crime*, 2nd edn, London: Sage. A clear introduction to the study of crime and the mass media, the first chapter provides a thorough overview of major theoretical perspectives on the media and how they relate to the analysis of crime.

McQuail D. (2005) *Mass Communications Theory: An Introduction*, 5th edn, London: Sage. This standard text provides extensive coverage of theories of the media and is now in its fifth edition.

CHAPTER 3

The Media and Moral Panics – Theories and Examples

Moral panic is such a well-established term, both in academic and everyday vocabulary, that it is surprising to recall it has only become widely used since the work of Stan Cohen in the early 1970s on youth subcultures. Since then the term has been regularly used in the media to refer to all sorts of antisocial and/or criminal behaviours. Essentially, a moral panic refers to an exaggerated reaction, from the media, the police or wider public, to the activities of particular social groups. These activities may well be relatively trivial but have been reported in a somewhat sensationalized form in the media; and such reporting and publicity has then led to an increase in general anxiety and concern about those activities. So a moral panic is an exaggerated response to a type of behaviour that is seen as a social problem – the term indicates an over-reaction on the part of the media and/or other social institutions. Furthermore, this over-reaction magnifies the original area of concern. Indeed, it leads to the social group (and, as a consequence, the behaviour and activities they engage in) being viewed by the wider society as 'folk devils' – another term coined by Cohen. Indeed, Cohen's book on the Mods and Rockers of the 1960s was titled *Folk Devils and Moral Panics: The Creation of the Mods and Rockers* and therefore, as Newburn (2013) puts it, has 'the distinction of containing two terms, *folk devils* and *moral panics*, which have subsequently entered popular terminology'.

Given the status of Cohen's studies in this area, we will start by considering his analysis before looking at examples of media reporting of moral panics from before his work through to more contemporary examples.

COHEN: *FOLK DEVILS AND MORAL PANICS*

Cohen's study started out as his doctoral thesis and was an attempt to offer a sociological explanation for a particular and immediate concern – the delinquent behaviour of (and between) two deviant youth subcultures – the Mods and the Rockers. However, Cohen was aware that his analysis had implications beyond the immediate subject matter. In the preface to the first edition of the book, written in 1971, he asks 'who on earth is still worried about the Mods and Rockers?' And in an extended introduction to the second edition (1980) he points out that the book was 'out of date even when it originally appeared in 1972'.

Cohen sets out the basis of his argument in the first paragraph of his study – a paragraph which has been extensively quoted and which provides what has become the generally accepted definition of a moral panic. As with more recent scholarly work on moral panics (for example, Critcher 2003; Jewkes 2004; Newburn 2013) we will start our brief overview with the following quote.

> Societies appear to be subject, every now and then, to periods of moral panic. A condition, episode, person or group of persons emerges to become defined as a threat to societal values and interests; its nature is presented in a stylized and stereotypical fashion by the mass media; the moral barricades are manned by editors, bishops, politicians and other right-thinking people; socially accredited experts pronounce their diagnoses and solutions; ways of coping are evolved or (more often) resorted to; the condition then disappears, submerges or deteriorates and becomes more visible. Sometimes the object of the panic is quite novel and at other times it is something which has been in existence long enough, but suddenly appears in the limelight. Sometimes the panic passes over and is forgotten, except in folk-lore and collective memory; at other times it has more serious and long-lasting repercussions and might produce such changes as those in legal and social policy or even in the way society conceives itself.
>
> (Cohen 1972, p. 9)

Cohen then points out that there have been recurrent moral panics in post-war Britain over various forms of youth culture whose behaviour is deviant or delinquent – including the Teddy Boys, Mods and Rockers, Hells Angels and Skinheads. These groups have been seen as distinctive social types or groups, not just in terms of their behaviour but also in terms of their style. As the quote above suggests, the panics associated with such groups have been transient and soon forgotten. This is further illustrated by Cohen's comment:

> At the beginning of the decade (the 1960s), the term 'Modernist' referred simply to a style of dress, the term 'Rocker' was hardly known . . . Five years later, a

newspaper editor was to refer to the Mods and Rockers incidents as 'without parallel in English history' and troop reinforcements were rumoured to have been sent to quell possible widespread disturbances. Now, another five years later, these groups have all but disappeared from the public consciousness.

(1972, p. 10)

In terms of its theoretical stance, Cohen's seminal study on moral panics was clearly based on the labelling or interactionist perspective – an approach with a strong focus on how society labels rule-breakers as belonging to particular deviant groups and how once a person or group is labelled, the actions they undertake are viewed and interpreted in terms of this label. A key part of the labelling process involves the mass media – and its role in defining and shaping social problems:

The media have long operated as agents of moral indignation in their own right: even if they are not self-consciously engaged in crusading or muck-raking, their very reporting of certain 'facts' can be sufficient to generate concern, anxiety, indignation or panic.

(Cohen 1972, p. 16)

Given that the media devote a massive amount of space and time to deviant behaviour, it is not surprising that a large part of Cohen's study is spent examining the role of the mass media in creating moral panics and folk devils (an area we will consider in more detail below, pp. 50–52).

In order to do justice to Cohen's argument, we need to look briefly at the actual events his study was attempting to explain – the clashes between the rival youth group, Mods and Rockers, at seaside towns in the mid-1960s. Our brief review will lean on Critcher's (2003) more detailed analysis. The Essex resort of Clacton was the scene of the first 'event' over Easter 1964. Groups of young people from London and other parts of south-east England, some of whom were identifiable as Mods and others as Rockers, gathered at Clacton on this wet bank holiday weekend. There was little for them to do and a few minor scuffles and incidents occurred; after two days of relatively mild violence the press were full of blaring headlines on 'the terror' wreaked by 'wild ones' (see the question break below) and newspaper editorials called for government action. The next bank holiday, Whitsun, police, journalists and youths were expecting trouble at other southern coastal towns (with Brighton, Margate and Eastbourne the venues selected by the Mods and Rockers). Again a series of minor incidents provoked sensationalized newspaper reporting; with police forces coordinating massive police operations – including turning back youths as they arrived at seaside towns and arresting those who showed any resistance. After a few more such weekends, the seaside gatherings declined as the youth cultures (particularly the Mods) petered out or developed into other subcultural groupings, such as Skinheads and Hippies.

Cohen argued that the social reaction engendered by these events depended on the sort of information available in the public arena; and that as most people have no first-hand knowledge of deviants they are reliant on the media. The media are particularly important in the early stages of the social reaction through their producing of the images that the wider public will assimilate. Cohen highlights three processes which set up and establish the social reaction and consequent moral panic. First, there is an exaggeration or distortion of the events themselves – through exaggerating the numbers involved and the extent of violence and damage that occurred. Second, through predicting that such events will recur; and third, through symbolization – using language so that, for instance, Mod, comes to stand for a whole form of youth style and status.

QUESTION BREAK

Mods and Rockers jailed after seaside riots

Scores of youths have been given prison sentences following a Whitsun weekend of violent clashes between gangs of Mods and Rockers at a number of resorts on the south coast of England. Yesterday two youths were taken to hospital with knife wounds and 51 were arrested in Margate after hundreds of teenagers converged on the town for the holiday weekend . . . Three offenders were jailed for three months each and five more sent to detention centres for up to six months.

In Brighton, two youths were jailed for three months and others were fined. More than 1,000 teenagers were involved in skirmishes on the beach and promenade last night. They threw deckchairs around, broke them up to make bonfires, shouted obscenities at each other and at passers-by, jostled holidaymakers and terrified elderly residents . . .

In Margate, there were running battles between police and up to 400 youths on the beach early yesterday morning. Bottles were thrown and two officers were slightly hurt. Later, on the high street, around 40 young men smashed council flat windows and vandalized a pub and hardware shop. Last night, hundreds of young men and girls were still wandering around the resort long after the last train had left . . .

There were further clashes at Bournemouth and Clacton.

(From: BBC News Online *On This Day*, 18 May 1964)

The concept of Mods and Rockers actually crystallized in the public consciousness at a specific place and time: Clacton-on-Sea, Essex, during the Easter Bank Holiday weekend of 1964. After two days of comparatively mild violence in the wet seaside resort – the worst was a shop window being broken – the newspapers were full of blaring headlines – 'Day of Terror By Scooter Groups', 'Youngsters Beat Up Town – 97 Leather Jacket Arrests', 'Wild Ones Invade Seaside'.

It was under this glare of publicity that the idea of scooter gangs – Mods – versus motorbike gangs – Rockers – really flourished. Until then they had not been rigidly separate groups . . . In truth, especially in cities, the groups were often inter-related, often from the same housing estates: only separated by fashion or generations, older brother/younger brother, etc.

(www.the59club.com/public_html/mockers.html)

QUESTIONS

- From the accounts above, what evidence is there of the media 'amplifying' the panic over Mods and Rockers?
- What youth subcultural groups have hit the headlines since then?
- Research a more recent youth subcultural group and describe the media coverage of them. What similarities and differences can you suggest between this coverage and that of the Mods and Rockers in the 1960s?

Cohen's work was clearly more focused on moral panics and the social and media reaction rather than the actual deviant and delinquent behaviour and explanations for it – a point he acknowledges in introducing the second edition of his classic study, 'the book was more a study of moral panics than of folk devils' (Cohen 1980). So, before we turn to a brief look at other examples of moral panics it would be helpful to consider Cohen's comments on the links between the media and deviant behaviour. He was well aware that his study did not attempt to explain deviance and that the social reaction he examined was, as he put it, 'the "effective" rather than "original" cause of deviance'. In other words, his work did not attempt to provide a theoretical explanation for this type of delinquent behaviour.

Cohen highlights different strategies for studying social reaction, such as sampling public opinion on particular types of deviance and constructing ethnographic and historic accounts of the reactions to such behaviour. However, in order to understand the reaction to deviance by the public and the authorities, it is vital to consider the nature of information that they receive. In modern societies, most information is received second hand, usually processed by the mass media and so subject to their definitions of what constitutes 'news' and how it is presented. And this information is also affected by the constraints that newspapers and broadcasters have to operate under – both commercial and political constraints. It is clear from studying media responses to deviant behaviour that the media can play on the concerns of the public and can create social problems quite suddenly and dramatically. The media reaction to deviant behaviour can lead to a process of deviance amplification (see the section below for a fuller explanation of this process), whereby media attention increases the isolation of the deviant groups who are forced to continue and develop their deviant behaviour and so on. Certainly, the way the media reported the behaviour of the

Mods and Rockers had a major influence on public social reaction to those groups. As Cohen puts it:

> The public image of these folk devils was invariably tied up to a number of highly visual scenarios associated with their appearance: youths chasing across the beach, brandishing deck chairs above their heads . . . sleeping on the beaches and so on.
>
> (1980, p. 20)

Cohen emphasizes the importance of the growth and spread of a generalized belief about a particular form of behaviour or group of deviants and points out that, for the most part, such generalized beliefs are spread through the mass media.

Of course, social reaction does not solely rely on the media. There is also initial, on-the-spot reaction from people who are part of or witness to the particular behaviour and there is also the organized reaction of the system of social control, often the police. Nonetheless, the 'transmission and diffusion of the reaction in the mass media' is, for Cohen, a crucial element in explaining moral panics.

YOUNG: DRUG USE AND MORAL PANIC

At around the same time as Cohen's original research and study, Jock Young, a fellow sociologist and criminologist (and indeed a co-author with Cohen of later studies, including *The Manufacture of News* in 1981), explored the moral panic that developed around the drug use of 'hippies' in the mid- to late 1960s. Indeed, Young's findings were first published as a chapter in a book edited by Stan Cohen, *Images of Deviance* (1971). In particular, he examined the social reaction to the use of marijuana in the Notting Hill area of west London and described the process of 'deviance amplification'– a process that occurs as a consequence of a moral panic over a specific type of behaviour. Basically, deviance amplification is a reinforcing and snowballing effect that happens as a result of a negative social reaction to such criminal or deviant behaviour. So, Young's study is an examination of the effects of the moral panic about drug use on this behaviour in London in the late 1960s. The title of Young's study was 'The Role of the Police as Amplifiers of Deviancy' and we will look at it briefly before going on to consider an evaluation of Cohen's analysis of moral panics.

As implied in the title to his study, Young considers the effect of the beliefs and stereotypes held by the police about drug users and the conflict between the police and the drug user. However, in terms of our focus on social reaction and moral panics, it is Young's examination of the notion of deviance amplification and the relationship between society and the deviance that is most pertinent. Young describes the interaction process between the police and drug user in a sequential manner that is worth reproducing from the original:

(i)   the police act against the drug users in terms of their stereotypes;

(ii) the drug user group finds itself in a new situation, which it must interpret and adapt to in a changed manner;

(iii) the police react in a slightly different fashion to the changed group;

(iv) the drug users interpret and adapt to this new situation;

(v) the police react to these new changes; and so on.

(Young 1971, p. 33)

Young goes on to look at how the mass media present information about deviant groups, and in this case drug users, using extracts from the popular press, including this from *The People* of 21 September 1969:

Hippie Thugs – The Sordid Truth: Drug-taking, couples making love while others look on, rule by a heavy mob armed with iron bars, foul language, filth and stench, THAT is the scene inside the hippies' fortress in London's Piccadilly. These are not rumours but facts – sordid facts which will shock ordinary decent family loving people.

He argues that 'our knowledge of deviants not only is stereotypical because of the distortions of the mass media but is also one-dimensional'. The information that is available about deviants is based on a 'gross misperception' because of stereotyped information 'purveyed via the mass media'. He goes on to suggest this leads to a social reaction based on stereotyped fantasies, rather than accurate knowledge and information; and 'because the criterion for inclusion in the media is newsworthiness it is possible for moral panics over a particular type of deviancy to be created by the sudden dissemination of information about it'.

Of particular interest to our area of study, Young also considers how the amplification of deviance (in this case drug use) leads to the fantasy being translated into the reality. He argued that, over time, the police action against marijuana users led to the intensification of their deviant behaviour that included a change in their lifestyle, so that 'certain facets of the stereotype became the actuality'. We will finish our review by summarizing Young's description of the main aspects of the social world of the marijuana user and how this leads to amplification and intensification of their deviant behaviour. First, intensive police action increases the cohesion and organization of the drug-using community, with drug users uniting in a common sense of injustice at how their behaviour is treated by the police and portrayed by the media. Second, this police action leads the drug user to segregating himself (*sic*) from the wider society of non-drug users. Third, the more the drug users accept their deviant identity and norms, the less chance there is of them re-entering mainstream society. Fourth, as the deviant behaviour becomes more entrenched so police concern with and reaction to that behaviour increases, and drug use becomes more of a secretive activity. And as a side effect, drug use becomes a symbol of rebellion against an unfair and unjust system. Fifth, increased and more severe police action leads to the price increase of marijuana; and as the profits to be made from selling increase so professional dealers begin to emerge, and other criminal activities, including the selling of different drugs, overlap with marijuana use. Sixth, the reactions and developments described above increase levels of suspicion and, in the context of perceived police persecution, encourage feelings of paranoia amongst the drug users.

In this 'us and them' context, the marijuana user and the user of 'harder' drugs, such as heroin, will feel some sort of common identity as victims of police persecution.

Finally, as the mass media excites and exacerbates public indignation and panic over marijuana use, pressure on the police to prevent such behaviour increases. This leads to the police arresting more marijuana users and, consequently, the mass media and public reacting to the new higher figures of drug offenders with even greater panic.

Young's study, then, paints a very clear picture of how social reaction to a type of deviant behaviour can lead to a moral panic that actually increases and intensifies that behaviour. His diagrammatic representation of deviance amplification is reproduced below.

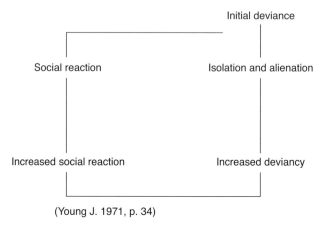

(Young J. 1971, p. 34)

EXPLAINING MORAL PANICS: GOODE AND BEN-YEHUDA

Before turning to an evaluation of Cohen's work, we will look at Goode and Ben-Yehuda's study on moral panics, published in 1994 and dedicated to Stan Cohen. They differentiate moral panics from social problems and moral crusades – according to Critcher (2003) the former (social problems) lack 'folk devils or wild fluctuations of concern' and the latter (moral crusades) are 'organized agitations initiated by moral entrepreneurs' (Critcher 2003). Goode and Ben-Yehuda highlight five key criteria of moral panics:

- There has to be a heightened level of concern over the behaviour (and the consequences of that behaviour) of a certain group.
- This leads to increased levels of hostility towards the group who engage in the behaviour.
- The concern and hostility have to be met with a certain degree of consensus from society as a whole that the threat caused by the group's behaviour is real and serious.
- The behaviour is reacted to with a sense of disproportionality; as Goode and Ben-Yehuda put it, 'the concept of moral panic rests on disproportionality' with public concern being in excess of what is appropriate given the objective harm done by the behaviour.

- By their very nature, moral panics are volatile – they erupt quickly and subside suddenly.

Goode and Ben-Yehuda then offer three different explanations for moral panics. First, a grassroots model that suggests panic originates with the wider public when they are worried or concerned about an issue. Second, an 'elite-engineered' model, whereby an elite group deliberately promotes a campaign to generate concern and panic in the public over an issue that may not in itself be terribly harmful to society as a whole; and this is done to divert attention away from other problems or issues that elite do not particularly want brought into the public arena. Third, the interest group model suggests moral panics emanate from 'the middle rungs of power and status', from groups such as professional associations, religious groups, police departments or the media themselves. Goode and Ben-Yehuda argue that it is a combination of grassroots and interest group models that offers the best explanations – without a grassroots feeling a moral panic would have no foundation and without interest group involvement it would have no means of expression (Critcher 2003).

COHEN: *FOLK DEVILS AND MORAL PANICS* – A CRITIQUE

In an evaluation and critique of the 'moral panic model', Jewkes (2004) considered the processes involved in establishing a moral panic that were highlighted by Cohen and then raised some problems with his model. The analysis of moral panics developed by Cohen was clearly focused on youth subcultures and the symbolism associated with them. And since his study, moral panics have been developed around a wide range of youth subcultures or groups, including punk rockers, muggers, ravers and ecstasy users, lager louts and hoodies. In spite of the diversity of these and numerous other groups, Jewkes points to some key factors identifiable in most moral panics. Although we will only consider some of these factors here, it is useful to list the five 'defining features of moral panics' which she defined:

- Moral panics occur when the media turn a reasonably ordinary event and present it as extraordinary.
- The media, in particular, set in motion a deviance amplification spiral, through which the subjects of the panic are viewed as a source of moral decline and social disintegration.
- Moral panics clarify the moral boundaries of the society in which they occur.
- Moral panics occur during periods of rapid social change and anxiety.
- Young people are the usual target of moral panics, their behaviour is 'regarded as a barometer to test the health or sickness of a society'.

(Jewkes 2004, p. 67)

Cohen paid particular attention to the role of the media in constructing moral panics according to their criteria of 'news values' – as he put it, 'much of this study will be devoted to understanding the role of the mass media in creating moral panics and folk devils' (Cohen 1972, p. 17). Exaggeration and distortion were seen as inevitable in order for a potential news event to become an actual story; and there will also be a degree of predictability that the event/issue being described will inevitably happen again. In terms of deviance amplification, journalists and newspaper editors are seen as 'moral entrepreneurs' who, along with politicians, pressure groups and others, set in motion the spiral by which deviant groups become criminalized and marginalized. The deviance-amplification process describes how, as the negative reaction from society towards particular groups escalates, so the 'deviants' become more isolated and, as a consequence, more criminally oriented. While the spiral may last for months, it never spirals out of control because, in time, media and public interest will wane and the particular subject of the panic, the folk devils of the time, will become more familiar and so will be perceived as less of a threat.

Jewkes also makes the point that identifying a group as a threat establishes a division or boundary between 'us' and 'them' – between the decent, moral and respectable and the deviant and undesirable outsiders. This fits in with Durkheim's classic theoretical position on deviant behaviour (1895), whereby such behaviour is seen as establishing moral boundaries of right and wrong that strengthen the 'collective conscience' of a society. So, moral panics can be seen to draw communities together in a sense of collective outrage and can also make the 'respectable' feel more sure that they are 'good' in comparison to others who are much worse. The final point Jewkes makes is about the tendency for moral panics to target youth. She points out that, although the category of 'youth' came into its own in the 1950s and after, young people have been perceived as a social problem for many years – and well before the 1960s (see Pearson 1983, and pp. 9–12).

Before moving on to consider other examples of moral panics, it would be helpful to consider some of the problems or flaws with the notion of moral panics. Jewkes (2004) raises a number of areas of ambiguity and contention in the definitions, terminology and application of the moral panic model. First, there is a lack of clarity over the defining characteristics of a moral panic; in Cohen's work moral panics are seen as short-lived episodes that fade away after a few weeks or months; however, some areas of concern may last for considerably longer – concerns over juvenile delinquency, for instance, have been present for hundreds of years (see Chapter 1). Although moral panics define moral boundaries of acceptable and unacceptable behaviour, there is little or no focus on why groups step outside of those boundaries and behave the way that they do in the first place. Linked with the issue of moral panics and history, there is an assumption that the rapid pace of social change in recent decades leads to more frequent moral panics, although there is no real evidence that the pace of change is any more rapid than it was 100 or 200 years ago.

Second, Jewkes questions the assumption that the deviant groups involved in moral panics are economically marginalized and behave as they do as a result of boredom and/or financial hardship, as Cohen suggested in the case of the Mods and Rockers. However, youth subcultures of the 1960s could equally be interpreted as a product of the rising affluence of British society and youth, in particular, in the 'swinging sixties'. Also, the moral panic 'thesis' tends to overemphasize the centrality of the media, with analysis focusing on the media rather than the actual deviant behaviour – on the reaction rather than the causes and long-term effects.

This, Jewkes suggests, leads to a 'superficial analysis' as well as encouraging a shift in the media towards 'sensationalized reporting and public entertainment'. In later editions of his study, Cohen discussed some of the shortcomings of the moral panic model, a point acknowledged by Jewkes, who concludes her commentary with the following comment and reference to Cohen:

> Ultimately, perhaps, moral panics should be regarded in the way that Cohen intended – as a means of conceptualizing the lines of power in society and the ways in which we are manipulated into taking some things too seriously and other things not seriously enough.
>
> (Jewkes 2004, p. 85)

In his introduction to the second edition of *Folk Devils and Moral Panics* (1980), and as mentioned earlier, Cohen acknowledged that the book was out of date as soon as it was written. He also makes the point that the rather pessimistic ending to the first edition has been more than justified in the intervening years – the first edition ended with the following comment:

> More moral panics will be generated and other, as yet nameless folk devils will be created . . . because our society as presently structured will continue to generate problems for some of its members – like working-class adolescents – and then condemn whatever solutions these groups find.
>
> (1980, p. i)

In these intervening years (basically the 1970s), Cohen points to the developments of the 'skinhead years, the brief glamrock interlude, the punk explosion, the revival of both the Teds and the Mods (and) the continued noise of football hooliganism'.

He also looks at other academic considerations of moral panics and the developing interest in the relationship between deviance and the media. In particular, he refers to the work of Hall and colleagues at the Birmingham Centre for Contemporary Cultural Studies on the phenomenon of 'mugging', published as *Policing the Crisis* in 1978. This study examined the moral panic about mugging in 1972 and 1973 but focused more on the role of the agencies of social control, rather than the emphasis on social reaction and labelling in Cohen's original work. The crime of mugging attracted a great deal of media attention in the early 1970s and Hall and his colleagues' work showed how issues of race, youth and crime were condensed into the image of the mugger as a 'violent black youth'. A number of individual 'mugging cases' were prominently reported in the media with stories highlighting what was described as a new and frightening type of crime on the streets of Britain. As mentioned, muggers were portrayed as black, which contributed to the view that ethnic minority immigrant groups were to blame for the breakdown of society. As Hall and colleagues could not find any real basis (from crime statistics) for this panic, they developed a Marxist, critical analysis that argued that the moral panic about mugging was encouraged by the government and the media as a way of deflecting attention away from other issues and problems in society, such as growing unemployment.

MORAL PANICS IN HISTORY

So far we have focused on the sociological concept of moral panic as it was developed by 'sociologists of deviance', led by Stan Cohen, in the 1970s. However, behaviour that has produced strong, and panicky, responses from the wider society has a much longer history than this. Before looking at more recent examples of moral panics, we will consider two earlier, historical examples of behaviour and responses to it that would most likely be seen as moral panics if they had occurred in contemporary society. In the first chapter of this book, we looked at Pearson's study (1983) of the history of juvenile delinquency and reactions to it and one of the 'respectable fears' he examined, the 'garotting' craze of the mid-Victorian period, will be our first example.

Then we will look at an example from the 1600s, the witch craze that swept Europe for a number of years.

Garotting

Pearson (1983), amongst other historians, shows us that for generations British society has been plagued by the same concerns and fears about criminal and deviant behaviour. In particular, he highlights the way that each generation tends to characterize the youth of the day, and particularly specific youth groups, as problematic, antisocial, deviant and so on. In his historical reviews of juvenile crime and delinquency, he refers to the panic in the mid-Victorian period, around the 1850s and 1860s, over a new variety of crime called 'garotting', a Victorian parallel with the more recent crime of mugging that involved strangling and choking the victim in the course of robbery. The press reacted in a way that helped amplify the concerns over this crime, with *Punch* magazine launching an 'anti-garotte' movement, advocating the use of a variety of rather bizarre anti-robbery devices, such as spiked metal collars. While this may have been slightly tongue-in-cheek, it is clear from the letters in the press of the day that there was a real panic over garotting. While the language of the day is rather less sensationalized than might be found in the popular press today, it is worth quoting at some length from letters to *The Times* to illustrate this reaction and panic.

> On Saturday, the 1st inst., when returning home at night, and as usual walking quick, I was, without any warning, suddenly seized from behind by some one, who, placing the bend of his arm to my throat, and then clasping his right wrist with his left-hand, thereby forming a powerful lever, succeeded in effectually strangling me for a time, and rendering me incapable of moving or even calling for assistance . . . whilst a second man easily rifled me of all he could find. I was then violently thrown to the ground, or rather I found myself lying there when I came to my senses . . . Now, this robbery was committed on one of the most frequented highways out of London, viz., Hampstead-road . . . and I am convinced that an application of this human garotte to an elderly person, or anyone in a bad state of health, might very easily occasion death.
>
> (Letter to *The Times*, 12 February 1851)

Observing in your paper of to-day a letter from a gentleman who was nearly strangled and robbed of his watch by this abominable practice, I think it right to say that about a month since I was treated in exactly a similar manner. This was also in a public thoroughfare, and within a few yards of a public house that was open.

(Letter to *The Times*, 17 July 1851)

I wish to add my testimony to that already given in your paper with respect to the cowardly system of Thugee now being carried on in the streets of London. About three weeks back I was returning home along the Haymarket about 12 o'clock at night, and, having occasion to turn aside up a court, I was suddenly seized round the throat by one ruffian, while another snatched my watch and struck me on the head . . . rendering me senseless.

(Letter to *The Times*, 19 July 1851)

As mentioned, in response to this street crime, *Punch* magazine published cartoons and adverts promoting protection from garotters (see advert in question break on p. 60). There was also a boom in the security/protection business with people offering their services as bodyguards, as illustrated in the following advert:

The Bayswater Brothers (whose height is respectively 6 feet 4 inches and 6 feet 11, and the united breadth of whose shoulders extends to as much as 3 yards, 1 foot, 5 inches) give, respectfully, notice to the Gentry and Public of Paddington, Kensington, Stoke Newington, Chelsea, Eaton Square and Shepherd's Bush, that they will be most happy, upon all social and jovial expeditions, such as dinner and evening parties, as well as tee-total meetings, to escort elderly or nervous persons in the streets after dark, and to wait for them during their pleasure, so as to be able to escort them home again in safety. No suburb, however dangerous, objected to, and the worst garotting districts well known, as the Brothers, both BILL and JIM, were for several months in the police force. Terms, so much per head per hour, according to the person's walk of life. A considerable reduction on taking a party of twelve or more. Distance no object. Testimonials, and ample security given. For further particulars, Apply to B.B, Royal Human Society, Trafalgar Square.

(*Punch*, 31 January 1857)

However, the reaction was not limited to the press; and the panic over this form of street crime led to hard-line approaches from politicians, as ever seeking public approval for being tough on crime. In particular, there was a call for a return to harsh physical punishment, such as flogging – a call that was reflected in the passing of the Garotters' Act in 1863. Although the Garotters' Act was not merely the result of the panic, it is clear that this new crime provided the impetus for such legislation. The Act also reflected a move away from the more reformative, humanitarian approach to punishment and imprisonment that had characterized the early nineteenth-century period (for instance, the religious emphasis on prisoners doing penance and emerging with purified souls, highlighted by John Howard and the early prison reformers of that period); and a consequent support for a more hard-line, repressive approach to dealing with criminals. Flogging, for example, had long been associated with the public school system and with life in the army and navy, and was widely supported by politicians and other leaders of the period, who had, of course, passed through those institutions themselves.

Certainly, the Garotters' Act, and the flogging of garotters, chimed with the mood of the day, as indicated in the following contemporary comment:

> A parliamentary return just issued affords us the gratifying information that the Garotter's Act of 1863, punishing attempts at robbery, accompanied by violence, with flogging, has not been allowed to remain a dead letter. In the first year of the operation of this salutary measure, under its beneficent provisions, according to the document above referred to, 19 prisoners were flogged in England . . .
>
> There are objections to public flogging . . . But one thing might be done to give the roughs, who are inclined to be Garotters, some idea of what the flogging inflicted on a Garotter is. An elaborate photograph of the face of every such criminal condemned to be flogged taken whilst he is experiencing the sensation excited by the scourge, at the moment when his features are contorted with their strongest expression. What a pretty portrait-gallery might thus have been derived from the nineteen Garotters who were flogged in 1863!
>
> (*Punch*, 8 April 1865)

QUESTION BREAK

Consider the letters to *The Times* above and the example of an advert for the 'anti-garotte' collar below.

DO YOU WISH TO AVOID BEING STRANGLED!!

IF so, try our Patent Antigarotte Collar, which enables Gentlemen to walk the streets of London in perfect safety at all hours of the day or night.

THESE UNIQUE ARTICLES OF DRESS

Are made to measure, of the hardest steel, and are warranted to withstand the grip of

THE MOST MUSCULAR RUFFIAN IN THE METROPOLIS,

Who would get black in the face himself before he could make the slightest impression upon his intended victim. They are highly polished and

Elegantly Studded with the Sharpest Spikes,

Thus combining a most *recherché* appearance with perfect protection from the murderous attacks which occur every day in the most frequented thoroughfares. Price 7s. 6d, or six for 40s.

WHITE, CHOKER, AND Co.

(*Punch*, 27 September 1856)

- How would you describe the way that the media portrays young people today?
- How might the crime of garotting be reported in contemporary newspapers?
- The 1860s was a very different society from today. From your knowledge of history, do you feel that London and other large cities at this period of time would be safer places to walk around at night than such cities nowadays? Give reasons for your answer.

The European witch craze

Although not limited to a short period of time, as with the examples of moral panics looked at so far, and in line with the definition offered by Cohen, there were elements of the European witch craze of the sixteenth and seventeenth centuries which merit it being considered as an early, historical example of this phenomenon. As mentioned at the start of this chapter, general usage of the term moral panic is only relatively recent. In his classic study of the European witch craze, Trevor-Roper (1967) saw it as part of a 'general crisis' and he was very clear that his subject of study was the 'witch craze' and not the belief in witches. He was interested in the inflammation and incorporation of the belief in witches into a 'bizarre, but coherent intellectual system which, at certain socially determined times, gave to otherwise unorganized peasant credulity a centrally directed, officially blessed persecuting force' (Trevor-Roper 1967, p. 9). Beliefs in witches and the casting of spells have occurred throughout history and in societies throughout the world; the 'witch craze' refers to the organized and systematic 'demonology' which Trevor-Roper suggested that the medieval Church constructed out of those beliefs and which, at this time in history, seemed to gather a momentum of its own.

While there was no definite starting date for the European witch craze, from the sixteenth century many Europeans developed a growing concern over the phenomenon of witchcraft, often seeing it as a sort of hostile and anti-Christian sect. This was reflected in governments, and local communities, organizing 'hunts' for alleged witches – accusing, torturing and executing thousands of people, almost exclusively women. The belief that women were sinful and had the power of the devil within them had developed from previous centuries – women were seen as having the ability to summon the devil for sexual intercourse. Most people accused of witchcraft were single women, usually poor and the hunts have been seen as an attempt to keep women 'in their place'. The witch-hunts were often instigated by hysterical women and children who accused relatives and neighbours of outrageous crimes, with witnesses bribed or threatened in order to prosecute the accused.

As these witch-hunts increased so the confessions drawn from supposed witches became more detailed. And, as Trevor-Roper points out, it was hardly surprising that confessions were almost always secured from those accused of being witches:

> The ordinary rules of evidence, like the ordinary limits of torture, were suspended ... And the circumstantial evidence need not be very cogent: it was sufficient to discover a wart, by which the familiar spirit was suckled; an insensitive spot which did not bleed when pricked ... or an incapacity to shed tears. Recourse could even be had to 'lighter indicia', such as a tendency to look down when accused, sign of fear, or the mere aspect of a witch, old, ugly or smelly. Any of these ... might justify the use of torture to produce the confession, which was proof, or the refusal to confess, which was even more cogent proof and justified even more ferocious tortures and nastier death.
>
> (1967, p. 45)

The witch trials were run by genuine believers in witchcraft and their aim seemed to be to exterminate witches as evil conspirators who worked with the devil. Perhaps the largest witch-hunt in Europe was held between 1645 and 1647 in East Anglia and led by Matthew Hopkins, a self-appointed Witchfinder General (see question break below for more information on Hopkins and his witch-hunting). Witch-hunting spread in England after 1542 after the passing of a statute against witchcraft, with estimates of 1,000 people, mostly women, being hanged for practising witchcraft. Women were invariably accused of witchcraft – they were seen as the weaker sex and more liable to fall under the spell of the devil.

Once established, the stereotype of the witch created its own folklore, which then became a centralizing force in establishing the craze or panic, as with other stereotypes linked with moral panics. As Trevor-Roper puts it: 'Once the folk-lore had been created and had been impressed by the clergy upon every mind, it served as a psychological as well as a social stereotype' (1967, p. 120).

Various theoretical explanations have been offered for the European witch craze and it would be useful to mention some of these briefly. In providing an overview of the main historical theories, Pavlac (2006) suggested there were 'ten general historical theories'. Here, we will mention those that relate to the notion of moral panic. Mass hysteria theory saw witchcraft as a sort of illness and that certain peasants became clinically neurotic and even psychotic over witchcraft and in a group panic went after witches – with sources of the panic including illnesses that seemed to have no cause. A more conspiratorial explanation saw devil worshipping as existing as a subversive attack on the ruling Christian order and church, with the tortured confessions of witches taken at their word. Witchcraft was also seen as a continuation of pagan religions that was misinterpreted by Christian witch-hunters as satanic.

More sociologically based theoretical explanations include the argument that witch-hunts can be beneficial for a society as they help define what is right and wrong, what is acceptable and unacceptable, and so help to reinforce social boundaries or moral, acceptable behaviour. This positive approach, a social functionalist position, contrasts with more critical, social control explanations, suggesting that governments of the period exploited the fear of witchcraft in order to centralize authority and expand government intervention.

Of course, this brief account has only provided a very general overview. The intensity, duration and viciousness of witch-hunts and trials varied from place to place. The witch craze itself died out in the later seventeenth century, with the weakening in the absolute power of the Church and clergy, the Enlightenment period and the developments in science.

QUESTION BREAK

Witchfinder General

During the period of the witch craze, an Essex man, Matthew Hopkins, became known as the Witchfinder General. Hopkins was an East Anglian lawyer who made it his mission to rid that area of witches. He waged a crusade against witches and his notoriety spread far and wide. Hopkins earned a fortune from his activity – up to 20 shillings a witch (compared to the average wage of two pence a day). Historians have suggested he was allowed to carry on virtually uncontrolled because of the civil war, a time of general religious and political upheaval and chaos. By about 1647, people were becoming tired of Hopkins's behaviour and he returned to his home town of Manningtree, Essex and died in that year. A film made about him, starring Vincent Price and released in 1968, has become a cult horror classic. Although only a low budget film, the magazine *Total Film* named it the fifteenth greatest horror film ever made.

Consider the questions that follow on the brief account of Matthew Hopkins and his activities.

Matthew Hopkins's reign of terror lasted from 1645 to 1647. Little seems to be known of Matthew Hopkins prior to his becoming the self-appointed Witchfinder General. One of the first cases instigated by him was against Elizabeth Clarke. She was apparently a one-legged widow and Hopkins soon had a confession out of her stating she was familiar with her 'familiars' – generally considered to be demons in the guise of animals or pets (cats, goats and so on). Women were often searched for a third teat as proof of satanic connections – as this third teat enabled them to nurture demons. Other signs were from various marks that might be on the body – beauty spots or even slight skin imperfections. In all it is suspected Hopkins was directly or indirectly associated with as many as 200 executions of witches.

▌ RECENT MORAL PANICS

There is a danger that the notion of media panic can be applied somewhat indis-criminately to all sorts of quite transient examples of youthful behaviour and/or delinquency; and in our discussion we are keen to keep the focus on the social reac-tion as led by the mass media. Having said that, there have been many recent exam-ples of youthful behaviour that could be considered as having produced a moral panic. In his book that focused solely on the media and moral panics, Critcher (2003) discussed a range of such recent examples, including the rave/ecstasy culture of the late 1980s and early 1990s, the reaction to video nasties in the 1980s and 1990s, new age travellers in the mid-1980s and, periodically, child abuse in families. Of course not all of those examples relate just to youth. In the next section, we will discuss one more recent example, the panic surrounding 'hoodies', and we will relate this to the more general concerns and panics over youthful behaviour. Then we will finish the chapter by looking at one of the examples of moral panics that was exam-ined by Critcher, paedophilia, and briefly consider this in relation to the recent sexual abuse allegations made against Jimmy Savile and other media celebrities.

Hoodies

A recent example of a style of dress worn by young people, rather than what could be termed a youth subculture, that has excited some degree of panic and paranoia amongst the wider population, has been the wearing of hooded sweatshirts, or hoodies. Of course, hoods on garments of clothing have been worn throughout history, with images of monks in the Middle Ages wearing hooded cowls coming to mind. Hooded jackets were particularly popularized in the 1970s as part of the hip-hop music scene and as a result of being worn by Sylvester Stallone in the *Rocky* films. However, it was not until the 1990s that the term 'hoodies' was generally used to describe these garments, when they became associated with the emergence of what were termed 'chavs', disaffected working-class youths, in this country; and were spread by their use by young skateboarders. And it was not until 2005 that the press and public were referring to the 'hoodie culture'.

It is particularly in the UK that hoodies have been regarded and reacted to in such a negative way – exemplified in them being banned from shopping centres such as the Bluewater retail park in Kent. This banning of hoodies and baseball caps (officially stated as 'wearing clothing that obscures the face – hooded tops, baseball caps – will not be allowed') brought the hoodie culture into the public arena; and raised the irony of shoppers being prevented from wearing an article that was still on sale in shops within the centre. The move was, though, welcomed by many, including the then prime minister, Tony Blair, and the deputy prime minister, John Prescott, who saw it as an attempt to clamp down on antisocial and threatening behaviour. By contrast, 'defence' for the wearing of hoodies came from the leader of the opposition at the time, David Cameron, who suggested the hoodie was not worn as an offensive act. In a speech made in July 2006, which was parodied by the government as the 'hug a hoodie' speech, Cameron said:

> In May last year hoodies became political . . . The Bluewater shopping centre banned them and the Prime Minister said he backed the ban . . .
>
> But debating the symptoms rather than the cause won't get us very far. Because the fact is that the hoodie is a response to a problem, not a problem in itself . . . For young people, hoodies are often more defensive than offensive. They're a way to stay invisible in the street. In a dangerous environment the best thing to do is keep your head down, blend in, don't stand out . . .
>
> For some the hoodie represents all that's wrong about youth culture in Britain today. For me, adult society's response to the hoodie shows how far we are from the long-term answer to put things right.
>
> (BBC News, 10 July 2006)

The banning of hoodies from the Bluewater shopping centre in 2005 excited a great deal of media interest and debate. It led to the 'meaning' of the hoodie being examined by journalists and academics. As Gareth McLean (2005) pointed out, although only a sweatshirt with a bit extra, the hooded top strikes fear into the heart on most people, 'a lone figure behind us on the walk home – hood up, head down – and we quicken our step . . . a group of hooded teenagers on the street and we're tensing our shoulders, clenching our fists'. His article in *The Guardian* reports the vice-chair of the British Youth Council, Rachel Harrington, as saying that the Bluewater ban 'demonstrates a growing demonization of young people . . . and over-reacting to any behaviour by young people'. While Angela McRobbie is cited in *The Guardian* (Ainley 2005) as highlighting the hoodies' anonymity and air of mystery as explaining its appeal and also the anxiety it produces in others. She goes on to say that:

> leisurewear and sportswear adopted for everyday wear suggests a distance from the world of office (suit) or school (uniform) . . . (The hooded top) is one in a long line of garments chosen by young people, usually boys, and inscribed with meanings suggesting that they are 'up to no good'. In the past, such appropriation was usually restricted to membership of specific youth cultures – leather jackets, bondage trousers – but nowadays it is the norm among young people to flag up their music and cultural preferences in this way, hence the adoption of the hoodie by boys across the boundaries of age, ethnicity and class.

Ainley (2005) makes the point that the moral panic over hoodies is almost a continuation of a previous panic over chavs – working class, white boys who had underachieved in school and who, in the face of a bleak future in terms of respectable employment, turn to antisocial, delinquent behaviour. Of course, we have been here many times before, from the Victorian garotting mentioned earlier, through a variety of (typically) male working-class youth subcultures. And, as before, the rest of society resents and fears such groups; as Ainley puts it, the 'respectable working middle class live in fear and loathing of the hooded, chav "underclass"'. Indeed, it was this resentment and response that led to the banning of hoodies from the Bluewater centre; and it was a response not just from 'respectable' society but from other teenagers:

> Street rats, says Ainsley, 17. 'That's what they're called.' 'They sit on the streets and drink', explains Lauren, 16 . . . The teenagers from Bexleyheath describe the disrespectful youths of today as they glide along the Bluewater shopping centre in Kent. Street rats wear hooded tops and baseball caps.
>
> (Barkham 2005)

The moral panic about hoodies was part of a wider concern about the antisocial behaviour of youths and, as with other panics, the reaction has been criticized by academics and those working in the criminal justice system as excessive. As Shapland (cited in Barkham 2005) commented, 'I'm not sure if it's always a good idea to see youth as a problem . . . Hooded tops are a problem if you are relying on cameras and policing at a distance rather than face-to-face personal security.' While, in a report in *The Guardian*, Barkham refers to the director of the Crime and Society Foundation think tank, Richard Garside, suggesting that the government's drive for respect could amplify perceptions of antisocial youths and to the West Midlands Police service complaining that they are being inundated with calls from the public about 'innocuous antisocial behaviour'.

Raising the spectre that society is in danger of creating 'folk devils' out of Hoodies, Rod Morgan, chair of the Youth Justice Board, advises against extreme responses, asking:

> Would we be wise to exacerbate the problem by making certain forms of dress or behaviour even more attractive by damning them? We have to be careful we don't demonize them. Having said that, if young people are engaged in serious anti-social behaviour, destroying the quality of life in neighbourhoods, it needs to be dealt with.
>
> (Barkham 2005)

However, in spite of the differing political comments around the reaction to hoodies, the media reporting of 'hoodie culture' has been both hostile and scare-mongering, in line with the way the media has responded to other, previous moral panics. Even though at the same time as exciting this hostile reaction, the hoodie is a widely popular item of clothing that is in the wardrobes of millions of people, and is sold in the millions by firms such as Nike, Adidas and Gap. As the examples below indicate, recent murder cases have referred to the hoodie in their headlines, irrespective of whether this was a key aspect of the particular crime:

Justice for Dad Killed Tackling Hoodies

A teenager was facing life in jail last night for shooting dead a young father who stood up to a gang of hoodies.

(Daily Express, 28 March 2007)

Named: The 'Hoodie who shot dead Rhys'

. . . Rhys was shot dead in a pub car park in Croxteth Park, Liverpool, more than two months ago as he walked home from football practice with two friends. Police believe the hooded gunman was firing at a rival gang but missed and hit innocent Rhys.

(Daily Express, 30 October 2007)

In similar vein, reporting of the August 2011 riots linked the rioting behaviour with hoodies:

Reflection on London Riots: The Real Danger of Hoodies and Folk Devils

Those who were following the London riots must have seen protesters dressed in hooded sweatshirts. They were basically everywhere. The mere sight of hooded young boys was enough to spark moral panic.

(Jakarta Globe, 23 August 2011)

QUESTION BREAK

In his report on teenage hoodies, Barkham highlights how older people have always commented critically and negatively on the behaviour of youth. And how these older people often forget that they were involved in behaviour that was reacted to and panicked over in similar vein.

'There isn't the respect now that there used to be', says a pensioner, Wendy Wadeson, from leafy Pratt's Bottom, near Bromley . . . Her husband Colin says: 'In the evening when you're out and there's a group of youngsters in a dark area it can be threatening'.

When asked if they were mods or rockers in their youth, Mr Wadeson responded: 'Mods, I suppose' and when asked if he went to Brighton where the Mods and Rockers clashed: 'Oh, there were those days. People were drawn into it. It's easily done'.

(Barkham 2005)

QUESTIONS

- Why do you think older generations feel that 'things were better in their day'?
- From your knowledge of previous and current youth subcultures, do you feel that recent examples of antisocial behaviour from young people are more serious?

As mentioned above, the panic over hoodies reflected a more general concern and panic over youthful behaviour, a concern which goes back throughout history. Indeed in discussing youth and crime it is commonplace to hear references to 'feral youth' and 'feral children'. Feral children have been a subject of fascination (and fantasy) for hundreds of years. Essentially a feral child is a human child who has lived away from human contact from a very young age and has received little or no human care, love or language. There have been hundreds of reported cases of such children.

In recent years it has become almost fashionable for young criminals and delinquents to be called 'feral youth'; and for their offending and antisocial behaviour to be explained in terms of lack of sustained (and proper) human care and contact. For instance, the *Daily Mail* reported on research from Cambridge University which suggested it was not opportunity that makes the thief but rather (lack of) morality under the headline: 'Truth about Britain's Feral Youth: Small Core of Youngsters Commit Staggering 86 crimes by age 16' (*Daily Mail*, 24 June 2012).

The article referred to the study's findings that, out of a sample of 700 teenagers, a tiny minority of 3.8 per cent of teenagers committed 47 per cent of the 16,000 juvenile crimes examined. When asked about their attitudes to crime and what offences they had committed, a lack of moral compass, rather than opportunity to commit crime or social background, was seen as the most important factor in youthful law-breaking.

Although critical of this view of youth, a survey by the charity Barnado's in 2011 found that although the majority of children were well behaved, of the more than 2,000 people questioned, 44 per cent said young people were becoming feral and 49 per cent felt children were 'beginning to behave like animals' ('Many Adults Think Children are "Feral", Survey Finds', BBC News Online, 3 November 2011). The Barnado's charity itself said that young people who end up in custody often come from difficult backgrounds and the Barnado's project worker who commissioned the report, Natasha Cripps, said the use of the word 'feral' indicates a 'complete desertion of young people' and that 'to us that word feral is really quite scary', adding 'it's easy to demonise young people and use them as a scapegoat for social difficulties'. Barnado's chief executive, Anne Marie Carrie commented that, 'we seem to have forgotten the fact that most children are well behaved and . . . are unquestionably accepting a stereotype of young people as criminal and revolting'.

Paedophilia

In his discussion of paedophilia as a moral panic, Critcher (2003) that there are few academic and secondary sources of information on paedop... that an examination of newspaper coverage is the clearest way of showing how the panic emerged and developed. He categorizes various phases of this development, even though the term paedophilia was rarely used before the 1990s. First, in the late 1970s and early 1980s, the term was introduced in relation to child pornography and the notion of organized paedophile rings. By the later 1980s, he argues that paedophiles became associated with the abduction and murder of children, illustrated by the police investigation 'operation stranger' into 14 children who were murdered or missing between 1978 and 1986. The panic surrounding this crime peaked in the 1990s, fuelled by the media coverage of sexual offences against children in Ireland and, later, Belgium. The Irish context involved the publicity over Roman Catholic priests who were accused of sexual offences against children; while a 'bigger surge in coverage' concerned the case of the Belgium paedophile, Marc Dutroux. Dutroux was given early release, in 1992, from a thirteen-and-a-half year prison sentence he received in 1989. Subsequently he kidnapped, tortured and sexually abused six girls aged between 8 and 19, four of whom died. He was arrested in 1996 and has been in prison since. This case sparked public outrage in Belgium and led to the tightening of the parole criteria for convicted sex offenders, partly as a result of public pressure – indeed in October 1996 more than 300,000 people dressed in white marched through Brussels, the capital, demanding major reforms of the judicial system.

By the late 1990s, the press coverage of paedophilia reached what might be termed moral panic level. Critcher cites 25 headlines referring to child abusers and paedophiles in one month in one newspaper, the *Daily Mail*. He cites a *Daily Mail* editorial arguing against the release of paedophiles, asking 'what kind of law is it that plays Russian roulette with the lives of our children?' (13 March 1998). By 2000, the coverage of paedophilia in the British press had reached unprecedented levels following the sexual murder of Sarah Payne, an eight-year-old girl who had been missing for two weeks. Photographs and stories about Sarah and her anguished family appeared every day in the media; and following the discovery of her body thousands of people made their way to the field to lay wreaths. This murder, in July 2000, encouraged a media-orchestrated outcry, led by the *News of the World*.

The role of the *News of the World* in promoting the moral panic over paedophiles is worth considering briefly. This paper is part of Rupert Murdoch's News International corporation and, along with *The Sun* and other tabloid papers, was a vociferous supporter of and campaigner for hard-line measures being taken against criminals. Following the murder of Sarah Payne, it campaigned to force the Labour government to introduce stricter sentences against sex offenders. Using the fact, that, as a result of the 1997 Sex Offenders Act, sex offenders have to register their names and addresses with the police, the *News of the World* started to publish the names, photographs and approximate whereabouts of 200 individuals on the Sex Offenders Register. Although the police and welfare agencies warned that such a practice might well endanger children by driving sex offenders into hiding, it continued to publish the list as, it put it, a matter of 'public concern'. The *News of the World* claimed that there were thousands of paedophiles preying on young children and was joined by other papers demanding action against paedophiles. As a front-page article in the *Daily Mirror* put it, 'Hanging these bastards really is too good for them.' The panic orchestrated by the British press encouraged an atmosphere that sparked a series of brutal attacks on suspected paedophiles. The violence and lynch mob atmosphere on the Paulsgrove housing estate in Portsmouth led to prolonged rioting and innocent families being forced out of their homes and into hiding. Elsewhere in the country, a number of people were wrongly identified as sex offenders and subjected to arson attacks on their homes. And, rather than condemning the *News of the World*, the government, aware of the panic and mood of the general population, organized compromise meetings with the paper, relatives of Sarah Payne and children's agencies. As Hyland (2000) argues, even though sex abuse is a matter of great concern, 'this does not legitimize the hysteria over predatory paedophiles being whipped up by the media . . . all this has accomplished is to induce panic and fear amongst many parents'. (The question break below considers the *News of the World*'s 'name and shame' campaign.)

In a detailed study of the 'Paulsgrove riot', Williams and Thompson (2004) highlighted a number of problems and inaccuracies with the media accounts of it. After a year-long ethnographic study, they found that the Paulsgrove 'riots' were not provoked by the *News of the World*'s campaign. The residents of the estate had planned a peaceful demonstration to express concerns about Victor Burnett, an offender who had been exposed by the *News of the World* and whom residents had previously complained about. It was the failure of the authorities to act upon these complaints that led to a peaceful demonstration against the local housing department. Williams and Thompson concluded that:

> While some of the marches saw clashes with the police; what is important . . . is to note that the demonstrators were neither out to cause personal injury or damage property, as was commonly alleged; and they were not vigilantes. Contrary to what the press assert . . . no one, paedophiles or 'innocent' residents, was personally attacked.

There was evidence that some teenagers did throw stones at some houses, but there was no planned attack on anyone, paedophile or otherwise. And no one was arrested, charged or convicted of such an act either.

QUESTION BREAK

The following extracts refer to the *News of the World*'s campaign in 2000 to 'name and shame' paedophiles in response to the murder of Sarah Payne; and subsequent 'naming and shaming' in *The Sun*. Read them before considering the questions below.

In response to the murder of Sarah Payne, the News of the World *'named and shamed' scores of people it said were guilty of sex offences against children . . .*

'If you are a parent you must read this', said Sunday's News of the World. *The tabloid newspaper went on to publish the names and photographs of dozens of people it said had perpetrated sex attacks on children. Some 88 per cent of us want parents to be told when a convicted paedophile moves in to their area, says a poll commissioned by the paper.*

Since September 1997, moves have been made to monitor the whereabouts of convicted sex offenders. However, the information is restricted to the appropriate police force, the probation service and the local MP. Under the Sex Offenders Act, those found guilty of crimes such as rape are obliged to report their name and address to a local police station within 14 days of their conviction or release from custody . . .

Anyone failing to register risks a six-month prison term or a £5,000 fine. The register contains some 12,000 names; a compliance rate of 97 per cent says Tony Butler, of the Association of Chief Police Officers . . .

Some 250,000 Britons have been convicted of a sexual offence – 110,000 have targeted children. However, those convicted or released before 1997 are not compelled to join the register. Nor are those given conditional discharges for more minor sexual offences, such as the possession of child pornography.

Pressure groups, such as End Child Prostitution, Pornography and Trafficking (Ecpat), also complain that the register fails to include Britons convicted of sex crimes abroad. Also, names on the register are not shared with foreign authorities if the offender decides to leave the country, says Helen Veitch of Ecpat. 'The monitoring process falls down when the offender goes overseas . . .'

Despite its plans to tighten controls, the government remains adamant that it will not follow the American lead, and give the public access to its register . . . However, American courts are concerned leaks of the names, addresses and car registration numbers are all too common . . .

Naming and shaming can also tar the innocent. The Daily Mail *reports a Manchester man was wrongly targeted by a mob following the* News of the World *campaign. With many paedophiles targeting children within their own family, public notification may also stop many victims from seeking a conviction in the first place, according to the American Civil Liberties Union. 'One reason attacks are not reported is the shame'. Perhaps not the 'shame' the* News of the World *was hoping to produce.*

(BBC News, Monday 24 July 2000, http://news.bbc.co.uk/2/hi/uk_
news/848759.stm)

Executives of the News of the World *have agreed to meet police and probation chiefs who have led criticism of its campaign to publish the names and photographs of paedophiles. The newspaper denied it was giving ground last night and issued a robust statement saying that it would give an audience to its critics tomorrow but if necessary restate the objectives of its campaign. However, an article published in yesterday's* News of the World *acknowledged that police chiefs and others had 'valid reasons' for opposing the publication of paedophiles' names and addresses in newspapers and said their expert opinion would be listened to.*

Ahead of the meeting, requested by Tony Butler, Chief Constable of Gloucester and the police chiefs' spokesman on child protection, probation officers led a fresh attack on the newspaper by accusing it of driving sex offenders underground. The Association of Chief Probation Officers (Acop) wrote a letter of complaint, copied to the Press Complaints Commission, claiming the 'naming and shaming' of sex offenders was hindering work to supervise offenders by driving them underground. The tactic also risked identifying innocent relatives of offenders and encouraged violence, Acop said . . .

The National Association for the Care and Resettlement of Offenders (Nacro) backed up the accusation by saying driving paedophiles underground was counter-productive and actually heightened the risk that they would re-offend . . .

Ministers also appealed to the newspaper to heed police warnings that it was better that sex offenders remained at registered addresses where they could be monitored by officers. Chris Smith, the Secretary of State for Culture, Media and Sport, said he was 'very worried' by the public naming of paedophiles although he recognized it was done with the 'noble motive' of protecting children . . . Paul Boateng, a Home Office Minister, also warned against creating a 'climate of fear' and emphasised the need to avoid 'panic and hysteria'.

(The Independent, 31 July 2000)

The Sun *has been forced to make an embarrassing apology after naming and shaming the wrong man as a sex offender. Owing to a mix up by a picture agency, the tabloid mistakenly used a photograph of David Gazley in place of a picture of Christopher Harris, who has been banned from going near children for life after groping young girls in Great Yarmouth. An apology to Mr Gazley – whose portrait appeared in Saturday's* Sun *above the headline 'Face of kid ban pervert' – is published in the tabloid today. 'We sincerely apologise to Mr Gazley for the hurt and embarrassment caused by our report', said the newspaper.*

Rebekah Wade, who replaced David Yelland as editor of The Sun *in January, pioneered a 'name and shame' campaign against convicted sex offenders when she was editor of the tabloid's Sunday stable mate, the* News of the World. *The campaign fought under the banner 'Sarah's Law', following the murder of eight-year-old Sarah Payne, aimed to name all 110,000 sex offenders in Britain in a bid to change the law to give public access to the Sex Offenders Register. However, critics said Wade's campaign was responsible for inciting mob violence and forcing paedo-philes to go into hiding.*

(The Guardian, 31 March 2003)

- List the arguments for and against the media publicizing the names and personal details of convicted sex offenders. (Try to think of beneficial and negative effects for the victims and the wider public.)
- What dangers with the over-publicizing of crimes and criminals are indicated by the extracts? Can you think of any others?

Critcher (2003) finishes his account by considering whether the notion of moral panic can be applied to paedophilia, in particular given the prolonged nature of the panic. Certainly paedophilia does meet all the major aspects and criterion of a moral panic – there are identifiable 'folk devils'; there is widespread agreement, and strong emotional passions, amongst the public, media and politicians about the extent and danger of such behaviour. However, the focus on the 'folk devil' paedophile as a stranger who preys on children does not present an accurate picture of the variable nature of sexual offenders. Although 'stranger danger' seems to be the biggest worry for parents, and while it is this aspect of sexual offending that excites media and public opinion, it is well established that it is abuse within the family, or by an adult who is trusted by the child, that is the most common form of sexual abuse and offending. The numbers of children abducted and killed in Britain by a stranger have remained at between five and ten annually for many years, with a very small percentage of sex offenders falling into the category of predatory paedophiles. As Critcher points out, the paedophile label contributes little to our understanding of the frequency or nature of sexual abuse, 'moral panics distort our capacity for understanding, even when they appear to recognize a genuine problem'.

In a recent study that highlights the difficulties with categorizing and applying taxonomies to popular fears, Cavanagh (2007) looks at the panic around Internet paedophilia. As we have seen, a demonized group or individual (the folk devil) is a central aspect of the phenomenon of a moral panic, and the scapegoating of those people involved acts to reaffirm the communal boundaries of the wider group or society. In applying this to Internet paedophilia, Cavanagh recognizes that there is a recognizable folk devil in the form of a 'shadowy paedophile lurking in the chatroom to seduce the unwary'; there are also various other 'candidates for blame'. For instance, there are the Internet service providers and the issue of whether commercial bodies should share some responsibility for regulating what is available on the Internet. And should the state and other institutions be blamed for failing to police the problem?

As Internet paedophilia, and paedophilia in general, became more widely reported and panicked about, there emerged moral entrepreneurs who aimed to channel public support against the folk devils. Groups such as Internet watch and child welfare organizations, along with more traditional moral entrepreneurs such as the churches, emerged alongside technical experts as spokespeople against the new threat. Indeed, fears about the specific illegal materials provided on the Internet merged with fears of the Internet in general as an invasive and addictive media (see Chapter 7 for a fuller discussion of cybercrime).

Concerns over paedophilia and the sexual abuse of children hit the media headlines in late 2012 with sexual allegations made against the former TV personality Sir Jimmy Savile. Revelations about Jimmy Savile's sexual offences against children and youths, including rape, came to light in October 2012. It transpired that Savile had been committing serious sexual offences for many years, stretching back to

the 1950s and until shortly before his death in 2011. However, partly due to his status and position, Savile was knighted in 1990 for his services to charities, allegations and complaints against him were ignored or not followed up with any conviction for years. Indeed an investigation into sexual abuse claims against Jimmy Savile which was being prepared for a documentary for Newsnight on BBC1 for airing in 2011 was dropped on the advice of its editors, due to the supposed lack of evidence.

Complaints and allegations against Savile were followed up in 2012 under 'Operation Yewtree' and their findings were reported in a joint report from the Metropolitan Police and the NSPCC (Gray and Watt 2013). The report, entitled 'Giving Victims a Voice', detailed the almost unbelievable extent of Savile's sexual offending. In its concluding remarks the report commented that: 'Jimmy Savile was one of the UK's most prolific known sexual predators. Indeed the formal recording of allegations of crime on this scale is, to the best of our knowledge, unprecedented in the UK.' Overall the police said that Savile committed more than 200 sex crimes, including 34 rapes, over more than half a century and all over the country, with most of the victims children and teenagers.

REVISITING THE NOTION OF MORAL PANICS

In this chapter we have considered a range of behaviours and reactions to them under the broad term of moral panics; and there are many more examples that we might have looked at. In doing this, we have used the notion of moral panic very broadly and in concluding it would be useful to say something about the term. At the start of the chapter we said that moral panic is a well-established term; however, that does not mean it is a clear-cut one. In a recent paper on the panic surrounding paedophilia and the Internet, Cavanagh (2007) makes the point that 'applying taxonomies to popular fears' is a task fraught with difficulty. Indeed, the term has been used so indiscriminately by the media that it has become almost 'a term of abuse to refer to the activities of journalists . . . so the idea of a moral panic is elaborated as an elaborate media scam, a deliberate attempt to "spin" social problems.' What Cavanagh is suggesting is that the moral panic has become a regular aspect of media reporting of antisocial and criminal behaviour, so that 'moral panics are a direct product of the mundane practices of journalists'. The essential point here is that public anxieties and concerns are only able to take on a public form through the media.

Nonetheless, there are key elements apparent in any moral panic. As Cavanagh (2007) puts it, the moral panic reflects social anxieties and concerns about behaviour that is seen as some sort of moral threat. The concerns are then exaggerated in regard to both scale and frequency, they are symbolized in terms of them being a threat to traditional values and are emphasized by groups of 'moral entrepreneurs' who reframe the particular problem in terms of the solutions that they favour. And it is important to be aware that moral panics are not myths but are the result of actual behaviour and real events. So the analysis of moral panics 'is focused on the observation of distortion and exaggeration in presentation of this factual problem'.

The idea of a moral panic is based on their being a disproportionate reaction to the particular behaviour and event(s), as Goode and Ben-Yehuda (1994) comment, 'the concept of moral panic rests on disproportionality'. In this chapter the various examples we have considered certainly all fit this description.

However, and in relation to this notion of disproportionality, there may be occasions when the reaction to particular criminal behaviour may well be justified. Indeed when considering whether the term moral panic is applicable when the behaviour, for instance paedophilia, is a real and serious criminal offence or when there is a massive number of instances of such behaviour it could be argued that the 'panic' is justified – in other words the reaction may not be disproportionate. In this context, Coward (2012), when commenting on the Jimmy Savile case and particularly the fact that Savile's behaviour was to some extent protected because of his celebrity status (see above), highlighted how paedophilia did not always get taken as seriously as it might. He referred to a complaint he had made about a glowing tribute that had been printed in *The Guardian* newspaper to a well-respected musician who had been found guilty of sexual abuse of children. In response to his complaint he had been told the tribute focused on the man's public life; in much the same vein as those who had complained about Jimmy Savile had been told to look at all the good things he does in public and in his charity work. Coward criticizes the view which suggests sexual abuse is an exaggerated problem and makes the point that, 'sex abuse only seems exaggerated until it affects you or people you directly know, until you see its devastating effect'.

FURTHER READING

Cohen S. (2002) *Folk Devils and Moral Panics*, 3rd edn, London: Routledge. We have referred extensively to Stan Cohen's class study in this chapter but there is nothing like reading the original. The first edition of this book was published in

1972 and the second in 1980 and either of these is well worth looking at along with the more recent third edition.

Critcher C. (2003) *Moral Panics and the Media*, Milton Keynes: Open University Press. This study critically evaluates the usefulness of moral panics models and the role of the media in creating such panics. It examines a number of case studies, including child abuse, paedophilia, video nasties and AIDS.

Goode E. and Ben-Yehuda N. (1994) *Moral Panics: The Social Construction of Deviance*, Oxford: Blackwell. This work acknowledges the importance of Cohen's work and discusses a number of different theoretical explanations for moral panics.

Young J. (1971) 'The Role of the Police as Amplifiers of Deviancy', in Cohen S. (ed.), *Images of Deviance*, Harmondsworth, UK: Penguin. This study of drug use in 1960s London looks at the role of the police in fuelling a moral panic.

The Media Portrayal of Criminals

Explanations and theories of criminal behaviour are as old as the types of behaviour themselves – debate and discussion about why people break laws have excited public interest throughout history; and most people hold their own views as to what causes such behaviour. And these views probably all contain elements of truth even without being complete explanations – so inherited defects, overcrowding and poverty, getting in with the 'wrong' crowd and poor parental supervision, have all been seen as causes of criminal behaviour. Given the massive interest in crime and criminals, and the wide range of behaviour that the term 'crime' encompasses, it is not surprising that a wide and diverse range of theoretical explanations have been put forward; and from a number of different academic disciplines, including biology, psychology, sociology and philosophy. Early theorists and researchers tended to try identifying biological and psychological causes of criminal behaviour – arguing that certain individuals are predisposed to such behaviour because of their genetic make-up. Particular criminal individuals were seen as having either inherited or developed specific characteristics that encouraged such behaviour. More recently, sociologically based theoretical explanations have focused on the social context in which crime occurs and have argued that crime and criminals can only be fully understood in relation to the social structure, to specific social conditions and processes. Theoretical explanations see the criminal as someone who is biologically, psychologically or socially different – even if their 'difference' is only by virtue of the fact that they have been caught and labelled by the criminal justice system as criminal. Before looking at how the media has portrayed criminals, the question break below asks you to consider your views of the criminal.

QUESTION BREAK

Although early theories suggesting that some people were born criminal have been rejected by more recent theorizing, the notion that there is a 'criminal type' is still widely held.

What do you consider to be the sort of characteristics that form the common perception of the 'criminal type'? (Think of both individual and social characteristics.)

Look at the list below. If you had to picture the typical criminal how would it fit each of the headings below?

* Social class
* Gender
* Ethnicity
* Age
* Location

Although we cannot predict the answers you might have given to the question above, it is a fair guess to assume that most people's picture of a 'typical criminal' would not be a middle-class, old, white woman living in a small rural village.

In this chapter, we will move away from the media portrayal of crime and look at how criminals (or more specifically those most often convicted of criminal behaviour) are represented. We will consider how the different categories of criminal are shown and reported by the media. In particular, the chapter will consider:

* The role that age plays in the portrayal of criminals; and changes over time in the way the media have reported on young offenders.
* The role that gender plays in the portrayal of criminals – how are women criminals shown and what are the main differences within the portrayal of women criminals?
* The role that ethnicity plays in the portrayal of criminals – how are black offenders shown compared to white and Asian offenders? And what about other ethnic minorities such as Eastern Europeans?
* The role of location – how different communities are portrayed by the media as being 'safe' or crime-ridden. As well as different geographical communities, we

will also look at 'virtual communities' such as Internet chat rooms and email groups.

- The role that class plays in the portrayal of criminals – comparing middle- and upper-class criminals, including corporate criminals, with working/under-class criminals.

The chapter will also consider the extent to which these areas overlap – for instance, the degree to which young, male, black, working-class people living in run-down communities particularly are prone to negative reporting and portrayal across the media.

THE MEDIA, AGE AND CRIMINALS

In this section, we will consider the ways in which the age of criminals influences media representations. Given that crime is strongly linked with age, and young people are much more likely to be convicted of crimes than other age groups, the focus will be on how young offenders, both children and youths, are portrayed. In particular, we will look at whether differences in media portrayals of criminals, and the degree of 'sympathy' for them, varies according to age – for instance, are younger offenders (and perhaps elderly offenders too) portrayed in a different manner to adult offenders? Arguably age is, on the face of it, more significant in terms of the media portrayal of victims of crime (see Chapter 5, pp. 118–121) – those victims who are seen as perhaps less able to look after themselves tend to gain greater sympathy from the public and the media than other categories of victims. So attacks on children and old people, especially old women, receive a good deal of media publicity; this emphasizes their (relatively) defenceless state and makes crime against them seem even more horrific. Here, though, we are examining the media representation of criminals and, as such, there are not the same issues of vulnerability and defencelessness, so this representation is liable to be less sympathetic.

As mentioned, the focus of this section will be on the media and young offenders; however, we will look briefly at the way elderly criminals are portrayed and if criminals who are considered to be old are shown in a different light to others. As regards youthful offenders, it seems that once an offender is classified as an adult then age is a factor which has little influence on how the media describes him or her – in other words, whether a criminal is 22 or 52, for instance, is not likely to be a major issue for the media to base their coverage around.

With regard to the media portrayal of criminals in relation to youth, we need to start by considering at what ages young criminals are portrayed differently to others. To some extent, this relates to the legal and justice systems, which treat young offenders separately to older ones – in this country, we have separate youth courts and custodial institutions for young offenders. In England and Wales, for children the age of criminal responsibility is 10 and children below that age cannot be found guilty of a criminal offence. From 10 to 18, young offenders are dealt with in separate, youth courts which are less formal in style than adult courts (and they are not open to the public as with adult courts). As Newburn (2013) puts it, 'this system reflects, in crude terms, the distinctions made between three life stages: childhood, adolescence and adulthood'.

Of course, the age of criminal responsibility is a relative concept in that it is a social construction rather than a biological fact, so it is not surprising that there has been regular debate about what is the appropriate age or that different countries and administrations have set different ages of criminal responsibility. For instance, in October 2012 the justice minister, David Ford, stated that he was 'committed to pressing for an increase in the age of criminal responsibility' (www.bbc.co.uk/news/uk-northern-ireland-20043029, 22 October 2012). He referred to a report he had commissioned to review the youth justice system in Northern Ireland which had been published in 2011 and had recommended increasing the age of criminal responsibility to 12. In similar vein, a report from the Royal Society in 2011 referred to how advances in neuroscience suggested that 10 years was too low for the age of criminal responsibility, arguing that parts of the brain connected with decision-making and judgement were still developing at that age (www.bbc.co.uk/news/uk, 13 December 2011). Indeed the age of criminal responsibility is far higher in most other European countries, for example, 12 in Holland, 13 in France, 14 in Italy, 15 in Norway and 16 in Spain. However, in other countries the age is set lower – 7 in India and also 7 in certain states of the USA. Having highlighted these differences, it is still important to consider how young offenders are dealt with by the criminal justice system.

It is not necessary to go into the development of our juvenile justice system in detail here, but some of the changes and developments have been influenced, at the very least, by public and media concern over youth offending. The notion of separating young offenders from adult offenders did not emerge until the mid-nineteenth century and the Young Offenders Act of 1854, which established reformatories for children between 7 and 14 who had been convicted of vagrancy. Juvenile courts were formalized by the 1908 Children Act and Borstals for offenders between the ages of 16 and 21 were set up at the same time. During the twentieth century, issues of child welfare came to the fore and the Children and Young Persons Acts of 1933, 1963 and 1969 emphasized the welfare and care requirements of young offenders rather than punishment. In his review of youth crime and youth justice, Newburn (2013) highlights a shift away from a welfare-based to a more punitive approach to juvenile offending in the 1980s and 1990s. The Conservative government of Margaret Thatcher adopted a very strong 'law and order' position and introduced new practices to reflect this – in 1980, for instance, the 'short, sharp, shock' treatment was introduced in detention centres, an approach which adopted a sort of quasi-militaristic approach to young offenders which emphasized hard work and discipline and aimed to instil respect for authority. This shift is illustrated by the *contemporary* media portrayal of crimes committed by young offenders. There were regular media storylines in the early 1990s over joyriding, 'certainly the press was full of stories of young people stealing cars and then using them for spectacular . . . shows of bravado', and over youngsters who were offending so regularly that they were dubbed 'one-boy crime waves' in the popular press (that being a headline used by the *Daily Mail* on 10 September 1992). This concern reached almost fever-pitch levels in 1993 after the abduction from Bootle shopping centre, Liverpool, and the subsequent murder of two-year-old Jamie Bulger. The abduction of Bulger by two young boys was captured on CCTV and shown on national television, with the subsequent arrest, charging and (later that year) conviction of two 10-year-old boys encouraging a media-led panic about young offenders (the Bulger murder and the media reaction to it is examined in more detail in Chapter 2, p. 28). Newburn (2007) notes that in the days after the trial of Thompson and Venables in November 1993, there was massive and extremely hostile media coverage – the *Daily Mail* had almost 40 stories in the three days after the trial and *The Guardian* and *The Daily Telegraph* had 22 and 23 stories respectively.

Jewkes (2004) sees the Bulger case as providing a watershed in relation to youthful offenders and criminal justice. Thomson and Venables were tried in an adult court and the case led to a massive expansion in the use of CCTV cameras in the UK (see p. 142). It also highlighted the issue of childhood – and how the significance, and even existence, of childhood has varied throughout history. Jewkes points out that 'by and large, childhood has been seen as fundamentally separate from adulthood, and children regarded as requiring nurture and protection'. As we have seen, media reporting of the conviction of Thomson and Venables emphasized the themes of childhood horror and evil rather than childhood innocence; and is seen by Jewkes as 'the apex of a wave of hysteria that, in the early 1990s, incorporated joyriders, truants, drug users, burglars, gang members and, memorably, "Ratboy", a child of 14 with a string of offences to his name who had absconded from local authority care and was reportedly living in a sewer'.

After the Labour government came to power in 1997, there were an array of new initiatives relating to youth crime, including youth offending teams, and in response to growing public and media concern over antisocial behaviour, ASBOs (Antisocial Behaviour Orders). ASBOs were introduced in the UK in 1998 by the Crime and Disorder Act of that year to deal with incidents that would not normally warrant a criminal prosecution and although not limited to youths they were certainly seen as connected with young delinquents. Typically ASBOs were court orders which told an individual aged over 10 how they must behave and they were widely used in the initial period after their introduction. However, after a Whitehall evaluation in 2007, which demonstrated that nearly half the orders had been breached and that being given an ASBO was widely seen by sections of the community as a 'badge of honour', support for them declined. Many in the police and other criminal justice agencies believed that their day was over and in 2010 the Home Secretary, Theresa May, announced plans to abolish the ASBOs and replace them with 'community-based' social control policies. This led to proposals in 2012 to replace ASBOs with two orders, the Criminal Behaviour Order and the Crime Prevention Injunction.

QUESTION BREAK

Portrayal of young people by the media

Read the following comments and consider the questions below:

I think the media has created a moral panic where they see young people as criminals wearing hoodies, going round attacking people and are always on the street . . . I think the media doesn't show enough the achievements of young people.

(Comment on BBC News, School Report, 28 June 2007, http://news.bbc.co.uk/2/hi/school_report/6241218.stm)

Media focus on youth drug addiction, vandalism, unprotected sex, as well as many other 'negative' issues, has led some people to view young people in terms of stereotypes and gross generalizations . . . Negative media stereotypes can also influence young people themselves – a kind of self-fulfilling prophecy. On a broader level, young people can be discriminated against or treated suspiciously because of stereotypes.

(www.actnow.com.au)

QUESTIONS

- What are the typical words that people would use to describe young people today? Are they generally negative or positive?
- Can you think of examples of how negative media stereotypes have influenced people you know?
- To what extent do you think the above, rather typical, comments are fair?

It is well established that young people are more likely to be convicted of criminal offences than older people. Data on youthful offending shows that at least one-fifth of all those cautioned or convicted in any year are aged between 10 and 17 and over one-third are aged under 21; and estimates of the peak age for offending place it at between 15 and 18, with it being slightly higher for males than females (MORI 2004, in Newburn 2013).

Because of this high rate of offending it is perhaps not surprising that young people and youth have been seen as a social problem in Britain and elsewhere for many years. The fact that young people have been and still are a focus of adult concern is indicated by the terminology applied to young offenders – juvenile delinquents and, more recently, antisocial behaviour are terms that have been applied almost exclusively to younger offenders. The media have played a crucial role in the construction of 'problem youth' and, following the work of Brown (2005), we will consider the ways in which the media have been involved in the 'packaging and repackaging of problem youth'. In his study of the history of youth crime, Pearson (1983) gives numerous examples of the negative media reporting of youth and youth crime in particular (in Chapter 1 we looked at Pearson's argument that youthful crime had existed over hundreds of years). More recently, the notion of 'moral panics' developed from Cohen's work in the early 1970s highlighted the key role of the media in influencing the wider public's (negative) perception of youth and youth crime (in Chapter 3 we considered moral panics and how delinquent youthful behaviour and youth subcultures burst on to the public and media consciousness in the 1950s and 1960s). Studies of moral panics were initially focused on specific and discrete groups, who became seen as 'folk devils'. However, the Marxist-influenced work of Hall and colleagues in *Policing the Crisis* (1978) expanded the scope of moral panics to represent youth more generally (see p. 57).

Brown argues that in the 1980s there was a move away from the media portrayal of youth as a problem. This was the era of the 'yuppies' (young urban professionals); '"problem youth" in the media vied with images of "kids in the city"' (Brown 2005). However, with the rise in youth unemployment in the 1980s, by the later years of that decade and into the 1990s, the emphasis soon changed to seeing youth as a problem – as indicated by the subheading Brown used in her review of media representation of problem youth, 'A total panic? The media and young people in the 1990s'. Young people without jobs, involved in delinquency and drug taking, were high on the media agenda. And the decreasing age of young people involved in problem and criminal behaviour attracted media and public concern – a trend highlighted in the joyriding stories of the early 1990s and culminating in massive publicity surrounding the murder of Jamie Bulger by two 10-year-old boys in 1993 (see p. 81 above).

In looking at the media representation of offenders in relation to age, the focus has been on young offenders. In finishing this section, we will briefly consider how elderly offenders are portrayed – and whether there is a more sympathetic approach to law-breakers who are seen as old.

The media portrayal of elderly criminals has to be seen in the context of the increasing numbers of such offenders. Although there are many more offenders than prisoners, prison statistics can help illustrate trends in data on offenders. In the decade 1995 to 2005, the number of sentenced prisoners aged 60 and over in England and Wales rose by 169 per cent; and by March 2007 there were 2,080 such prisoners, including 1,036 over the age of 65 and more than 200 over the age of 70 (James 2007). The Prison Reform Trust report *Doing Time: The Experiences and Needs of Older People in Prison* (2008) pointed out that the prisoners aged over 60 are the fastest growing age group in prison and that this is largely due to sentences becoming harsher and longer. There is a similar trend in the USA, where a Human Rights Watch report, *Old Behind Bars* (2012) highlighted how ageing men and women are the most rapidly growing group in US prisons and that prison officials are hard pressed to provide them with appropriate care and living conditions. It found that the number of sentenced state and federal prisoners aged 65 or over grew at 94 times the rate of the overall prison population between 2007 and 2010. In 1995, 3 per cent of the prison population in US prisons were around or over 55 years old and by 2010 the figure had risen to 8 per cent and around 124,000 prisoners (Human Rights Watch 2012). Of course, it is still the case that the great majority of offenders are younger and as regards offenders in general, in 2005 in England and Wales, 6 per cent of all 17-year-old males were found guilty of, or cautioned for, indictable offences (the highest rate for any age group) compared to less than 1 per cent of men in each age group over the age of 43 (Social Trends 2009).

Of course, this increase in elderly offenders is not unexpected given the general ageing of the population – for instance, in 1950, 8.5 per cent of the population of the USA was aged 65 or over, in 2010 this figure had risen to 13 per cent and it is estimated that the figure will be 15.5 per cent by the year 2020. In the UK the picture is similar; in 1971, 13 per cent of the population were aged 65 and over, by 2005 this figure had risen to 16 per cent, and the 2011 census revealed that one in six of the population are aged 65 or over and that this figure will rise to one in four by the year 2050.

QUESTION BREAK

The ageing prison population

Prison is a poor place in which to grow old. The physical environment is often inadequate. Offending behaviour programmes and release and resettlement programmes are designed to meet the needs of younger people, which means that older prisoners suffer age discrimination.

(Age UK 2011)

Older people in prison raised concerns with PRT [Prison Reform Trust] researchers about a range of unmet health needs . . . We were particularly concerned that some older people entering prison had the medication they were receiving in the community stopped . . . A few prisoners interviewed suffered from incontinence and had trouble accessing sanitation facilities outside their cells . . . Almost half (48%) of the men interviewed had experienced bullying or intimidation either by staff or, more frequently, inmates.

(Prison Reform Trust 2008)

QUESTIONS

- What are the implications of the increasing numbers of elderly prisoners?
- What do you feel to be the major social and economic costs of this trend?

In terms of the sort of offences committed, elderly offenders cannot be seen as a homogeneous group. The habitual criminal, for whom prison is an accustomed experience, differs from the person who is first arrested when aged 60 or over – and some prisoners grow old due to serving long sentences. In their research into older prisoners, Collins and Bird (2006) found that theft and handling stolen goods (31%), followed by sexual offences (21%), were the commonest reasons for custodial sentences for older offenders; they also highlighted some unexpected trends, including drug trafficking by older females.

These increases in elderly offenders and, particularly, prisoners, have raised concerns about the needs of such criminals. Collins and Bird (2006) refer to a study of 203 prisoners over the age of 60, which found that 10 per cent were 'functionally disabled in activities of daily living, and most of them were unable to climb stairs'. In a report for the Prison Reform Trust, 'Old Inside', Sampson (2007) points out that the number of elderly prisoners will continue to increase due to the ageing of the population, trends in sentencing and better crime detection; and considers the problems of an ageing prison population. First, he highlights the problems for prisons themselves – there are no care assistants or the like in prisons and health and mental problems of elderly prisoners do not sit easily with running a disciplined regime. He refers to a review by the Prison Inspectorate that referred to prisoners not getting exercise as they could not get to the exercise yard and not washing because they could not stand unaided in the showers. Second, as regards problems for individual prisoners, he raises the question of how can prisoners reconcile themselves to the reality of growing old and dying behind bars; and how do they cope with major illnesses such as strokes when they are lying in a prison bed, with no relatives to care for them. Although older prisoners make up the fastest growing sector of the prison population, the prison service has no special measures in place to meet their particular needs. Of course, some may feel little sympathy for people who have committed serious enough offences to warrant a prison sentence; however, there are clearly some elderly prisoners who are not a threat to the community, who do not need bars on their windows as they cannot even walk unaided.

In terms of media coverage, headlines are often made when old people, with a non-criminal past, are found guilty and jailed for making a stand against the law – such as refusing to pay council tax bills. In such cases, the media seems to support and sympathize with the offender because of his or her (old) age. For instance, there was a good deal of media support for council tax protester, Sylvia Hardy, aged 73, who was jailed for seven days in 2005 for owing council tax arrears of £53.71. Indeed, the media coverage led to a mystery donor paying the fine and her being released from prison after two days. Mrs Hardy had refused to pay her bill, claiming that her pension could not keep up with the rises in council tax. A similar, recent case of an elderly woman being imprisoned for refusing to pay her council tax is mentioned in the question break below.

Look at the various media reports below – from *The Daily Telegraph*, the *Daily Mail* and *The Guardian* reporting on old-age offenders as well as a report from the Australian news network, ABC, on a serious crime committed by elderly offenders.

Miss Josephine Rooney, 69, of Derby, who has been jailed this week for nonpayment of council tax . . .

Here's what happened. Miss Rooney's street was once thought to be a lovely place, the kind of street where people knew their neighbours and everybody was safe. Two years ago, it became clear that something was wrong. Locals now referred to the same street as Crack Alley and a clean-up effort discovered 1,100 dirty needles in a single day. Miss Rooney was sick of the decline in her street and dismayed at the council's apparent unwillingness to do anything about it, so she refused to pay almost £800 in council tax, a decision that has led to her being imprisoned.

What a disgrace . . . What a slur on the democratic instincts of a good citizen, and what pathetic, craven adherence to the rule of law, even when confronted with the arguments of a person who is clearly in the right. Miss Rooney should become a hero to everyone who has ever been confronted by the intransigence and boneheadedness of a local council . . .

Miss Rooney's street, like so many in Britain, has been over-run by people fuelled by a mad sense of entitlement, by a vast carelessness and selfishness, and violence on their minds . . .

But my tolerance of the yobs has run out. Far from being a socialist cause, they are more like representatives of the extreme right. That is why I think the efforts of Miss Rooney are the opposite of criminal: her community spirit is such as any of us might follow.

You won't be surprised to hear that this Government – 'tough on crime, tough on the causes of crime' – saw fit to champion the same Miss Rooney not long ago. As part of its Respect Campaign, it gave her a Taking Stand award. Now that same old-age pensioner is languishing in jail because her council could not bear the stand she was taking, and couldn't find a way to listen to her and tackle the problems in her street.

(O'Hagan A., 'Josephine Rooney Deserves A(nother) Medal',
The Daily Telegraph, 28 June 2006, www.telegraph.co.uk)

A grandmother was jailed for two years yesterday after being caught at her home dismantling a cannabis farm that had netted her tens of thousands of pounds over four years. Police raided the Torquay home of Lynda Seager, 63, as she tried to get rid of her drug cultivation after a separate raid at her former husband's home in Sussex a day earlier. Officers found 197 cannabis plants and hydroponic equipment for growing plants without soil . . . Yesterday she was sentenced to two years in prison.

(Peachey P., 'Grandmother Tried to Hide Evidence of Cannabis Farm',
The Guardian, 4 November 2011)

Record numbers of pensioners are being criminalized for trivial offences by target-driven police. Officers arrest 40 senior citizens every day in Britain on average, official figures show. Their crimes range from failing to pay a fine for overfilling a wheelie bin to not wearing a seatbelt or chopping a neighbour's hedge without permission. Many are being punished for the first time after decades of abiding by the law. Critics say these 'easy collar' arrests are part of a cynical drive to meet police performance targets. Figures from forces around the UK reveal that a staggering 44,321 pensioners were arrested over the past three years. Previous estimates of 'grey crime' have attributed 2,000 offences a year to the over-65s.

(Bentley P., 'The Old-Age "Offenders": Generation of
Elderly Turned into Criminals', *Daily Mail*, 3 April 2010)

An elderly couple in Perth have been declared Australia's oldest drug traffickers and, as a result, they're set to lose all of their assets, including their house. Eighty-one-year-old David Davies and 77-year-old Florence Davies were convicted earlier this month of two counts of possession of cannabis with the intention to supply. They were both given suspended jail sentences, but today's announcement by the Director of Public Prosecutions could leave them with nothing.

The DPP's office says the case is tragic, but in the end, there was no choice and the confiscation has to go ahead. David Weber reports . . . The Davies' home was raided in 2002. Nearly 19 kilograms of cannabis was found hidden in a false ceiling. Another 300 grams was found in an ice-cream container under the bed. And more than $7,000 was found in the car. Police estimated the drug haul to be worth more than $260,000. But while there was a maximum sentence of 10 years or a $100,000 fine, the judge said the elderly pair had led an otherwise blameless life, and he gave them short, suspended sentences.

That was 10 days ago. Today, the Davies situation took a dramatic turn for the worse. The DPP's Director of Legal Services, Fiona Low, says efforts are now underway to take ownership of the Davies' property. Fiona Low: 'There may be some mitigating factors in terms of the process after the formal vesting. Yes, I mean age, health, are relevant considerations. However, what I think people need to remind themselves of is that this was a conviction for a large quantity of traffickable drugs and a jury found them guilty . . . The purpose of the legislation is to act as a deterrent. Anyone involved in trafficking drugs will be dealt with harshly . . . the trafficking of drugs is something that the community demands be attended to.'

(ABC News Network, 18 June 2004, www.abc.net.au/pm/
content/2004/s1135431.htm)

QUESTIONS

- What part does the age of the offenders play in the content and style of the different extracts?

- Do you think the crimes would have been reported differently if the offenders had not been so old?
- Can you think of other examples of elderly offenders being portrayed with more sympathy by the media?

THE MEDIA, GENDER AND CRIMINALS

As well as there being a strong link between age and crime, there is also a strong relationship between gender and crime. The stereotypical picture of the criminal is of a young male and the statistics support this picture. Men have done and continue to commit the vast majority of crime (or at least recorded crime) – in general terms, roughly 80 per cent of those convicted for serious offences in England and Wales are male. For instance, 251,901 women were arrested for notifiable offences in 2010 compared to 1,223,356 men (a figure that is just over 20%). Perhaps the most startling differences are revealed in prison population figures – in March 2013, of 84,505 prisoners in England and Wales, 3,958 were women, so at that time under 5 per cent of prisoners were female (Ministry of Justice 2013). In this section, we will look at how gender influences the way the media represent crime, in particular we will examine the media portrayal of female criminals. In this relatively brief discussion, our focus will be on how the media report violent women offenders, and particularly women found guilty of murder. Murder is the most serious of crimes and if crime is typically seen as a male preserve, then focusing on the media coverage of women murderers will provide an interesting angle on the media's representation of criminals.

Tuchman (1978) argued that media discourses regarding women are guilty of 'symbolic annihilation', that is, the media ignore, trivialize or condemn women. In particular, this aspect of the media has an effect on the way that news about offending women is reported. We have highlighted the fact that men still commit the majority of crime; however, about one-third of violent crime stories in the media are about female offenders. This raises the question as to why the media seem to be more interested in female offenders than males.

Views of and explanations for women and their involvement or lack of involvement in crime have ranged from exploring the inherently different natures of men and women to focusing on the socially constructed gender roles that influence men's and women's lives. And there has often been (and still continues to be) a widely held acceptance of 'common sense' assumptions of female behaviour. From an essentialist (naturalistic) point of view females have a different countenance to men. This naturalistic explanation renders anything that deviates from the female norm as 'unnatural'. The acceptable female norm is closely linked to female biology. For example, women are seen to be closer to nature as they give birth and are subject to the menstrual cycle. It is widely assumed then that women are naturally caring, emotional and maternal.

This view of women has been criticized by many as assuming that what is natural is morally right and desirable. But, even more important, especially to feminist thinkers, is the view that these attributes are accepted as natural and not socially constructed and, importantly, that this 'evolutionary' explanation naturalizes and justifies the continuation of sexist attitudes to and perceptions of female criminals.

In recent years, the media have helped in the formation of strong biological interpretations of female behaviour, which have found their way into explanations for female criminality, for example, premenstrual syndrome (PMS), battered woman syndrome, post-natal depression and infanticide. This has resulted in more sympathetic treatment by the media and the criminal justice system as it denotes a form of diminished responsibility. As an example of this, PMS has been used successfully in courts as a mitigation for crimes varying from shoplifting to murder. A famous case was that of *R. v. Craddock* in 1980 and *R. v. Smith* in 1981 (Craddock and Smith being the same person). Craddock was working as a barmaid and killed a co-worker. In court it was successfully argued that she suffered from acute PMS and this was accepted by the judge as a mitigating factor and probation and medical treatment were recommended. The following year Craddock (now Smith) attempted suicide and threatened to kill a police officer; again the judge accepted PMS as a mitigating factor. Since those cases, PMS has continued to be used as a mitigating factor in the British court system.

However, by rooting offending women behaviour within biological and psychological explanations, we are in danger of creating an over-simplistic view of female criminality. Interpretations of female criminality which have focused on biological and psychological differences between men and women have also been used to explain women's relative lack of involvement in crime. However, sociological and feminist-based explanations emphasize the social construction of gender identity and how this influences behaviour, including criminal behaviour. So, for instance, girls and women have fewer opportunities for crime as girls tend to be more constrained and regulated by their families when growing up.

Common-sense assumptions about gender roles and the 'appropriate' behaviour for men and women are reflected in the way the media report crime and criminals and their use of these stereotypical views of women. The language or discourse used by the media is a key factor here. Discourse is an important concept when discussing the media portrayal of the female offender. Indeed, Foucault argued that 'Social control depends on language. Discourses of sexuality, sanity and criminality are transformed into a technology of power formulated in terms of the law' (1978, p. 87).

The narrative within the media is in essence a form of storytelling. Within news media, items are often referred to as 'stories'. This is most apparent within newspapers and TV crime news in which journalists construct news stories that can be evaluated easily by the audience. News and the selling of newspapers then are reliant on a number of 'stock stories' that follow a well-established path. Ericson, Baranek and Chan (1991) go as far as to argue that, even when new evidence or profiles present themselves, journalists are reluctant to change their stories' direction; this seems to be particularly true of female offenders and is evidenced in the accounts of female murders that we look at below. The idea of the stock story within mainstream journalistic portrayals of female offenders has been much documented during the last 20 years. Often these stock stories come in the form of binary classifications steeped in gothic storytelling, for example, the virgin or vamp (see Benedict 1992). On the one hand is the Lady Macbeth figure (the unnatural monster and manipulator) or the Pygmalion; on the other hand is the dupe, the woman who is willing to do anything for love and resorts to killing as a way of cementing her relationship with a man (see Cameron and Fraser 1987). Other narratives focus on appearance and contrast the ugly duckling with the femme fatale. Finally are those stories that focus on women's biology and psychology and emphasize the mad and the bad, which gives recourse to the so-called link between femininity and madness and evil (see Frigon 1995).

Bronwyn Naylor (2001) examined the reporting of violence in the British print media and found significant differences in the intensity and nature or the reporting of violent male and female offenders. Again, narratives used in female accounts pointed to the emotional and irrational nature of female crime, while male violence was presented as 'normal' and 'natural'.

THE MALE GAZE

The concept of the 'male gaze' was first introduced in media studies by Laura Mulvey in the 1970s to describe how the audience is forced to view women through the eyes of the heterosexual man (Mulvey 1975). Although first used in film theory, the concept is often applied to other kinds of media, for example, advertising and journalism. The male gaze points to the fact that the image of females within the media are framed for the benefit of the 'male', therefore images stress the importance of physical attractiveness. As we see later, this idea can be seen in the way that, when female offenders are portrayed, the offender's physical appearance, rather than the offence itself, often become the focus of attention.

In their book *Media and Body Image*, Wykes and Gunter (2004) argue that the media is guilty of socially constructing femininity. Powerful messages that are unrealistic yet persuasive are used within the media to encourage women to fit the feminine stereotype. For example, women are encouraged and expected to be forever slim, youthful, feminine and heterosexual. In terms of female offenders, their appearance, unlike their male counterpart, is subject to intense scrutiny.

Physical appearance becomes an important aspect in the reporting of female offenders. Rather than the offence being described, the female offender becomes the central focus. The male gaze becomes an important tool when analysing the content of newspaper articles. Most reports of female offenders are dichotomized into those who fit the male gaze, those who are physically attractive and those who are the opposite and physically unattractive. This dichotomy is popularly reflected in the contrasting images of the ugly duckling and the femme fatale.

In the rest of this section, we will look at how the media have represented some of the most well-known female criminals of recent years; and as we mentioned at the start our discussion will focus on women murderers. Below are examples of three (in)famous female killers and the iconic images that often accompany media reporting of them and also of Amanda Knox who was convicted of murder in Italy in 2009 but whose conviction was overturned in 2011. We will briefly consider these cases in relation to media reporting and the male gaze.

Karla Homolka

In 1993, Karla Homolka was convicted of manslaughter in the rape and murder of two teenage girls and for the drugging and rape of her younger sister Tammy. Her accomplice, husband Paul Bernado, was convicted in 1995 for two murders and two aggravated assaults. Homolka was sentenced to 12 years' imprisonment and was released in 2005. Despite the severity of the murders, media attention focused on Homolka's physical appearance. Newspapers at the time were obsessed with Homolka's conventional attractiveness; *The Washington Post* described her appearance on her wedding day. 'Karla Homolka was resplendent on her wedding day, 29 June 1991. Garlands of baby's breath adorned her hair and fluffy veil; her long flounced dress made her look like Cinderella' (*The Washington Post*, 23 November 1993).

On her release 12 years later, media attention once again returned to her physical attractiveness. Journalist Georgie Binks (2005), in her reflections on the case, discusses how male investigators and reporters were mesmerized by Homolka. Christie Blachford, a reporter at the time, states that 'in the days of her trial, there were some male reporters who were titillated by the fact she was so sexually compliant. I remember a colleague saying to me "imagine coming home to that everyday"' (cited in CBC News, 10 June 2005). Homolka used the 'pretty girl syndrome' to her advantage, as Binks commented, 'you can't really blame Karla for batting her eyelashes when it counted, because it worked. You can only blame a society that puts the pretty girl above all else.'

Tracie Andrews

In 1997, Tracie Andrews was convicted of the murder of her boyfriend Lee Harvey, whom she stabbed to death in 1996. Previously she had stated that her boyfriend had been the victim of a road rage incident and even appeared in press conferences appealing to witnesses to come forward. Reports at the time focused on Tracie's physical appearance and described her as 'former model Tracie Andrews' and 'blonde Tracie Andrews'. On her subsequent arrest *The Sun* newspaper's headline read 'Death Quiz Tracie in Glamour Poses'. The article features numerous glamorous photographs of Tracie Andrews at a photo shoot, stating 'Sexy Tracie Andrews looks every inch the glamorous model in carefree poses snapped before the nightmare of her fiancé's road rage murder'. On the day of her conviction (30 July) the tabloid newspaper *The Daily Star* ran headlines that read 'The Blonde From Hell' and 'Looks That Could Kill'. Clearly tabloid newspapers became obsessed with the fact that Tracie had been a former model and much of the text within the articles focus on her attractiveness rather than the case in hand.

Rose West

In 1995, Rose West was found guilty of the murders of 10 young women and girls, including her 16-year-old daughter. Her husband Fred West escaped trial as he had committed suicide while on remand in prison on 1 January 1995. Newspaper reports, both at the time and since then, have focused on Rose West's 'frumpy' appearance. The fact that she did not fit society's examples of feminine beauty have been used by the media to explain her crimes. The tabloids, for example, surmised that she took part in the killings as she was insecure about her looks and afraid of losing her husband (who had already had affairs). Thirteen years on and the media still focus on her lack of conventional beauty and her attempts to 'tidy' herself up. Recently the *Daily Mirror* newspaper ran the headline 'The New Face of Rose West' and stated 'Frumpy Rose, 51, has trimmed her hair to a shorter, neater style and has lost two stone. She has also replaced her bulky glasses for NHS contact lenses and wears pastel colours' (*Daily Mirror*, 5 May 2005). Indeed, the victims of Rose West's crimes are almost ignored by the media's obsession with her.

Amanda Knox

Amanda Knox was convicted in 2009 of murdering Meredith Kercher, an English student, two years previously in Perugia, Italy. She was sentenced to 26 years' imprisonment and served four years under what was termed 'cautionary detention', as under Italian law she would not be considered guilty until the verdict was confirmed by a higher court. During her appeal at the second level trial in October 2011, the murder conviction was overturned and she was released. The media coverage of the murder, the initial trial, the appeal and release of Amanda demonstrated some quite divergent approaches. There was a good deal of strong criticism of Amanda but, especially after her conviction, there was some strong media support for her. Also the media reporting focused on Amanda's sexuality and her appearance and behaviour as much as on the case itself. Amanda's boyfriend Raffaele Sollecito, who was also convicted of the murder and then released, received far less media coverage and, presumably as a consequence, is a much less known figure than Amanda. As an illustration of the different ways in which this case was reported, the British tabloid press in particular christened her 'foxy Knoxy', with headlines such as 'Foxy Knoxy: Inside the Twisted World of Flatmate Suspected of Meredith's Murder' (*Daily Mail*, 6 November 2007). However, in the USA in particular there was a good deal of media orchestrated support; Seattle-based residents (Amanda's home town) founded the 'Friends of Amanda' support group in 2008; and headlines such as 'Amanda is Innocent of Brutal Murder, Retired FBI Agent Claims' (ABC News 2010) were commonplace. The ambivalent attitude towards Amanda Knox is illustrated by the account given by CNN after her release:

> **Amanda Knox Freed, but Truth About Student's Slaying Elusive**
> **Who is Amanda Knox?**
>
> Is she a two-faced she-devil, angelic and compassionate to some but Satanic and Lucifer-like to others? That's what Carlo Pacelli, the lawyer for a man Knox falsely accused in the 2007 murder of her roommate, Meredith Kercher, called her as he summed up his case last week. Is she 'Foxy Knoxy', as the British tabloid press leered and sneered at her . . . or is she the fresh-faced girl from Seattle she still appears to be, even after spending nearly four years behind bars before her conviction was quashed? Is Knox simply the victim of character assassination, painted falsely as a 'femme fatale' by prosecutors and media the world over?
>
> (http://edition.cnn.com/2011/10/03/world/europe/
> italy-knox-analysis/, 4 October 2011)

QUESTION BREAK

The iconic image below is of British murderer Myra Hindley. She was sentenced to life imprisonment in May 1966 for aiding her then lover Ian Brady in the rape and murder of five children between 1963 and 1965. She eventually died in prison in 1992 after a battle with cancer.

Investigate the way in which the media have portrayed Myra Hindley.

What does the media (including newspapers, Internet, books) say about her looks and her personality?

How do your findings relate to the concept of the male gaze?

INTIMATE PARTNER KILLINGS AND VICTIM BLAMING

In recent years there has been a fascination by the media on the reporting of intimate partner killing. This is most notable when a woman is the murderer. In 2006/2007, 757 deaths were initially recorded as homicides by the police in England and Wales, 75 per cent of which were male. However, only 11 per cent of males were killed by their partner, ex-partner or lover compared to 65 per cent of females (Povery *et al.* 2008). Within press reports, the gender of the actors involved in intimate killings holds more news value than the role that they played in the crime as either victim or offender; the focus tends to rest on the female's role in the case. The female's private life is scrutinized. Her role as mother, wife, lover and so on are explored and her sexual preferences discussed and held up as an indication of her 'culpable' nature, whether as the victim or the offender. Below we consider two British cases of intimate partner killings and how the media reported them.

In April 1991, New Zealand student John Tanner murdered his then girlfriend Rachel McLean and buried her body under the floorboards of her Oxford flat. Tanner appeared on *Crimewatch* to re-enact his last sighting of Rachel and appealed to the public for any information regarding her disappearance. Her body was discovered nearly three weeks later and Tanner was arrested and charged with murder. The focus of media attention rested on the idea that Tanner had killed Rachel in a fit of jealous rage as he had suspected that she had been unfaithful. Subsequent newspaper coverage focused on Rachel's alleged infidelity and Tanner's uncontrollable jealousy. *The Daily Telegraph* headline after the trial stated, 'Lover Strangled Student in Jealous Rage' and the *Daily Mirror* went with 'Jealous John Tanner Strangled His Unfaithful Girlfriend'. These headlines almost exempt Tanner from his behaviour as this violence is suggested as being 'out of control'. Conversely, Rachel is described as contributing to her own death; she is a culpable victim, contributing to her own victim status due to the fact that she was unfaithful and so deserved (or was at least partly to blame for) her plight.

The most famous British case of intimate partner killings occurred in 1989 when Sara Thornton murdered her husband as he lay in a drunken stupor. The case became famous due to the work of women's groups. Thornton alleged that she had been the victim of sustained abuse. It was argued in court that her behaviour was the result of battered woman syndrome, although it was stated that this was inadmissible in court. Thornton was given a life sentence in 1990; on appeal the case was retried and she was found guilty of manslaughter on unspecified grounds and sentenced to five years in prison but was freed because of the length of time she had already served. Despite unprecedented support from women's groups, the media portrayal of Thornton was largely unsympathetic and focused on her role as a wife and mother. In a letter to *The Independent* in 1991 Sara argued, 'because I dared to fight I am being ignored . . . If Malcolm had killed me they would have used everything they are using against me now in his defence. I'd have been portrayed as a woman who nagged him over his drinking, who didn't always wear knickers, who went off to a conference and left him.'

The focus of media attention then is often on the woman; success at fulfilling her role as a mother, housewife, wife and not the crime in question.

SEXUALITY

Benedict (1992) argued that women are categorized as either virgin or vamp, in other words, women are categorized as either saintly madonnas who are sexually inexperienced or even frigid, or those who are sexually promiscuous or sexually deviant in their preferences, for example, lesbians and those who engage in deviant practices such as sadomasochism. These ideas are most noticeable in media coverage of female offenders. In her book, Hart (1994) investigates the origins of the link between lesbians and criminals; she suggests that the categorization of women is reserved for the white, middle-class heterosexual female. This leads to the binary classification of normal women and 'other' in which the lesbian and the criminal fall – they are outside the boundaries of normality. Hart postulates that these ideas emerge from the work of Victorian sexologist Havelock Ellis who discusses the female invert. Not necessarily lesbian but linked to lesbianism due to the aggressive masculine form her desire takes. 'It is, moreover, noteworthy that a remarkably large portion of the cases in which homosexuality has led to crimes of violence, or otherwise come under medico-legal observation, has been among women' (Ellis 1937, first published 1905). Hart argues 'if the "normal" woman was man's opposite, the invert as the opposite of the normal woman became man's double. Imagining the female invert as inhabiting his sexual subject position effected a rupture in sexual difference that also established her as a powerful threat to his exclusive claim to masculinity' (1994, p. 8).

These ideas around sexuality are still evident in media coverage of female offenders and have been most noticeable in the case of Aileen Wuornos.

Aileen Wuornos

Aileen Wuornos was convicted of the murder of seven men. The murders took place between November 1989 and December 1990. She was sentenced to death in 1992 and died a decade later by lethal injection. Working as a prostitute, Wuornos had claimed that the men had raped or had attempted to rape her and that the crimes had been in self-defence.

The media portrayals of Wuornos focused on her life as a prostitute and lesbian. In her book, Hart argues that the excessive negative media attention around Wuornos arises from these two factors. Her prostitution and lesbianism posed a threat to the heteropatriarchal. Heteropatriarchy is the idea that power within society belongs to the white male who is heterosexual and masculine, able-bodied and financially secure.

Due to Wuornos's prostitution and lesbianism it is said that she crossed the boundaries of the archetypal feminine woman and therefore became the 'outsider'.

Her unconventional lifestyle had a devastating effect on the media portrayal of her trial. Her plea of self-defence was ridiculed and weakened due to the fact that she was a prostitute. It would seem that the right to self-defence is negotiable and a prostitute who sells sex for money has no negotiation.

Wuornos's lesbianism became linked to men-hating behaviour. In an article written for *Glamour* magazine, former FBI agent Robert Ressler states:

> There may be an intrinsic hatred of males here, as well as an identification with male violence which helped push her across the line into what has been considered a 'male' crime . . . In stark contrast to the complex motives attributed to male serial murderers, and the evocation of those male murderers as essentially unsolvable mysteries, Wuornos's motives are presented with absolute clarity: she is a lesbian; *therefore* she hates men and *therefore* she killed them.
>
> (cited in Schmid 2005)

FICTIONAL REPRESENTATIONS

In concluding this section it is worth briefly discussing the use of the fictional and 'real' female offender within TV and film. Over the last two decades, a genre of Hollywood films has emerged depicting female offenders. The narrative of such films tend to construct the image of the female offender through her sexuality mental state. Many of the films depict the deranged woman who is driven insane and threatens the family unit (especially the mother and the children); for example, *Fatal Attraction* (1987), *The Hand that Rocks the Cradle* (1991) and *Basic Instinct* (1992). Other films focus on the male-hating female offender, such as *Single White Female* (1992).

Despite society's condemnation of female offenders, especially murderers, there does exist a multi-million pound industry around them. Because of TV and film, these women often become stars/celebrities in their own right. The Aileen Wuornos story, for example, has spawned, up to now, two documentaries, 'Aileen Wuornos: Selling of a Serial Killer' and the TV Movie *Overkill: The Aileen Wuornos Story*; and, most famously the Hollywood smash-hit *Monster*, which earned an Oscar for Charlize Theron's depiction of the killer.

Holmlund (2002) considers the emergence of a cycle of films featuring the lesbian as a sexy female killer coining the term 'Hollywood's deadly lesbian dolls'. In his account, Holmlund examines the fact that 'audiences are both fascinated by, yet uncomfortable with, violent women . . . [and] a murmured fear of lesbianism lurks beneath the general discomfort with violent women' (2002, pp. 74, 75).

QUESTION BREAK

Look at the publicity for the film *Monster* (see websites for this film about Aileen Wuornos, such as www.imdb.com).

Think of other women criminals in film or television dramas. How would you describe the way they are portrayed? To what extent is their appearance emphasized in the roles they play?

THE MEDIA, ETHNICITY AND CRIMINALS

Another important aspect of the pattern and trend in crime figures relates to the ethnic background of offenders. It is a common stereotype that young males, and especially young ethnic minority and particularly black males, are especially prone to criminal behaviour. And a range of crimes are widely seen as typically committed by young black males. Since the 1960s, for instance, drug use and supply, and 'mugging' or street robbery have been popularly associated with black people and more recently carjacking and gangland violence have been characterized in a similar way. Illegal immigration and asylum seeking have also been associated with ethnic minority groups – although this has tended to be associated with Asian and/or Eastern European groups rather than black. Indeed, this highlights the danger of lumping all ethnic minority groups together when examining 'race and crime'.

With regard to this characterization of certain types of crime as typically the preserve of 'black' or other ethnic minority groups, in the 1980s and 1990s 'mugging' was seen as a crime almost exclusively committed by black youth. Indeed, the Metropolitan Police Commissioner Sir Paul Condon controversially stated that the majority of muggers in London were black. Similarly, there has been recent comment and concern about the upsurge in gangland violence and shootings in British cities, which have been associated with black people.

However, if we look at the official data on ethnicity and the criminal justice system, it is apparent some of these widely held, 'populist' views are not based on any hard evidence. Official Home Office statistics on race and the criminal justice system are produced annually as a consequence of the Criminal Justice Act of 1991. As regards the percentage of the population from different ethnic groups, figures from the 2011 census can be used as a comparative baseline. The 2011 census showed a significant rise from previous censuses in the percentage of the populations who were foreign born, with 3.3 per cent of the general population black (black/African/ Caribbean/black British), 7.5 per cent Asian and 1 per cent 'other'. These proportions need to be kept in mind when looking at the proportions of different ethnic minority groups involved with crime and criminal justice. Data from the Ministry of Justice showed that in 2010 there were higher rates of stop and search for all black and minority ethnic groups than for the white group and that while the overall number of arrests had decreased in the previous five years, arrest of those in the black and Asian groups had increased, with black people arrested 3.3 times more than white people. Indeed, black people were seven times more likely to be stopped and searched than the white population, although it should be borne in mind that over 40 per cent of all stop and searches are done by the Metropolitan police forces and a much higher percentage of ethnic minority groups live in the area served by the Metropolitan police (Ministry of Justice 2011).

In terms of sentencing and punishments, in 2010 a higher percentage of those in the black and minority ethnic groups were sentenced to immediate custody for indictable offences than in the white group (white 23%, black 27% and Asian 29%). Furthermore, the proportion of ethnic minority groups in prisons are massively greater than would be expected by the general population figures. The Ministry of

Justice data showed that on 30 June 2010 out of a total prison population in England and Wales of 85,002, just under 26 per cent (21,878) were from black and minority ethnic groups – a proportion that had remained much the same for the previous four years (Ministry of Justice 2011).

So ethnic minority groups are clearly dealt with by the criminal justice system in a manner that indicates that they are seen as more 'crime prone' than other groups. Explanations for these differences include arguments that the black crime rate is over-exaggerated by the statistics and that the criminal justice system is biased against ethnic minority groups. It is not our brief to go into those arguments here (see, for instance, Marsh *et al.* 2011), but we will look at how the media reporting of crime reflects these differences.

Before looking at some examples of the media reporting of crime and ethnicity, we will look at two reports into 'race' and crime in the news, one from the UK and the other from the USA. In an examination of 'race' and violent crime in the press entitled 'A Tale of Two Englands', the Runnymede Trust (2008) explored the reporting of violent crime in relation to the ethnicity of the victims and the offenders, in an attempt to explore the 'ways in which popular understandings of race and crime influence reporting in the media and vice versa'. Amongst the key findings were that the patterns of press reporting on violent crime were 'strongly informed by notions of race' and that 'in essence, England is conceived as two-fold: an England consisting of a law-abiding and morally superior Us; and an England inhabited by criminal and pathological Others'. The report found that journalists were very imprecise when discussing ethnic minority groups and veered towards either the stereotypical associations of particular groups with specific crimes, such as Eastern European bag-snatchers and Jamaican crack dealers, or lumping all different, ethnic groups together as 'standing in direct contrast to white middle-class England'. Certainly they found that the typical gang member was seen as being black and that murders covered in the news were 'more likely to be assumed to be "gang related" if there was black youth involved than if all involved were white'.

In similar vein, a study into 'youth, race and crime in the news' by the Building Blocks for Youth organization in the USA (Dorfman 2001) provided a detailed content analysis of crime news by searching criminal justice databases. It found that the 'depictions of crime in the news are not reflective of either the rate of crime generally . . . (or) the proportion of crime committed by people of color'. It also found that a disproportionate number of offenders covered by news reporting were from ethnic minority groups, especially African Americans. In particular black and Hispanic groups were over-represented as violent offenders and white people under-represented on evening news programmes. In concluding, the report makes the point that news organizations routinely watch and 'borrow' from each other and that this encourages them to repeat distortions, including 'the distorted picture of crime, race and youth from the news'.

As we have seen throughout this book so far, it is through the reporting of crime by newspapers and on television that messages reach the wider public about the extent and pattern of crime. And it is the way that headlines are phrased and the content and style of the narrative that is used in stories about crime that help to shape public attitudes. In considering the way that the ethnicity and cultural background of criminals influences, if not determines, the way that those criminals are portrayed and represented, it is important to look at examples of media reporting. At the start of this section we pointed out that certain ethnic minority groups are seen as particularly likely to be disproportionately involved in crime (groups such as black youths and Eastern European asylum seekers, for instance) and that certain crimes are closely associated with specific groups (so, for example, black youths are associated with violent robbery – 'mugging'). In the question break box below we have included newspaper reports on young black criminals and on Eastern European criminals to illustrate the way that the news reporting of crime and criminals helps to establish and then confirm stereotypes about ethnic background and crime.

QUESTION BREAK

Read the extracts on black and East European/'foreign' criminals before considering the questions below them. Extracts 1 to 4 relate to black criminals; the first three are from mainstream newspapers, while the fourth is from *The Epoch Times*, an independent news media company that was established in 2003 as a web-based organization before becoming a printed newspaper in 2004; it is based in New York but with a global network of reporters. Extracts 5 to 10 relate to asylum seekers and East European criminals and are from various popular British newspapers.

1. Black Men 'to Blame for Most Violent City Crime' . . . But They Are Also Victims

The majority of violent inner-city crime is committed by black men, police figures suggest. But the statistics also show that black men are twice as likely to be victims of such crimes. Police hold black men responsible for more than two-thirds of shootings and more than a half of robberies and street crimes in London, according to figures released by Scotland Yard. The statistics released under Freedom of Information laws have provoked a debate about the racial make-up of violent crime in the capital. The data, which provides the ethnicity of the 18,091 men and boys who police took action against in London during 2009–10, looked at both violent and sexual offences. It found that 67 per cent of those caught by the police for gun crimes were black. Among those proceeded against for street crimes, including muggings, assault with intent to rob and snatching property, 54 per cent were black males . . . The statistics also suggest that police hold black women accountable for a disproportionate amount of violent crime. On knife crime, 45 per cent of suspected female perpetrators were black.

(Camber R., *Daily Mail*, 27 June 2010)

2. 70% of Muggers are Black in Robbery Hotspots

Black suspects make up more than 70 per cent of muggers in some of the worst hotspots for street robbery in England and Wales, according to new research. A study published yesterday by the Home Office showed that up to 87 per cent of victims in Lambeth, South London, told the police that their attackers were black. Nearly 80 per cent of the victims were white. Black people account for 31 per cent of the population in these areas. 82 per cent of victims on the London underground and 70 per cent of victims on commuter railways around London also identified their muggers as black.

(Tendler S., *The Times*, 10 January 2003)

3. Are Young Black Kids to Blame for the Gun and Knife Crimewave?

Tony Blair yesterday admitted that political correctness has hampered the fight against violent black gangs and called for a change in crime policy . . . 'We won't stop this by pretending it isn't young black kids doing it', he said, conceding that he has undergone a change of heart over multi-cultural policing.

(*Daily Express*, 12 April 2007)

4. Youth Gangs Running Wild in England

Young black teenagers in Britain are falling into criminal gangs because of family breakdown and lack of positive role models, community workers say. Since January there have been 17 shootings and stabbings in London alone, as police warn that the rise in teenage gangs is the worst problem facing Britain, after terrorism.

(Jones S., *Epoch Times*, 16 August 2007)

5. Migrants Send Our Crime Rate Soaring

Police are struggling to cope with a wave of violent crime caused by the arrival of hundreds of thousands of immigrants, one of Britain's senior officers has warned. Mike Fuller, Chief Constable of Kent, says his force is being stretched to the limit by the huge numbers flocking into the UK. He blames these 'migration surges' for a 35 per cent rise in violent crime in his county. His worries are voiced in a letter to Home Secretary Jacqui Smith which was leaked at the weekend.

(Fagge N., *Daily Express*, 28 January 2008)

6. Romanian Gangs 'Are Flooding London with Pickpockets, Prostitutes and Beggars' Ahead of Olympic Games

Romanian crime syndicates are flooding London with hundreds of pickpockets, prostitutes and beggars ahead of the Olympics. Coachloads of penniless migrants are arriving in the capital every day, many already armed with maps directing them to the best patches, which they have been ordered to defend from rivals. Council workers are already having to clear around 60 Romanian nationals sleeping rough on the streets around Marble Arch and Oxford Street every night and they fear the situation is getting worse.

(*Daily Mail*, 24 April 2012)

7. Eastern European Criminals Blamed for Surge in Migrant Offences

Eastern European criminals see Britain as 'rich pickings' and are thought to be behind a surge in offences caused by migrants last year. Foreign nationals being arrested for crimes including robbery, burglary and theft have more than doubled in the period, figures show. In general, crimes committed by those born abroad has increased by 53 per cent. An investigation has discovered increasing numbers of foreign nationals being detained by West Midlands Police, the country's second biggest force . . . Khalid Mahmood, MP for Perry Barr, said: 'There are a lot more undesirables coming in now. They see rich pickings in Britain because there are no controls'.

(Alleyne R., *The Daily Telegraph*, 12 September 2012)

8. Fugitive Eastern European Criminal Entered UK Legally and Raped Two Women in Knife-Point Attacks

A fugitive Eastern European criminal exploited EU 'open door' border laws to enter Britain and rape two women in terrifying twin attacks. Mindaugas Butkus, 23, fled his native Lithuania over a vicious knife-point robbery – yet he was allowed to come to the UK legally and without permission saying he wanted to work here to support his family back home. Just weeks after arriving in Liverpool, he stalked two women before beating one across the face and threatening the other with a knife in two separate rapes . . .

Paul Nuttall, UKIP North West MEP, said: '[This case] shows we cannot protect our borders. How can anybody say that not being able to keep criminals out of this country is in our national interest? I would like the victims to be able to sue the government'.

Vicious thug Butkus had originally been jailed for six years in Lithuania for a robbery in which he slashed a victim above the eye with a knife.

(*Daily Mail*, 14 January 2013)

9. The Killer Asylum Seekers

Two members of the armed gang which killed PC Sharon Beshenivsky were Somali asylum seekers with a catalogue of criminal convictions . . . Yusuf Abdillh Jama and his older brother Mustaf could not be deported back to their homeland because the Home Office ruled it was too dangerous. Yet after the murder Mustaf went on the run – back to Somalia . . .

Yesterday, the officer's heartbroken husband Paul said: 'It is absolutely disgusting that this man – a criminal who acts like an animal – is shown human rights. What about my kids, my wife, my family?' . . . Mr Beshenivsky expressed his fury at the system that put the needs of his wife's killers above those of her family . . . He said: 'If they are violent and they are asylum seekers in this country, they shouldn't be allowed to stay here, full stop'.

(Greenhill S., Seamark M. and Sims P.,
Daily Mail, 19 December 2006)

10. Swan Bake: Asylum Seekers Steal the Queen's Birds for Barbecues

Callous asylum seekers are barbecuing the Queen's swans . . . East European poachers lure the protected royal birds into baited traps . . . Police swooped on a gang of East Europeans and caught them red-handed about to cook a pair of royal swans.

(*The Sun*, 4 July 2003)

QUESTIONS

- How would you describe the reporting of black youth in extracts 1 to 4?
- How would you describe the portrayal of East Europeans in extracts 5 to 10?
- What sort of messages do these extracts promote about those ethnic minority groups?
- What particular phrases might help establish stereotypical views of such groups?

As a follow-up to the newspaper extracts included in the question break above, an important point to consider when looking at media reporting of crime and their role in establishing stereotypical pictures of different ethnic criminal groups is that the media can and do exaggerate stories; and there is little that can be done to reverse any negative portrayal that might have been created. For instance, the story in *The Sun* about East Europeans eating royal swans was shown to be inaccurate, yet the comments will still remain in the readers' minds. Indeed, the independent media watchdog, the Pressurewise Trust, accused *The Sun* of 'urban myth-making' by printing the story of asylum seekers stealing and eating swans. Pressurewise asked the police about the alleged incident and found that no one had been charged with any such offences and although *The Sun* was forced to print a clarification to the story, Pressurewise felt this was not enough. As a spokesmen for them said: 'There is no solid evidence to support a sensational story that has entered the public imagination, yet five months later *The Sun* is simply obliged to run a disclaimer that it confused conjecture with fact' (www.pressgazette.co.uk).

THE MEDIA, CRIMINALS AND 'CRIMINAL COMMUNITIES'

This section does not strictly refer to how the media portrays criminals but rather focuses on the way that different communities are represented in the media; and in particular the negative representation of certain communities as 'criminal areas or communities'. However, given that this chapter has examined how the media has presented some of the key social and environmental characteristics of the criminal, it would seem appropriate to look also at geographical environment in relation to the media reporting of crime and criminals.

In recent years, in particular, 'local leaders', including politicians and decision-makers, have emphasized the importance of their cities or areas having a positive, attractive image. It is believed that public image, which is largely spread via the different forms of media, can and does have major implications for their area – a positive image can work in terms of attracting business and money, new residents and cultural developments; while a negative one can have the reverse effect. Indeed, a negative image is seen as an obstacle that will work against a better future for the city or area. While many different factors will influence the image of an area, crime rate is one of the most significant – a high crime rate, or even the perception of an area as having a high crime rate, leads to bad publicity and a negative effect on the area. The American city of Chicago was heavily associated with gangland crime in the early years of the twentieth century – infamous for the exploits of Al Capone and others in the 1920s and 1930s. And even though the crime rate in Chicago was one of the lowest amongst American cities by the later years of the twentieth century, it is still generally perceived and referred to as a city of crime and violence – in other words, the stereotype, perpetuated by the media in films and books, persists.

Before looking at the way different areas are portrayed by the media, the question break below asks you to think about how areas you know are represented by the media.

QUESTION BREAK

Consider the areas around where you live (or have lived). Can you think of areas that have a negative image? What part does the amount of crime play in promoting this image?

Which cities in the UK have a positive image and which negative? Can you suggest reasons for these images?

Criminology as an academic, scientific discipline developed in the early twentieth century, and much of early criminological theorizing focused on explaining why crime occurred in urban areas and cities. Indeed, as Crutchfield and Kubrin (2007) put it, 'early twentieth century criminology might reasonably be considered the criminology of urban places'. And a concern about the effects of urban and city living on crime rates did not begin with criminologists; many of the great early social theorists and sociologists such as Durkheim, Weber and Tönnies wrote about the changes to society and social relationships that resulted from the transition of societies from rural, village-based ones to urbanized and industrial ones. They talked about and analysed the dislocation and disorganization that would result as a consequence of the massive social changes brought about by the move to urban living; and that part of this disorganization would take the form of increased criminal behaviour.

However, it was in the 1920s and 1930s that social scientists based at the University of Chicago explored the notion that modern, industrial and urban societies would bring with them greater social disorganization and a growth in social problems, including crime. The approach and theorizing of these sociologists became known as the Chicago school. Chicago grew at a phenomenal rate in these early years of the twentieth century, becoming a massive metropolis with a diverse population, including European immigrants from Ireland, Germany and Eastern Europe and black Americans from the southern states of the USA. It has been described as a vast social laboratory and so it is not surprising that the first university sociology department in the USA was established there in 1892. The Chicago school was interested in examining and explaining the variations in crime levels within different areas of cities, observing that some areas of cities had consistently higher crime rates than others regardless of who populated those areas (Crutchfield and Kubrin 2007). They argued that social life in certain neighbourhoods was chaotic and pathological and that in such contexts crime was to be expected as a normal response.

One of the key figures in establishing the reputation of the Chicago school was Robert Park. Park and his colleagues believed that cities should be studied as ecological systems, with different areas and neighbourhoods within them developing at different times and in particular ways. Some neighbourhoods were relatively stable and well organized, others were more socially disorganized, and it was in those that crime, and other social problems, tended to be concentrated. Another leading figure of the Chicago school, Ernest Burgess, developed the ecological approach by mapping out different zones of Chicago. These zones formed concentric circles covering the whole city – at the centre was the business zone containing banks and offices, beyond this were the residential zones, starting with the 'zone of transition', just outside the business zone, then the zone of working men's homes, then the residential zone and finally the commuter zone. The zone of transition was the one where crime and other social problems were concentrated – in this zone the housing tended to be run down, the population was transient, the inhabitants were often immigrants and others who could not afford to live elsewhere. Two Chicago sociologists, Shaw and McKay (1942), examined patterns of juvenile crime in that city and found that the extent of crime was inversely related to the wealth of the area of the city – and the further away from the centre the wealthier were the areas. They found that crime rates were highest in the 'slum' areas, regardless of who lived in those areas, thereby developing the argument mentioned above that it was the nature of a neighbourhood, rather than the people and groups who lived there, that determined the extent of criminal behaviour.

Go back to the question break above and consider the extent to which your findings matched those of the Chicago school.

Divide the area or cities you considered into different zones – are there zones which you know to be particularly prone to crime?

The notion of criminal areas, then, is one which has been developed by social theorists and criminologists and so it is perhaps not surprising that the media portray certain cities, areas and neighbourhoods in such a light. And these representations are accepted and used by other bodies. Insurance companies, for instance, vary the premiums they charge people for insuring against theft according to the area in which people live. As an example, the Endsleigh insurance company analysed its claims data covering tens of thousands of households across Britain and published on its web page a list of the cities with the highest risk for burglary, and those which were safest from burglary. The company found that Leeds was the city where you are most likely to suffer a burglary (with a burglary rate 99% above the national average), followed by Hull and Nottingham, with Edinburgh, Cardiff and Swindon the least burglary-prone cities. Other Internet sites refer to crime rates in promoting or not a particular area – so in relation to house buying, for example, an American site, www.ezinearticles.com, highlights 'signs of a bad neighbourhood', including broken windows, graffiti and abandoned cars. It suggests that a less obvious indication is whether there are people walking around on a warm evening or at weekends and, if so, it means that the area is likely to have little crime; another indication being the number and regularity of police patrols.

More recently, in the UK a new online crime map was set up by the Home Office in 2011. This map and its related website (the national police site www.police.uk) were set up so that the public can access crime rates for their street or postcode and it can also allow the public to hold their local police to account, as it provides details of the neighbourhood policing teams and how to get hold of them. At its introduction to the public it led to a street in Preston being branded the most crime-ridden in England and Wales; however, on closer investigation it appeared that although 150 offences were recorded there in one month the crimes were actually committed across the whole of Preston city centre, rather than just the one street. Nonetheless such information and websites, deemed as official as they come from the government and police, can certainly lead to the labelling of certain areas as criminal.

In the UK, Liverpool is one of a number of northern cities that is portrayed in the media as crime-ridden, and is regularly the butt of jokes to that effect. Amongst others, Boris Johnson, the Conservative MP and more recently Mayor of London was forced to apologize for making unflattering comments about the city, as was TV presenter Anne Robinson for joking about thieving Scousers on *The Weakest Link* game show. Writing in *The Independent*, Jonathon Brown (2006) commented that the

British national media have 'written off the country's second most famous town as a shell-suited, hub-cap-nicking "self-pity city"'. He refers to the editor of the local paper, *The Liverpool Echo*, Alastair Machray, commenting that Liverpool gets a rough ride from the rest of the country, with a combination of bad news and Liverpool guaranteed to generate special coverage and excitement in the London-based media:

> Negative stories always get followed up by the nationals and all newspapers are guilty of focusing on the negative. But . . . if something bad happens it makes it a better story if it happens in Liverpool, rather than Leeds or Colchester. That is bewildering.
>
> (Brown 2006)

In considering these ideas on the importance of the image of cities and towns, the success of and publicity around the book *Crap Towns* (Jordison and Kieran 2003) is worth considering briefly. While the title hardly suggests this is an academic source, it is important to bear in mind that the role of the popular media is probably more important in influencing public perceptions – and the popular media includes books, as well as newspaper, television and the Internet. The idea for *Crap Towns* came after Simon Jordison wrote an article in *The Idler* (a magazine for people who enjoyed their leisure) criticizing his home town, Morecambe, for its 'desolate' promenades. This led to him being sent comments and opinions on different towns from all over the country, which he and his friend Dan Kieran edited into the book (they had previously produced a book on *Crap Jobs* which had been quite successful). They felt that everyone had either grown up in, or at least visited, a town they despised and the replies from readers suggested they were right. The subtitle of the book was *The 50 Worst Places to Live in the UK* and the authors found that Hull came out at the top – one former resident of Hull describing it as 'a sad story of unemployment, teenage pregnancy, heroin addiction, crime, violence and rampant self-neglect'. The local media's response to this illustrates the importance attached to how the image of location is represented. The *Hull Daily Mail* got on to the story and invited the writer of the above quote to have a look around Hull and ran a front-page article on his experiences and his subsequent comments that he 'actually quite liked the place'. The book certainly touched a nerve and the authors found themselves insulted on Radio Wales and joked about in *The Sun*.

QUESTION BREAK

Although only light-hearted, *Crap Towns* (2003) certainly gained a good deal of wider media publicity. Listed here are the ten towns which came out as worst – before considering the questions below, make your own list.

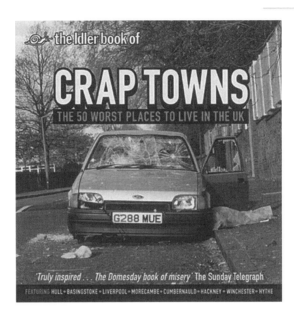

The top 10 worst towns:

Hull, Cumbernauld, Morecambe, Hythe, Winchester, Liverpool, St Andrews, Bexhill-on-Sea, Basingstoke, Hackney.

(Jordison and Kieran 2003)

QUESTIONS

- If you were describing your 'worst' town/city, what factors would influence you?
- What role, if any, would crime play in your decision?

The negative media portrayal of certain areas and towns is further evidenced by looking at the opposite end of the spectrum – peaceful, small-scale, rural-based areas are, in contrast, represented as places where crime is unusual. Indeed, so much so that when crimes, and particularly serious crimes, occur in such areas, they tend to make bigger news than if they had occurred in more 'expected' places. Murders in rural areas or villages invariably attract comments about 'sleepy villages being shocked' – both in terms of the media reporting and representation of real crime and fictional crime. Starting with fictional portrayals, the popular television series *Midsomer Murders* (a series which has been running since 1997) plays on the fact that it reverses the stereotypical of English village life. Based on the detective novels of Caroline Graham, and filmed in the English countryside, the programme uncovers and probes the criminal undercurrents that lie beneath the idyllic surface of village life in Midsomer. Part of the programme's attraction and certainly its surprise element is that, behind the peaceful and picturesque facade of this prosperous village, all sorts of vices and intrigues are afoot.

In terms of the media reporting of real-life crime, those crimes that occur in rural areas are typically described in relation to the backdrop of their supposedly peaceful environment. The following headline from *The Independent* illustrates this tendency, 'Typical English Village, Except for the Paedophile Moving Back Home' (24 August 1998). Below the headline, the article continues,

> In a scene typical of any English village a group of carefree children laughed and joked this weekend as they rode their bikes outside the village post office in Sonning Common. But this group is unlikely to be allowed out on their own for very much longer. In a couple of weeks, Rhys Hughes, a predatory paedophile with a 30-year history of abusing children, will be released from prison. He intends to return to his house in the scenic Oxfordshire village from where he terrorized children, including a five-year-old girl who lived nearby . . . And because the 65-year-old retired gardener was sentenced three months before the introduction of the 1991 Criminal Justice Act he cannot be made to conform to any supervision . . . He can come and go as he likes from the house he still owns.

In one of the most widely reported and harrowing of child murders in recent years, the abduction and murder of 10-year-olds Holly Wells and Jessica Chapman in August 2002, the nature of the location of the crime, the Cambridge village of Soham, was regularly commented on by the media. The following extract is from BBC News 24:

> On visiting Soham the first thing that strikes you is how small it is . . . Soham feels sleepy, safe and typically English . . . it's the kind of place where parents could let their children out unsupervised without undue concern.
>
> (17 December 2003)

Although such crimes are reacted to with outrage and anger wherever they occur, the fact that they have occurred in rural areas or villages adds an extra, almost sensationalized, element to the way that they are reported in the media.

Other more recent cases of child abduction have also led to media comment on the area from which the children were abducted in terms of image of the particular area. For example, in 2008 Shannon Matthews was reported as missing from her home on the Moorside council estate in Dewsbury, West Yorkshire, England. The search for her became a major missing person police operation with massive media coverage, including regular comments on the estate where Shannon lived. *The Sun* described it as 'like Beirut – only worse' while a more reflective article in *The Guardian* considered how it had 'come to symbolize all that is feckless and disreputable about the working class' (Wainwright 2008). The fact that Shannon was found after three weeks and had, in fact, been abducted by her uncle, with the knowledge of her mother, Karen Matthews, fuelled the negative picture of the particular estate and its residents; a picture that has continued in the years since Shannon's fake disappearance as the following extract from an article in *The Sun* newspaper indicates:

Vile mum of Shannon Matthews begins new life with a makeover

This is loathsome Karen Matthews – slimmer and disguised with a new short hairdo but still recognisable as the monster mum who staged the fake kidnap of her little daughter Shannon.

(*The Sun*, 13 April 2012)

In concluding this brief review of the part that geographical location can play in the media representation of crime and criminals, it would be useful to consider the links between the media and fear of crime in relation to location. In his recent research examining the media and fear of crime in a local context, Banks (2005) highlights the neglect of spatial context in research into the way the audience receives the media coverage of crime and argues for the development of more 'place sensitive' research. In particular, Banks analyses the way in which media representation of crime relates to the day-to-day lives of two middle-class households in Manchester. Even though ignored in much of the media coverage of crime, Banks argues that where people live and how people feel about those areas can have a major impact on the way that images of crime and criminals are interpreted. 'Sense of place' is one of the key variables that should be taken into account in examining and establishing the link between the media and crime. The two households he researched were the 'Kents' and the 'Henshaws', both white, middle-class families from similar social and educational backgrounds, living in the relatively prosperous suburb of Manchester, Didsbury. One family, the 'Kents' consumed a great deal of crime news and crime drama, from both television and the local press. Even though they had suffered break-ins they felt little sense of fear of crime. Banks suggests this is because they had lived locally for years, and had an extended family and friendship network living nearby – they 'felt connected and confident in their environment'. In this context, the media emphasis on crime was accepted and absorbed as a manageable risk. By contrast, the 'Henshaws' were not born and raised locally and had few family or social ties in the area. They tended to avoid watching and reading about crime in the media. They were a much more insulated family and, even though they had not been victims of crime, the impression they gave was of a household 'somewhat fearful and under siege from crime, both "real" and represented'. So, in spite of similarities in terms of background and where they lived, there were clear differences between the two families in terms of how they used the media and their attitudes and responses to the media presentation of crime and criminals – differences that seemed to reflect different approaches to how they viewed their communities and localities.

THE MEDIA, CLASS AND CRIMINALS

Here we will consider the extent to which the social class background of criminals influences the media representation of them. In many ways, however, social class is a less straightforward area to examine and analyse than, say, age, gender or location, all of which are relatively easy to measure. The measurement, and indeed concept, of social class has been an area of considerable debate, both in academic circles and more generally. While people are aware of their age, gender and where they live and are able to give specific answers when asked, the situation with class is less clear cut. People might classify themselves as working, middle or upper class, for instance, by referring to a range of criteria – perhaps their occupation, their wealth, their family background or their education. Having said that, social class is generally measured by social scientists by reference to occupation. Although it is not necessary to go into the academic debates over the meaning and measuring of social class, a few brief comments before discussing it in relation to the media and criminals would be helpful.

As mentioned, most social scientists see class position as largely determined by an individual's place in the economic system in terms of their occupation; and most would regard modern industrial societies as being stratified on the basis of social class. Although there have been different classifications of occupation in terms of class, in Britain class has typically been defined using the Registrar-General's scale of social class (see Table 4.1 below). This consists of six major class groupings, with class 3 sub-divided into non-manual and manual occupations; and in terms of social class groupings, middle class referred to groups 1, 2 and 3a and working class to the rest, from 3b to 5.

Table 4.1 The Registrar-General's scale of social class and socio-economic groups

1. Higher level professionals, managers and administrators
2. Lower level professionals, managers and administrators
3a. Lower level white-collar workers
3b. Skilled manual workers
4. Semi-skilled manual workers
5. Unskilled manual workers

While there have been more sophisticated attempts to classify different occupations in terms of class, with regard to examining media representations we will refer to upper, middle and working class in relation to broad occupational categories – so that upper class is associated with ownership of property, in particular land; middle class refers to those with non-manual occupations; and working class to those with manual occupations.

Although crime is committed by individuals from the whole range of social backgrounds, official statistics do show a strong association between social class and criminality, and that this is especially so with crimes of violence. And this link has led to a massive range of theorizing about why certain groups and individuals commit crime – and whether or not it reflects biases in the detection and prosecuting of offenders. However, those theoretical debates and issues are not our interest here, rather it is on how the media reports and represents offenders from different social backgrounds. In particular, we will look at how middle-class offenders are represented – by focusing on the media portrayal of white-collar crime (almost by definition middle-class crime) and white-collar criminals.

The key figure in the development of the study of white-collar crime is American sociologist Edwin Sutherland, whose work in the 1940s and beyond aimed to move criminology's attention away from crimes committed by those from lower social classes and towards those crimes committed by 'respectable' members of society. However, his work, and indeed that of later criminologists, has encountered difficulties in trying to provide a tight definition of white-collar crime. As Newburn (2007) points out, Sutherland's use of the term white-collar crime refers to three different types of crime – 'crimes committed by people of high status . . . crimes committed on behalf of organizations . . . [and] crimes committed against organizations'. It is the first of these, the social status of the offender, that will be the focus of our discussion of the media.

Partly because of the nature of white-collar crime – for instance, the fact that it generally takes place in private, the offenders will usually have a legitimate reason for being at the scene of the crime and that often there is no obvious victim or complainant – it is likely that white-collar crime is under-recorded in official crime statistics to an even greater degree than more 'conventional' crimes. Furthermore, relatively few white-collar offenders are dealt with by the criminal justice system, so that information on their social backgrounds is not easy to find. Newburn (2013) suggests that the higher status white-collar offenders are especially likely to enjoy considerable protection from prosecution because of their status. He refers to the prosecution for fraud in 2007 of Conrad Black, a British life peer and owner of *Telegraph* newspapers, as an 'exception to the more general trend in which elite offenders tend to manage to avoid prosecution and conviction'. So, given these characteristics of white-collar crime, it is not surprising that white-collar offenders, as well as crimes, get relatively little coverage in the media.

In an analysis of crime stories in national and Sunday newspapers, Tombs and Whyte (2001) found that the reporting of conventional crime stories was far greater than that of corporate crime; and that 'the overwhelming focus upon "conventional crimes" is greatest in the tabloids, while the imbalance is less stark in broadsheets, and particularly in the more liberal *Observer* and *Guardian*'. Also, that those corporate crime stories that were covered were unlikely to be in the first few pages of newspapers, but rather tended to appear away from headline news and in more specialist sections such as 'business' or 'finance' pages. Tombs and Whyte are somewhat pessimistic about corporate and white-collar crime and criminals getting more media coverage in future, as they put it:

> It is sixty years since Edwin Sutherland's attempts to free the discipline of criminology from the grip of dominant definitions of 'crime' handed down by the powerful. Is it not time that a few more of us started to redress this grossly distorted story?
>
> (Tombs and Whyte 2001, p. 22)

In considering how the media present and 'construct' white-collar crimes, Levi (2006) argues white-collar crimes and fraud, more generally, are treated by the mass media as what he terms 'extensions of infotainment'. Such crimes tend to be reported by the media if they involve celebrities being in some kind of trouble and turning to criminal activity to deal with it. For instance, celebrities or other 'successful' well-off people turning to drugs or gambling or committing financial frauds such as tax evasion. Levi argues that the media publicity accorded to middle-class crime has to be understood in relation to the cult of celebrity – in other words, the media focus on defendants of which their readers and viewers will have heard. He provides numerous examples of such cases, such as the American 'middle-class homemaker icon', Martha Stewart, jailed in 2004 and British politicians Lord Jeffrey Archer and Jonathon Aitken who were jailed in 2001 and 1999 respectively. Sports stars who are found guilty of criminal offences are also given a particular focus – jockey Lester Piggot was jailed for tax evasion in 1987, in 1998 soccer coach Terry Venables was banned from acting as a company director and jockey Kieran Fallon was banned from racing in 2006 over a race fixing scandal.

We have spent some time considering the ambiguous nature of white-collar crime and how it is responded to. It seems clear that the reporting of white-collar, business crime and criminals raises questions that, according to Nelken (2007), differ from those posed by other types of criminal behaviour, such as 'Why do they do it when they have so much to lose?' It would certainly seem to be the case that people (and, presumably, the media) have difficulty in seeing supposedly 'respectable' people with well-paid and well-regarded jobs as also being criminals. In concluding this brief discussion, we will look at the media portrayal of two (in)famous white-collar criminals whose offences cost their employers a small fortune – Jerome Kerviel and Nick Leeson.

Jerome Kerviel is the trader who cost the French bank, Societe Generale, something like £3.7 billion in the biggest fraud in financial history, discovered in January 2008. The newspaper reporting of this fraud portrayed Kerviel as either a 'genius' or emphasized his relative ordinariness, with quotes from his previous tutors suggesting 'he was a student just like others . . . and he didn't distinguish himself from others' (*International Herald Tribune*, 25 January 2008). The scandal led to a flurry of clips and comments on the web, with many defending and even glorifying Kerviel:

> Jerome Kerviel may have lost Societe Generale £3.7bn, but he is also rapidly becoming a hero among the viral video community.
>
> (*The Guardian*, 1 February 2008)

And this scandal has led to a resurgence of interest in and comment on previous rogue traders, notably Nick Leeson. Nick Leeson's risk-taking cost Barings Bank £800 million and led to its collapse in 1995. It also led to him being sentenced to six and a half years in jail in Singapore. Leeson was released after three and a half years, in 1999, and, having survived that, has since become something of a media celebrity – a film based on him, *Rogue Trader*, starring Ewan McGregor was released in 1999, he has his own website, speaks regularly at conferences and dinners and published an autobiography, *Back from the Brink: Coping with Stress* in 2005. The public and media reaction to large-scale fraudsters such as Kerviel and Leeson does seem to contain a good deal of admiration, if grudging, that sits at odds with the way 'conventional' criminals are responded to (an issue explored in the question break below).

QUESTION BREAK

Read the following extracts – taken from Nick Leeson's website; the *Daily Mail*'s comment on middle-class crimes, the CNN's (Cable News Network) selection of the top 10 British villains; and the *Daily Mirror*'s article on which offenders have their honours taken off them and which do not.

Nick Leeson website

Welcome

Welcome to the official website of Nick Leeson – the rogue trader whose unchecked risk-taking caused the biggest financial scandal of the 20th century. The collapse of Barings Bank (personal bank to HM The Queen) in 1995 and Nick Leeson's role in it, is one of the most spectacular debacles in modern financial history. How could one trader bring down the banking empire that had funded the Napoleonic Wars?

. . . Following Barings' collapse Nick Leeson was sentenced to six and half years in a gang-ridden Singaporean jail, in conditions that defy belief, while at the same time, his wife left him and he was diagnosed with colon cancer.

Against all odds, Nick Leeson survived and, now fully recovered from cancer, lives happily in Ireland with second wife Leona and three children. In 2005 Nick was appointed General Manager of Galway United FC. Nick Leeson continues to speak regularly at conference dinners and June 2005 saw the release of his new book *Back from the Brink: Coping with Stress*.

Minor 'Crimes' of the Middle Classes Raking in £400m Fortune for Cash-hungry Councils

More than £400 million a year is being raised by police and town halls targeting minor 'middle-class' crimes. They are hitting millions of people with tickets for speeding, parking, litter and even putting out bins on the wrong day. The 'offenders'; are being caught using a range of increasingly advanced surveillance techniques.

(*Daily Mail*, 18 January 2010)

The Screening Room's Top 10 British Villains

According to Hollywood, nothing says 'I'm an evil mastermind' like a cut-glass British accent . . . as one of the movie world's favourite stereotypes, this month we celebrate the London Film Festival by picking our top 10 British villains . . .

1. Laurence Olivier as Richard III (*Richard III*, 1955)
2. Peter Cushing as Grand Moff Tarkin (*Star Wars*, 1977)
3. Christopher Lee as Dracula (*Dracula*, 1958)
4. Ian McDiarmid as Emperor Palpatine (*Return of the Jedi*, 1983)

5=. Alan Rickman as the sheriff of Nottingham (*Robin Hood: Prince of Thieves*, 1991)

5=. Basil Rathbone as the sheriff of Nottingham (*The Adventures of Robin Hood*, 1938)

7. Malcolm McDowell as Alex de Large (*A Clockwork Orange*, 1971)
8. Carl Boehm as Mark Lewis (*Peeping Tom*, 1960)
9. Ian McKellan as Magneto (*X-Men*, 2000)
10. Terry-Thomas as Raymond Delauney (*School for Scoundrels*, 1960)

(www.cnn.com/entertainment, 26 October 2007)

This is a Gong Wrong

Tory apologists have been quick to enter the row over Naseem Hamed having his MBE stripped while Jeffrey Archer is allowed to remain a lord. 'It's not an establishment stitch-up', one said on the radio. 'It's simply because no laws exist to eject convicted criminals from the House of Lords'.

And he's right. But what about disgraced dames and knights? How about saying to a gerrymandering voterigger who committed perjury in trying to cheat the British taxpayer out of £42 million that you can no longer call yourself Dame Shirley Porter? How about saying to Mark Thatcher, who plea-bargained his way out of an African jail after helping to finance a failed coup, that we're taking back your inherited knighthood, ridiculously awarded to your dad for getting legless while smacked by your mother's handbag?

Of course, there's one rule for someone from a Sheffield council estate like Naseem (who was only given a piddling MBE to tick the ethnic/class box and make the shameless Honours List look all embracing) and another for Tory politicians and their offspring handed titles as establishment payback.

Naseem has been stripped like jockey Lester Piggot (taxfiddling) and darts player Phil Taylor (assault) because they are seen as scummy little oiks who should never have been allowed in the gentleman's club in the first place. Thatcher and Porter may have brought greater shame on Queen and country, but the powers-that-be have their lineage to think of.

(Reade B., *Daily Mirror*, 4 January 2007)

QUESTIONS

- Why do you think there is a degree of admiration for criminals such as Leeson?
- How does the media and public response to convicted large-scale fraudsters, for instance Nick Leeson, and middle-class criminals compare with that given to 'conventional' offenders?
- How would you describe the class background of the 10 film villains in the CNN top 10 British villains list?
- To what extent do you agree with the comments made by Reade in the *Daily Mirror* extract?

FURTHER READING

Jewkes Y. (2011) *Media and Crime*, Second edition, London: Sage. Chapter 5 of this excellent general text explores how the media respond to serious offending by women and analyses the stereotypical media portrayals of female criminals.

Mason P. (ed.) (2003) *Criminal Visions: Media Representations of Crime and Justice*, Collompton: Willan Publishing (see p. 226). An edited collection, part 2 of which focuses on how the media represents different types of criminal, including bank robbers, sex offenders, terrorists and serial killers.

The Media Portrayal of Victims

As we have seen throughout this book, the media, in all their various forms, are the vehicle by which the average person gets to know the world around them. It is pretty clear that the media play a major part in the developing, if not the actual social construction, of stereotypes – and most notably those that portray groups and activities in a critical or negative way. They have the power to criminalize individuals and whole sections of society and help to create moral panics around certain issues (see Chapter 3 on moral panics). And of course, the reporting of and writing about crime, in particular, allows and even encourages moral evaluations concerning what should be seen as good and what bad. It is not surprising, then, that the media can and do also contribute to the way we react to and perceive the victims of crime. This chapter will explore the links between the production and dissemination of the media's presentation of crime stories involving victims and the existing social and cultural norms.

Before examining the media presentation of victims, it is worthwhile first to briefly consider the development of academic victimology and the various theoretical strands within the discipline that have helped in the formation of our perception of victims of crime in general.

THEORIES AND METHODS OF RESEARCH IN VICTIMOLOGY

The term victimology was first coined by Frederick Wertham, who called for a 'science of victimology' (Wertham 1949). However, in terms of the historical development of victimology, it can be argued that Hans von Hentig and Bartholomew Mendelsohn are the theorists generally recognized as the 'founding fathers' of the sub-discipline. Both have been profoundly influential in establishing victimology as an academic discipline, but in quite distinct ways. Von Hentig's work is closely linked to criminology in that its concern and focus are with the victims of crime – so victimology is analysed as a part of criminology. In contrast, Mendelsohn's victimological theorizing is very much bound up in the philosophy of human rights – and victimology is seen as, essentially, an independent discipline. This division, and Mendelsohn's views in particular, help explain why victimology has been able to incorporate those who are best described as 'unconventional victims' – a particular area that has been crucial to the development of both radical and critical victimology (which we look at below).

However, despite these differences, both theorists are proponents of what has become widely known as positivist or conventional victimology. The key characteristics of positive victimology can be described as, 'the identification of factors which contribute to a non-random pattern of victimization, a focus on interpersonal crimes of violence, and a concern to identify victims who may have contributed to their own victimization' (Miers 1989). Miers, therefore, draws upon a number of influences which underpin positivist victimology, including a concern with the patterns and regularities of victimization and the development and application of the key concepts of 'victim precipitation', 'victim proneness' and lifestyle.

Arguably the first systematic study of the victims of crime was Von Hentig's book, *The Criminal and His Victim(s)*, published in 1948 (of course, the use of the male term was even more the norm in the 1940s). Von Hentig proposed a dynamic approach which discussed how the offender and the victim were involved in an interaction, thereby challenging the concept of the victim as passive. *The Criminal and His Victim* includes a chapter dealing with victims entitled 'The Contribution of the Victim to the Genesis of the Crime' in which the concept of victim proneness – the notion that some individuals might be more susceptible to victimization than others – is discussed. Individuals may be prone due to their social and/or psychological state. In other words there are characteristics which may have precipitated the offence through which they were victimized.

Mendelsohn (1963), on the other hand, argued that certain victims of crime were more or less culpable – an obvious example of greater culpability being the aggressor who through the fault of his own actions is killed. While both of these approaches tend to overemphasize notions of blame and vulnerability, they nevertheless provided the impetus for further research within the discipline of victimology. Furthermore, the idea of the blameworthy victim was to form the basis for theories of victim precipitation. Victim precipitation is based on the notion that there are certain situations in which the victim is a direct precipitator of the offence. So, for instance, in a murder case the victim may have precipitated the crime by having been the first to use physical force or a weapon.

Positivist ideas have led to a great deal of debate and have been strongly criticized, not least because of their attempts to cite the victim's role as a causal effect in their victimization. The use of the notion of victim precipitation and its connotations of victim blaming is highly controversial, but still remains a prominent feature in the formulation of explanations and reasons for crime which are employed by various agencies within the criminal justice system.

Radical victimology

In response to some of the criticism lodged against positive victimology, the radical victimological perspective emerged in the late 1960s and 1970s. As mentioned, radical victimology can be traced back to the work of Mendelsohn and his argument for a victimology of human rights that allows for exploration of the role of the state in defining who 'legitimate' victims are and, more importantly, how the criminal justice system is implicated in the 'construction' of victims and criminals. As a consequence, radical victimology acknowledges, in particular, those victims who have been rendered invisible. These victims have been best described by Quinney (1971) as 'victims of police force, the victims of war, the victims of the correctional system, the victims of state violence, the victims of oppression of any sort'. Radical victimology's holistic approach towards the victim allows issues relating particularly to women, such as rape/domestic violence, to enter the public arena. Moreover, the emphasis on the role of the state in the production of victims gives the corporate/white-collar victim a legitimate status.

What might be termed conventional radical victimology has, then, helped to expose the limited structural basis of victimization and therefore the problems facing the poor and the powerless. However, it did not contribute in any meaningful way to empirical research. And, as implied above, although positivist victimology generated much invaluable data, its research was based upon conventional constructions of crime and therefore neglected sexual and racially motivated crime and victims of corporate crime.

Critical victimology

Partly as a response to the shortcomings of other previous victimological perspectives and partly to build on the insights of feminism and left realist approaches, a new, 'critical' victimological approach has emerged in recent years. As with radical victimology, which it overlaps with in a number of ways, it is based on an essentially interpretivist, 'micro' approach to theorizing about social issues – in the context of victimology to theorizing about victims of crime. Critical victimology looks to include the 'hidden' victims of crime in its analysis and to consider and highlight the role of the state in perpetuating inequalities in the 'production of victims'.

The early critical victimological approach has been criticized and developed by Walklate (1989, 1990) amongst others. In particular, she has advocated a critical victimology that takes seriously the need for the (sub-)discipline to be based on empirical, objective research and to take close account of the structural context in which it is operating, but at the same time to do this without losing the real insights and strengths that can be offered by an interpretive understanding.

A key issue here seems to be the need to define what is the 'real' and to examine the processes which help provide an understanding of everyday reality. This issue is highlighted partly to take account of the fact that it is quite possible for victims not to know about their victimization and, therefore, the causes of it. It is for this reason that critical victimology advocates the need to examine the processes which 'go on behind our backs' in the context of defining victims. Critical victimology problema- tizes the relationship between the citizen and the state, it does not see the state as neutral, rather its mechanisms contribute to those victims we see and those we do not see. It is therefore not objective but self-interested and self-motivated. This, according to critical victimology, raises problems in relation to race, gender and class and how they are articulated in policy terms.

This theoretical approach to or refinement of critical victimology, developed by Mawby and Walklate (1994) amongst others, draws upon Giddens's (1984) theory of structuration in highlighting the importance of both macro and micro analysis – of structure and agency, as Giddens terms it. Structuration, as emphasized throughout critical victimology, allows the victim a voice. Critical victimology highlights the importance of people's ability to fight for themselves against their structural constraints, and quite often with surprising results.

Deserving and undeserving victims

These theoretical ideas have found their way into the world of the media, who have the power to socially construct the idea of the victim. The idea of the deserving and undeserving victim is a theme often found in media discourse, and ideas around morality are passed on almost unconsciously from the pages of newspapers and tele- vision reporting. Louis Althusser (1969) argued that our desires, values and prefer- ences are not innate but rather they are learned through ideological practice. We receive our ideological practice through what he termed 'ideological state appara- tuses', such as the family, the education system and the media.

His argument can be said to be closely related to the idea of propaganda. Alternatively, social psychological theories explore the role of the media in providing information to its audience; although a general theory of human behaviour, social learning theory, for example, has been used by theorists who are concerned with media effects. Albert Bandura (1977), for example, warned that 'children and adults acquire attitudes, emotional responses, and new styles of conduct through filmed and television modelling'.

The focus on the victim within media discourse is not merely to highlight society's moral code. Wherever a victim exists a crime has been perpetrated; and crime stories are the biggest sellers across the media, in films, on television, in the press and in books. Indeed, the idea that 'if it bleeds it leads' is often an accurate description of the way in which news is deemed as 'newsworthy'. Indeed the phrase 'if it bleeds it leads' has become associated with newsrooms and the media for a number of years, along with sayings such as 'sex sells', but has never been clearly attributed to any one individual. It illustrates the idea that the victim can be compelling; and ultimately television ratings and newspaper sales often rely upon the regularly gruesome descriptions of victims of crimes.

It can be argued that society in general and victimology as an academic discipline have managed to socially construct the idea of the deserving and undeserving victim. Feminist theorists have been particularly critical of positivist victimology and its attempts to cite the victim's role as a causal factor in his or her victimization. Through the use of such terms as victim precipitation, culpability and proneness, positivist or traditional victimology has created the idea of the deserving and undeserving victim.

QUESTION BREAK

What sort of victims might be seen as deserving and undeserving?

How does the media differentiate between the deserving and undeserving victim?

Victims of child abuse are most obviously and strongly presented by the media as deserving victims – for instance, tragedies such as that of the murder of Victoria Climbie in 2000, who was a victim of child abuse at the hands of her great-aunt and her boyfriend. In this case, the media portrayed the tragic circumstances of her life, evoking sympathy – she was the ultimate innocent, a trusting vulnerable child, as the extract from the BBC News coverage illustrates.

Girl, 8, 'Tortured' to Death

An eight-year-old girl, brought to England for a better life, died after suffering serious cruelty and neglect, a court has heard. Anna Climbie was beaten, burned with cigarettes and forced to sleep in a bin liner inside an empty bath, the jury at the Old Bailey was told. She died in hospital in February, suffering from hypothermia and malnutrition . . . A post mortem revealed 128 separate scars on her body including burns.

(BBC News, 22 November 2000,
http://news.bbc.co.uk/2/hi/uk_news/1035455.stm)

Another more recent victim of child abuse and murder was what has become known as the 'Baby P' case. Peter Connolly was 17 months old when he died in August 2007. He suffered more than 50 injuries after months of abuse from his mother, Tracey Connolly, her boyfriend, Steven Barker, and their lodger, Jason Owen. Aside from the horrific nature of this case, a particular aspect which received massive media coverage was the fact that Baby P had been seen repeatedly by social workers and had even been placed on the 'at risk' register. Also, Baby P had lived in the same part of London, Haringey, as Victoria Climbie, which led to widespread criticism of the child protection services in that borough and to a public inquiry and nationwide review of social service care.

As with Victoria Climbie, the media coverage of Baby P emphasized his vulnerability and innocence:

Nasty, Brutish and Short: The Horrific Life of Baby P
(*The Independent*, 16 November 2008)

Let Down by Everyone Who Should Have Cared: Report Reveals Appalling Failures That Led to Baby P's Brutal Death
(*Daily Mail*, 27 October 2010)

In an interesting study of the changes in the press coverage of child murders over the period 1930–2000, Wardle (2007) examined the visual representation of a number of high-profile child murders. She found that the content of the visuals changed over that period, from emphasizing the role of the criminal justice system in capturing and bringing to justice the murderers to a much greater focus on victims' families and the wider grief and emotions shown from society as a whole in recent years. Wardle starts by highlighting the massive media interest in crime news in general and the influence that media coverage can have on the public's understanding of crime. Without going into the role of and theory behind visual images and representations, it is clear that photographs can capture and help to create reality. Wardle found that the coverage of child murders increased over the period she was studying and that in the earlier part of this period, up to the 1960s, child abductions and murders were typically described as isolated and motiveless, whereas by the 1990s the sexual motives of the offenders were given greater prominence alongside the notion of 'predatory paedophiles' stalking communities. She also noted a change from photographs of the offender being the most regularly used images to photographs of the victim and victims' families being most common. Also, by the end of the twentieth century, photographs of public protests against paedophiles and of public displays of grieving were routinely used by newspapers.

QUESTION BREAK

Look at recent media coverage of murder cases – how many use photographs of the victims?

How would you describe those pictures?

With regard to the increased use of photographs of victims and their families, these photographs tend to be taken from past family album shots placed alongside contemporary pictures of grieving family members. By the 1990s, all of the newspapers looked at by Wardle tended to publish pictures of the victim as part of a loving family, in a way that, as she puts it, 'further underlined the tragedy of the crime by forcing readers to identify with the idyllic family album photographs, and to place themselves as part of the grieving family'.

Wardle also makes the point that children are not just represented in one manner – as innocent victims, but that they can also be shown as 'undeserving victims'. As well as being in danger, children are also seen as dangerous themselves; and she refers to Jewkes's (2004) comment that children can be represented at either end of a spectrum, as 'tragic victims' or, when offending themselves, as 'evil monsters'.

So far, in considering deserving or undeserving as categories of the way the media represents victims of crime, we have focused on child victims. However, in looking at women as victims of crime there has been some debate as to the differential portrayal of women victims according to their occupation and/or status – in particular the way that prostitutes who are victims of crime are represented in the media. And this raises another aspect of the deserving/ undeserving distinction – gender bias.

Marian Meyers (1997) argues that a gender bias exists within media reporting of male and female victims. Moreover, there is a fundamental difference between the 'innocent' and 'guilty' victim which feeds into the positivist concept of victim precipitation discussed earlier. Meyers goes as far as to suggest that the portrayal of female victims is 'a function of an underlying male supremacy that separates women into virgin/whore or good girl/bad girl categories based on cultural stereotypes, myths and assumptions regarding the proper role of women' (Meyers 1997).

Meyers further develops this dichotomy by stating that the innocent victim is cast in the vulnerable role whereas the guilty victim is held 'responsible for their status'. In analysing media responses, Meyers found that victims who were deemed as being wholly deserving of their victim status were typically very young or old and had often been tortured or murdered in a gruesome manner. This obviously taps into society's ideas around mental and physical vulnerability evoking sympathy. Visual and verbal cues were used to describe the frailty in comparison to the attacker; and neighbours and friends were called upon to comment on the innocence of the victim.

Those not in the vulnerable group were cast as in some way responsible for their own suffering. They were often described as drunk at the time of the incident, not cautious enough, involved in questionable activities or in behaviour outside of their *traditional* role. Meyers makes the point that in some crimes there seems to be a greater interest in considering the victim's position and role than in others. As she puts it:

> There is an interest in looking for the 'reasons' why a victim was beaten. That is similar to asking why a woman was raped, unlike in other crimes – for example, do people ask why a person was robbed?

> (Meyers 1997)

As mentioned, the idea of women victims being portrayed as either 'good' or 'bad', 'whores' or 'angels', is particularly apparent in the way the media reports crime against prostitutes – as the reporting of the recent murders of five women in Ipswich, Suffolk illustrates (the media coverage of the 'Suffolk rapist' is also discussed on pp. 15–18). In December 2006, the dead bodies of five women were discovered near and around the town of Ipswich in Suffolk. Media portrayal immediately focused on the fact that these women were prostitutes. Discourses around the case focused on the fact that the many of the women where drug abusers and had sex with men to feed their habit – this obviously fed into the notion that these women's lives were somehow less valuable and ultimately that they were in part responsible and even culpable for their deaths.

The style of popular journalism used to report the crimes in both the press and television led to a deluge of moral judgements. The past lives of the prostitutes became public property and were meticulously chronicled by the press. The prostitutes were distinguished from 'other' young women and consequently their evident 'culpability' raised.

A leading article in the *Daily Mail*, for example, stated:

> We do not share in the responsibility for either their grubby little existences or their murders. Society isn't to blame. It might not be fashionable, or even acceptable in some quarters, to say so, but in their chosen field of 'work', death by strangulation is an occupational hazard.
>
> (Littlejohn R., 'Spare us the "People's Prostitute" Routine',
> 18 December 2006)

Even when reporting the sentencing of Wright for the murders in Ipswich (see also Chapter 1, pp. 15–16), *The Sun* began its coverage with the comment, 'Serial killer Steve Wright today faces life behind bars for throttling five hookers . . .' (*The Sun*, 22 February 2008). Although the reporting focused on Wright's background, that first sentence does suggest that the victims are perhaps not as deserving or innocent as other victims may be.

The coverage of the Ipswich prostitutes resembled the case of the Yorkshire Ripper 30 years earlier in which detective Jim Hobson said: 'He (the Ripper) has made it clear that he hates prostitutes. Many people do. But the Ripper is now killing innocent girls.'

An article dating from the time of the Yorkshire Ripper stated that, 'the police describe the first two women as having "loose" morals and although both told us that they rejected that description, the sad truth is that they made themselves vulnerable' (*The Sunday Times*, 1980).

Of course, the reporting of the Ipswich prostitutes rested upon the fact that these women lived their lives outside of women's traditional role and therefore did not deserve the protection and sympathy that is usually evoked by the reporting of other victims. However, it should be mentioned that not all media coverage is so negative and a BBC dramatization of the murder and subsequent investigation of three one-hour programmes aired in 2010 and entitled *Five Daughters* tried to counteract this sort of journalism by portraying the real lives of the murdered women as mothers, daughters, friends and colleagues, although it could be argued the damage had been done by the earlier negative reporting.

QUESTION BREAK

Look at the examples of the reporting of murders of prostitutes.

He has murdered the five prostitutes – all were heroin addicts and three were mothers – in less than six weeks . . .

The bodies of three other vice girls – Gemma Adams, 25, Tania Nicol, 19, and Anneli Alderton, 24 – have been found over the past ten days.

(*The Sun*, 13 December 2006)

The five women murdered in Ipswich were tragic, lost souls who met a grisly end . . . No one with a shred of humanity would wish upon them their ghastly lives and horrible deaths. But Mother Teresa, they weren't . .

Frankly, I'm tired of the lame excuses about how they fell victim to ruthless pimps who plied them with drugs. These women were on the streets because they wanted to be. We are all capable of free will. At any time, one or all of them could have sought help from the police, or the church or a charity, or a government agency specifically established to deal with heroin addicts. They chose not to.

(Littlejohn R., 'Spare us the "People's Prostitute" Routine', *Daily Mail*, 18 December 2006)

During the 1970s and into 1980, Sutcliffe killed 13 women and left seven others for dead. The body of his first victim – 28-year-old Wilma McCann – was discovered in 1975, and, from the beginning, the West Yorkshire police were guilty of dragging their feet and bungling the investigation. Complacent police officers overlooked vital clues, and inadequate technology was used to collate the thousands of interviews and intelligence. Amidst all this, Sutcliffe just kept killing – with hammers, screwdrivers and knives – and police were no further forward by the time the body of his fifth victim, Jayne MacDonald, was discovered in 1977.

MacDonald's murder was described by police and press as a 'tragic mistake'. The previous victims had all been prostitutes, and therefore, in the eyes of many, complicit in their own demise. MacDonald was 16 though, and described by the police as 'respectable and innocent'. Victims were duly divided into deserving and not-so-deserving victims.

(Bindel J., 'Terror on our Streets', *The Guardian*, 13 December 2006)

Bradford Prostitute Murders: The Victims

Police have linked the cases of three prostitutes who have gone missing in Bradford and are questioning a man over their murders. Here are profiles of the alleged victims:

Susan Rushworth, 43: disappeared on June 22, 2009
Miss Rushworth, known as Sue or Susie, was a mother of three, with two young grandchildren, and had been receiving treatment for heroin addiction . . . Miss Rushworth, who suffers from epilepsy, is described by police as a 'street sex worker' . . .

Shelley Armitage, 31: disappeared April 26, 2010
Miss Armitage, who was reported missing by her boyfriend after she went missing from the streets of the red light district . . . was last seen on CCTV cameras at about 10pm on Monday, April 26, in Rebecca Street, close to the city centre. She had not claimed her benefit or used her mobile phone since she went missing. Miss Armitage also failed to attend a crown court hearing to be sentenced for an assault on a police officer last year.

Suzanne Blamires, 36: disappeared May 21, 2010
Miss Blamires has worked as a prostitute for at least a decade, living in different parts of the city. Her last known address was only three streets away from Miss Armitage, a friend of her, in the Allerton district of Bradford. It is believed that she also had problems with alcohol and drugs. In 2001 she was fined by magistrates after she propositioned a plain-clothes officer near Bradford University. She had been in several relationships over the past five years and was known to take both heroin and crack cocaine, as well as drinking large amounts of alcohol.

(The Daily Telegraph, 27 May 2010)

QUESTION

- What phrases do you think suggest that the victims in these crimes were perhaps to blame for their victimization and/or were less deserving of sympathy?

The notion of deserving and undeserving victims can also be related to the victims of corporate crime – which is sometimes not seen as 'real' crime or as 'victimless' crime. However, whether as consumers, workers, passengers, investors or residents, most people will become victims of some form of corporate crime. Despite this, victims of corporate crime remain relatively invisible and tend to evoke less sympathy than victims of 'conventional' crimes such as murder or abuse; and the media coverage tends to be less emotive. As Greer (2007) puts it:

The most notable thing about white-collar and corporate offending in the media is their general lack of prevalence and prominence relative to 'traditional' or 'conventional' crimes of interpersonal and sexual violence. This apparent lack of media interest can be related back to . . . [definitions of] newsworthiness.

In considering the media reporting of victims, the US organization, The National Center for Victims of Crime, points out that the media can inflict 'second victimization' on some victims by exacerbating their feelings of violation. This can occur in a number of ways, by searching for and reporting anything 'negative' about the victim, by inappropriately delving into the victims' past and attempting to interview victims at inappropriate times, such as during trials, or at funerals or in hospital settings. It is important to bear in mind that the great majority of crime victims will never have dealt with the news media; they are likely to be thrown into the limelight against their will because of crimes committed against themselves (or family members or friends in the case of secondary victims). And in high-profile cases the media coverage will be more intrusive and, potentially, distressing to the victim(s) – perhaps particularly when a combination of media sources are competing for scoops about the story. Indeed, the pressure to get a story can lead journalists to be overly aggressive to victims and their relatives. Another way in which the media can make things worse for victims is through the way that crime stories are presented – for instance, through filming or photographing bodies and body bags or through film footage of the crime and crime scene as a lead-in to a news item. An example of this was the media reporting of the kidnapping and subsequent beheading in Iraq of Ken Bigley, a British engineer, in October 2004. Bigley's kidnapping had become a political issue with the media reporting on videos released by Bigley's captors in which he was shown pleading for his life and for help from the British government. After his death, videos of the beheading were released and went 'viral', attracting massive publicity.

It is clear that one of the main issues relating to the media coverage of victims is the issue of secondary victimization. Kate Mulley (2001) states that the way the 'media interest is often experienced as a form of secondary victimization and can make individuals feel harassed, vulnerable, lacking in control and that their privacy has been violated'. Mulley also makes the point that many victims of crime just do not want their photographs or names to be published – at the moment anonymity is only guaranteed to child witnesses or when the person is a victim of rape or a sex offence.

Partly in response to these kinds of secondary victimization, the National Center for Victims of Crime (NCVC) in the USA has developed and published guidelines for crime victims who are interviewed on television talk shows and a suggested code of ethics for victim advocates in the media.

The positive influence of the media

As stated earlier, the media can be one of the most powerful tools and their potential for good must not be understated. The media in all its forms reaches a massive audience on a daily basis and news and messages and important information are exchanged. For the victims of crime this can aid their recovery and allow them to utilize the media. In her discussion of the way the media can further victimize victims, Mulley (2001) also mentions some positive aspects of media coverage of crime. Some victims and witnesses can and do derive a degree of comfort from media interest; talking to the media can help victims feel they are doing something to help with the investigation of the crime. And as Mulley puts it,

> Some individuals need to express their feelings and convey the hurt and anguish they have suffered. Others will want to tell their side of the story . . . or they may believe they want to set the record straight . . . Another strong motivation for cooperating with media interest is altruistic: to help and give strength to others who may have suffered a similar experience.
>
> (Mulley 2001, p. 30)

Victims may find that dealing with the media can be therapeutic at a time when they are suffering great loss and sadness. The media can draw attention to specific issues, such as highlighting victims' rights and even influencing government policy. The media can also provide a forum for the dissemination and exchange of important information, as in the case of missing children, for example. In the USA, for instance, the news media have played a significant role in promoting reform to the juvenile justice system that has included greater victim involvement in court proceedings.

It might be said that the media wields a double-edged sword in relation to the coverage of crime victims. Victims can be those either directly or indirectly affected by crime – and in those cases where the direct victims are dead, other 'victims' can include members of the dead person's family and social networks. On the one hand, media attention can further traumatize victims; once thrust into the public eye media coverage can often be unsympathetic, voyeuristic and psychologically damaging. However, on the other hand, for some the role of the media can be a positive influence.

The relationship between the media and victims of crime provides a potentially awkward and volatile mix – there are people doing their job as journalists talking with and interviewing people who are in the depths of despair. And these victims, especially in the cases of the most serious crime, will be living what seems to them a nightmare that they have suddenly been thrust into, unprepared and in a completely random manner. However, most victims do seem to accept that the media have a role to play and that some degree of media intrusion is inevitable.

One of the most renowned cases where secondary victims used the media to help change the legal system was that of Sarah Payne, who was abducted and murdered by known paedophile Roy William Whiting in July 2000. In response to her disappearance, the British media took up the campaign to highlight the issue. The public were bombarded with Sarah's image and her parents used news conferences and appeals to try to bring their daughter back safely. Unfortunately, Sarah was found dead three weeks later but this did not lessen the media and, in turn, the public's interest. The *News of the World* spearheaded a campaign which called for 'Sarah's Law', a law that would give all parents controlled access to the sex offenders' register. The parents also appeared on high-profile chat shows such as '*This Morning* with Richard and Judy' to gather public support for such a law. This echoed to some extent the role of the media in the USA after the murder of Megan Kanka in 1994 – media exposure of sex offenders being supervised in the community led to the passing of 'Megan's Law', which required sex offenders to be registered and for information about their location to be made available to relevant communities.

More recently, the media has been utilized in a similar way by the parents of Madeleine McCann, allegedly abducted in the resort of Praia de Luz in Portugal in 2007. The media campaign for the return of Madeleine has involved appeals for her safe return from celebrities such as David Beckham. In the hunt for Madeleine the World Wide Web has also played an important part. There is a dedicated official website, www.findmadeleine.com, which shows images of Madeleine McCann and even allows her father Gerry McCann to write a blog on his and his wife's personal feelings. The site also allows those who want to make a donation to a fund, which, at the time of writing, has received in excess of one million pounds. The sight attracted 25 million hits in its first day. Calum Macrae, Director of Infohost, said: 'In all my years in this business, I've never experienced anything like it. It's unbelievable. As the media hype spreads further and further across the globe, more and more people are visiting and posting messages' (*The Times*, 18 May 2007).

This case highlights the role of the most rapidly growing form of media today, the World Wide Web. There are thousands of websites that provide information and referral services for victims of crime – including online counselling services and sites that link victims with appropriate professionals.

However, media campaigns can backfire. In the case of Madeleine McCann, the media accounts have included suspicions and accusations about the parents. Indeed, two national newspapers, the *Daily Express* and *The Daily Star*, had to make front-page apologies to Kate and Gerry McCann (and make substantial payments to the fund set up to find the missing girl) for suggesting that they caused Madeleine's death and then covered it up. The apology in the *Daily Express* is shown below:

Kate and Gerry McCann: Sorry

The *Daily Express* today takes the unprecedented step of making a front-page apology to Kate and Gerry McCann. We do so because we accept that a number of articles in the newspaper have suggested that the couple caused the death of their missing daughter Madeleine and then covered it up. We acknowledge that there is no evidence whatsoever to support this theory and that Kate and Gerry are completely innocent of any involvement in their daughter's disappearance. We trust that the suspicion that has clouded their lives for many months will soon be lifted. As an expression of its regret, the *Daily Express* has now paid a very substantial sum into the Madeleine Fund. We promise to do all in our power to help efforts to find her. Kate and Gerry, we are truly sorry to have added to your distress. We assure you that we hope that Madeleine will one day be found alive and well and will be restored to her loving family.

(*Daily Express*, 19 March 2008)

Indeed criticism of Madeleine McCann's parents has continued to appear in the media since then, as the following extract from the *Leicester Mercury*, the McCann family's local newspaper illustrates:

McCanns Take Legal Action Against Ex-Solicitor over Madeleine Slurs

A former solicitor could be jailed for repeatedly accusing Kate and Gerry McCann of covering up the 'death' of their daughter Madeleine. Lawyers for the Rothley couple are taking civil action against Tony Bennett to try to stop him making allegations that they were involved in Madeleine's disappearance from the Portuguese resort of Praia de Luz in May 2007. Mr Bennett is secretary of an organisation called the Madeleine Foundation, which repeatedly claimed the three-year-old was not abducted.

(*Leicester Mercury*, 31 January 2012)

As a final comment on the positive influence and impact of the media in relation to victims of crime, we will refer briefly to the media's role in uncovering miscarriages of justice. Although not directly victims of crime, those who have been wrongly convicted of crimes could be seen as victims of the criminal justice processes and system. For the media, miscarriages of justice are seen as representing an innocent person being convicted of a crime they did not commit; usually the media presentation of such miscarriages includes a call for the legal system to remedy the injustice. Indeed, with the uncovering of a number of high-profile miscarriages of justice in the 1980s and beyond, such as the Birmingham Six, the Guildford Four, Judith Ward and Stefan Kisko, to name a few, the media represented the legal system in this country as being in crisis. The media role in these (in)famous cases is interesting in that initially there was generally a massive initial media interest in finding the offenders of the particular crime and in putting pressure on the police to come up with a suspect:

In cases like the Birmingham Six and Guildford Four, the media initially played a significant role in fanning the lynch mob-style atmosphere that resulted in the convictions.

(Donovan 2007)

However, after this interest, the media played a major role in uncovering and publicizing the miscarriages of justice, with programmes like *Rough Justice* (BBC) and *Trial and Error* (Channel 4) campaigning for cases to go to the Appeal Court.

As well as the press and television programmes, organizations and pressure groups campaigning against miscarriages of justice also make use of the Internet and World Wide Web. For example, Innocent is a Manchester-based organization that supports and campaigns for innocent people in prison. Its website aims to raise people's awareness of miscarriages of justice and provides copies of media articles and books that deal with such miscarriages.

Groups victimized by the media

Ethnic minorities as victims

It is well established that people from ethnic minority groups are more at risk of being the victim of crime than white people. The 2010/2011 British Crime Survey showed that the risk of being a victim of personal crime was higher for adults from a mixed ethnic background than for other ethnic groups; and that it was also higher for members of all black minority ethnic groups than for white groups. Over the five years from 2006 to 2011, there had been a statistically significant fall in the risk of being a victim of personal crime for the white population but this had not been the case for black minority groups. Furthermore, of the 2,007 homicides recorded from 2007/2008 to 2009/2010, 12 per cent of the victims were black and 8 per cent Asian – much higher percentages than the percentage of black and Asian population in general figures from the British Crime Survey 2011 (Chaplin *et al.* 2011). In this section, we will consider how victims of crime from minority groups are represented by the media.

It has been suggested that the portrayal of victims by the press is subject to certain prejudices – issues of race, class, sexuality, occupation and even attractiveness may affect the type, length and style of media coverage. Indeed, Sir Ian Blair, Metropolitan Police Chief Constable, accused the media of institutional racism in a statement in 2006. Taking two crimes as examples, Ian Blair highlighted the inconsistencies in the coverage of the murders of a white lawyer Tom ap Rhys Pryce and the Asian builders merchant Baliir Matharu. Both men were killed on the same day in brutal circumstances. Mr Matharu was mown down by a car after challenging two thieves who had broken into his van – he was dragged 40 metres. Mr Rhys Price was stabbed to death and mugged on his way home from Kensal Green tube station. While both were cowardly and heinous crimes the story of Mr Rhys Price attracted much more media coverage. Sir Ian Blair went as far as to suggest 'I actually believe that the media is guilty of institutional racism in the way they report deaths'.

The Guardian itself analysed the content of the national press coverage of the two stories over a two-week period. This produced a result of 6,061 words for Mr Rhys Price and 1,385 words for Mr Matharu. Further, *The Guardian* stated, 'if only tabloid newspapers are analysed, the difference becomes clearer. The murder of Mr Rhys Price was mentioned in 98 stories while Mr Matharis death was covered in just 14' (27 January 2006).

Asylum seekers as victims

The British media has attracted criticism from the United Nations High Commission for Human Rights for their attitude towards the reporting of asylum seekers. Antonio Guterres, UN High Commissioner for Refugees and author of the report, states in an introduction to 'Refugees: Victims of Intolerance', UN High Commissioner, that asylum seekers are an easy target:

> In some countries, deliberate attempts to dehumanize asylum seekers are continuing, always presenting them as menacing statistics, as criminals and bringers of disease, or as some other form of generalized abstract aberration that is easy to hate . . . In an increasing number of countries, asylum seekers – and the refugees among them – have become a tool for political demagogues, or have been turned into faceless bogeymen by an unscrupulous popular press.
>
> (Guterres A., 'Victims of Intolerance', 1 April 2006,
> UN Refugee magazine)

According to opinion polls, asylum continues to be one of the most important issues for the British public. Issues around asylum and asylum seekers are rarely out of the newspapers and are the subject of intense political and public debate. Reporting and commentary about asylum seekers and refugees is often hostile, unbalanced and factually incorrect. The extracts below are taken from The Refugee Council and look at the way the press use very negative terms to describe asylum seekers, such as 'stampede' and 'crooked tide'; they contrast specific recent newspaper headlines with the actual facts about the issue being reported.

The headline – 'JET SET ASYLUM SEEKERS: £3K TO QUIT AND FLY BACK'

The Daily Star, 1 May 2006

The facts – The Home Office has for some time operated a scheme to support asylum seekers who voluntarily return to their country of origin. As a pilot, this has been increased to a possible total of £3,000 – this is not all paid at once but in a series of grants as the individual shows that s/he requires support to set up in his/her country of origin – for example, they will often be homeless. It is not paid as cash and could not be used to fly back to the UK. In the event of a second application for asylum, the asylum seeker would not be eligible for this support. Even if the maximum amount were paid out, it would be three or four times cheaper than an enforced removal.

The headline – 'ASYLUM CRISIS AS AMNESTY DEAL FOR 15,000 TURNS INTO STAMPEDE'

Daily Mail, 28 December 2005

The facts – There was no crisis. Applications for the amnesty are made in writing – no one was stampeding anywhere. Since it was announced in October 2003, the Home Office has found that more families are eligible for leave to remain than they had originally expected, having been in the UK awaiting an asylum decision for over three years.

The headline – 'ASYLUM SEEKERS SENT TO MORE AFFLUENT AREAS'

Daily Mail, 23 December 2005

The facts – The reality is that most asylum seekers' accommodation is in 'ghettos' in deprived areas. They are housed in poor quality accommodation – often previously hard to let – sometimes in areas where research has shown they are more likely to face racial harassment. A Home Office report looking at the problems caused said there might be a case for changing the policy so that some asylum seekers would be sent to relatively less problematic areas.

The headline – 'BRITAIN IS THE ASYLUM CAPITAL OF THE WORLD'

Daily Express, 23 March 2005

The facts – The UK is home to just 3 per cent of nearly 9.2 million refugees worldwide. Two thirds of the world's refugees are living in developing countries, often in refugee camps. Africa and Asia between them host over 70 per cent of the world's refugees while Europe looks after just 22 per cent. In 2005, the UK ranked 14th in the league table of EU countries for the number of asylum applications per head of population.

The headline – 'HALT THIS CROOKED TIDE'

News of the World, 30 January 2005

The facts – A report by the Association of Chief Police Officers stated that the 'vast majority of people seeking asylum are law abiding citizens'. In fact, asylum seekers are much more likely to be the victims of crime than the perpetrators. A study conducted by Refugee Action found that one in five of their clients had experienced some kind of harassment while 83 per cent of asylum-seeking women do not go out at night for fear of being abused and harassed.

The headline – 'ASYLUM SEEKERS GIVEN VOTES TO GET LOANS'

The Mail on Sunday, 1 May 2005

The facts – Asylum seekers are not allowed to vote in local or general elections in the UK, nor do they have any access to loans. People can only register on the electoral roll if they are British, Commonwealth, Irish or EU citizens. Far from getting extra help, asylum seekers receive just 70 per cent of income support (£40 per week). They are not allowed work so are forced to live in poverty. In 2002, a joint Refugee Council/Oxfam report found that 85 per cent of organizations working with asylum seekers said their clients experienced hunger while 95 per cent said they could not afford clothes or shoes.

The headline – 'MIGRANT HEALTH THREAT TO BRITAIN'

Daily Express, 22 April 2005

The facts – The claim that asylum seekers are bringing in disease to the country is a primitive response to outsiders coming in. In September 2003, a pilot screening project conducted by the immigration service found that after testing 5,000 asylum seekers for infectious diseases, none carried TB, HIV or AIDS, nor any other serious diseases. Doctors did, however, find evidence of maltreatment and torture.

This sort of negative coverage has continued over the last few years as the following two extracts demonstrate:

Soft-Touch Britain, the Asylum Seeker Capital of Europe: We Let In More Than Anyone Else Last Year

Britain granted asylum to more people than any other European Union country last year, official figures revealed yesterday . . . Critics said the data confirmed that Britain is a soft touch when it comes to granting asylum.

(Daily Mail, 29 June 2012)

Asylum Seekers Cost £1.5m a Day

Britain's shambolic asylum system set taxpayers back more than £1.5 million a day last year. The Home Office had to fork out £583 million on 37,000 asylum claims, the Daily Express can reveal.

(Daily Express, 15 June 2013)

QUESTION BREAK

Rewrite the various newspaper headlines listed in the previous section to reflect more accurately the facts reported about asylum seekers.

Find out what you can about the numbers of asylum seekers and consider how accurate the extracts from the *Daily Mail* and *Daily Express* in 2012 and 2013 (above) are.

Look at the extract from Steve James's article below and highlight which parts or phrases refer to 'undeserving' and which to 'deserving' victims in relation to the reporting of asylum seekers.

UN criticises British media for scapegoating refugees

Twice this year, Britain's political establishment and media have attracted criticism from the United Nations High Commission for Human Rights for their attitude towards asylum seekers . . . The UNHCR was moved to complain against the scapegoating of immigrants in Britain, particularly by the national media. Referring to recent attacks on asylum seekers in Glasgow, which culminated in the murder of Kurdish immigrant Firsat Yildiz, UNHCR spokesman Kris Janowski said there was 'a linkage between the notoriously negative portrayal of asylum-seekers in the media and this kind of violence . . . "asylum-seekers" and "refugee" have even become a term of abuse in school playgrounds . . .'

Despite the volatile racial and social tensions in the area after the killing, Scotland's *Daily Record* tabloid launched a witch-hunt against the dead man, and any who protested his killing . . . On August 7, the paper led with a banner headline 'Madness – Refugees Bring Chaos to Glasgow', referring to the protest march held by asylum seekers against the racist killing, which was followed by a xenophobic counter-demonstration.

The next day, the *Record* went even further, effectively legitimizing Firsat's murder on the grounds that he had lied to the immigration authorities. 'Turk stabbing victim conned his way in as asylum seeker – The young Kurd killed in Glasgow was NOT a refugee who fled Turkey because of his political beliefs. He was a fruit and veg trader trying to build a better life in Britain', the *Record* alleged. It claimed that Firsat 'was a conman who came to this country to make a fast buck . . . we should not be blinded by political correctness' . . . .

The *Record* then moved on to target those who defended the rights of asylum seekers. On August 9, the Glasgow Campaign to Welcome Refugees (CWR) held a demonstration outside the *Record*'s offices . . . In a hysterical, full page editorial on August 10 entitled, 'Read this Scotland and Weep', the *Record* railed against those who were protesting its coverage. 'There are some political extremists who try to make capital out of any situation . . .' the paper opined, in what was in fact a more accurate description of the tabloid's own activities . . .

The *Daily Record* is not alone. Last month, Richard Littlejohn, a columnist in *The Sun,* Rupert Murdoch's daily tabloid, published a particularly vicious, racist novel entitled 'To Hell in a Handcart'.

Littlejohn's tract celebrates the anti-liberal and populist prejudices of an imaginary ex-policeman, Mickey French, who kills a Romanian asylum seeker involved in a robbery on his home . . . The racist prejudices and crude stereotyping in Littlejohn's first work of fiction can be read each week in his column in *The Sun* parading as fact.

(James S., 'UN Criticises British Media for Scapegoating Refugees', World Socialist Web, www.wsws.org, 2001)

The case study below illustrates how the sort of reporting on asylum seekers shown above clearly does not take account of the experiences that refugees have in their own countries prior to seeking asylum; and also affects their ability to settle in the UK if they are granted asylum.

How Negative Reporting on Asylum Seekers Made Morgan's Life a Misery

The story of Morgan Odhiambo, a refugee who chose Britain as a place of sanctuary, is sadly typical. In his native Kenya he suffered from corruption and brutality. After his car was stolen he suspected that police, after recovering it, made money by selling it on. When he challenged them about their fraudulent practices he was beaten and received threats that scared him enough to flee.

Like many people who live in countries once colonized by the British, and who become victims of corrupt political systems where the rule of law does not pertain, he decided to come to Britain. He arrived here in 2003 and immediately ran into rampant prejudice against people collectively known as 'asylum seekers'. Despite the fact that many British people were kind and welcoming, he ran up against plenty of scorn. Why? Gradually, he became convinced that it was due to negative press coverage. He says: 'People get their views from the newspapers. People look at you like you're a scrounger. They think you're just "one of them". They think you're here to take their money or their job. They just don't know the truth'.

(*The Guardian*, 1 November 2012)

The media, murder and secondary victims

In this section we will look at how people who are related to or linked with murderers convicted of particularly serious and shocking crimes can be demonized and victimized by the media representation of them. This is especially the case where women are seen as supportive of their male partners, as the two examples we consider below demonstrate – first Maxine Carr, girlfriend of Ian Huntley, and then Sonia Sutcliffe, wife of Peter Sutcliffe.

As an example of the power of the media in informing opinion and rendering some as victims of media attention, it is worth considering the media treatment of Maxine Carr more closely.

In August 2002, Ian Huntley, a school caretaker, murdered two 10-year-old girls, Holly Chapman and Jessica Wells, in the Cambridgeshire village of Soham. The case became one of the most high-profile murder cases in terms of media attention and the attendant massive public interest in (initially) the search for the two girls. At the time Maxine Carr, Huntley's girlfriend, provided him with a false alibi and later pleaded guilty to the charge of perverting the course of justice.

During the trial, Carr became the most hated woman in Britain, and media attention on her reached fever pitch. Maxine Carr's crime was a serious one, indeed she received a three-and-a-half-year prison sentence for it, but she had no role in the actual murder of the two girls. Nonetheless, her name has become synonymous with infamous female child murders such as Myra Hindley and Rose West. Indeed, press articles at the time likened Carr to Myra Hindley – despite the fact that she was not a murderer. In December 2003, *The Sun* and the *Daily Express* both reported on the fact that Carr's inmates in Holloway prison, where she was on remand, had dubbed her 'Myra Hindley mark II', with her picture appearing alongside that of Myra Hindley. Also in December 2003, the *Daily Express* carried the headline 'Sex-mad Maxine, the Myra of Soham'.

On release from prison, Carr was given a new appearance and identity and a court injunction which prevents her whereabouts from being revealed to the media. And this action has itself excited interest and debate in the media decision; the different sides of the argument as to whether Carr should be supported in being given a 'new life' after completing her prison sentence are illustrated in the extract from the BBC News online service from 14 May 2004, the date of her release.

Read the opinions of the two journalists below and state which you find most convincing. Give reasons for your answer.

Head to Head: Maxine Carr's Privacy

As Maxine Carr ends her prison sentence for involvement in the Soham murders, the media is expected to challenge a court ban on publishing details about her new life. The *Daily Mirror's* Sue Carroll and *Independent* columnist Deborah Orr explain their differing views on Carr's right to privacy.

Sue Carroll, *Daily Mirror*

Everybody is interested in Maxine Carr. The whole of the media are interested, so let's not pretend it's just a tabloid story. People are very disappointed and a bit aggrieved because they feel that she was probably treated fairly leniently. She didn't serve three-and-a-half years – that was accelerated . . .

I do agree that there is a pick-and-mix law at the moment, it's guess work, you don't know what anybody is going to get for any crime, but the public would perceive that she's been treated with kid gloves. I think that's a fair point, I think she has . . .

Nobody can invade her privacy, but she can invade her own because the story is that she is able tell her own story in her own words should she choose. I personally don't want to read it.

Deborah Orr, columnist for *The Independent*

If people would just accept that Maxine Carr committed a crime, she's now paid the price and now has to get on with her life, half of the anger that people feel would be immediately dissipated. I think people feel very angry at the idea that millions is going to be spent on keeping Maxine safe.

All of this wouldn't have to happen if people would just accept that she has spent some time in prison for what she did and now should be allowed to get on with her life . . .

What has happened to Maxine Carr even before the criminal justice system became involved is absolutely horrific. She will have to live with that for the rest of her life. She's young now and her understanding of what she did is going to get deeper and worse as she gets older. She is going to suffer forever no matter what other people do. I think what has happened to her is appalling. She's had her life taken away anyway without people running around shouting how she hasn't been punished enough. What has happened to her in her life is punishment enough.

(http://news.bbc.co.uk/2/hi/uk_news/3713861.stm,
14 May 2004)

Media attention on Maxine Carr has been and continues to be relentless. The image of Carr in the media (and an image that has largely been built by the media) is one of a selfish, arrogant, sex-mad liar and evil woman. In May 2004, *The Daily Telegraph* ran an article entitled 'Leave Us Alone, Say the Other 17 Maxine Carrs'. The hysteria over Maxine Carr had led those on the electoral register who shared her name to be in fear of their safety. The article even stated 'police forces up and down the country have prepared emergency measures to protect the namesakes, fearing that they could be attacked by vigilantes mistaking them for the former girlfriend of Ian Huntley, the man who murdered Jessica and Holly'. As mentioned above, her release from prison after serving 21 months (16 months of which were while she was on remand before trial) of a three-and-a-half-year sentence was widely criticized by the tabloid press. *The Sun* had successfully campaigned to ensure that Carr was not released earlier in 2004, congratulating itself with the headline 'Keeping Carr Caged Is a Victory for Us All', and commenting that the blocking of Maxine Carr's bid for early release was 'a huge victory for *The Sun* and its army of readers, who overwhelmingly voted in our "You The Jury" poll that she should serve her full sentence for lying to police about Ian Huntley and his role in the murder of ten-year-olds Holly Wells and Jessica Chapman'. It concluded, 'thank goodness justice and common sense have prevailed and Maxine Carr has been refused early release from prison'.

Much of the media portrayal has focused on the unthinkable idea that a woman should be associated with violence and abuse towards children. The role of her gender has played an important role in Carr's victimization. Stereotypical views of women and their feminine sensitive nature, compared to the animalism of man, have been used to illustrate Maxine Carr's extraordinary nature. In 2003, investigative journalist Nathan Yates launched his exposé on Ian Huntley aptly titled 'Beyond Evil'; his portrayal of Carr illustrates these stereotypical attitudes to women offenders. This view and the counter-argument that women offenders are demonized in a way that does not apply to all offenders are illustrated in the two extracts below. These extracts are lengthy but provide good examples of the excessive, if not obsessive, way that media coverage can increase the victimization of someone who had committed a crime but had served her punishment (they are included in the question break below).

QUESTION BREAK

Read the two extracts and consider the questions below them. The first is from a book by journalist Nathaniel Yates and the second from an article by Jo Knowles in The F-Word online magazine, which was established in 2001 and considers issues pertinent to contemporary UK feminism.

Beyond Evil: Maxine Would Cry Out for Sex

DESPERATE Maxine Carr would do anything to get a man. Filled with self-loathing, she would punish herself through starvation and sleep with anyone who asked in the hope that they might stay with her.

The woman who would give her boyfriend an alibi for double child murder was born Maxine Ann Capp on February 16, 1977 in Grimsby maternity hospital.

From birth she was isolated from the rest of her family, being by far the younger of two girls. Many who knew her believed this loneliness was the product of her difficult relationship with her father, Alfred Edward Capp.

Described on his daughter's birth certificate as a farm worker, he lived with her mother, Shirley Catherine Capp (nee Suddaby) in a small terrace house in Yarborough Road in the village of Keelby.

But by the time Carr was two-and-a-half, Alfred had split from his wife and he would play little part in the lives of his children. It seems he resented that Shirley had ordered him out of the house, and he decided to cut himself off completely from her and the girls.

From an early age, Carr felt anger towards her absent father, blaming him for all the ills in her life and in the lives of her mother and sister.

The little girl felt rejected and was already prone to severe mood swings . . .

It was around puberty that Carr's troubles erupted. She became acutely aware of the opposite sex. As she reached 13, she felt insecure about her appearance.

She thought she was unattractive to boys – too fat and spotty. The teenager became so unhappy she went on huge eating binges to try to bring herself some form of comfort.

Carr ballooned in weight to 10 st. and when she was 15 she began making herself vomit after eating.

A year later, the bulimia had turned into a habit of self-starvation. Carr became anorexic. Shirley was in despair at her younger daughter's condition.

Carr became so ill that she needed hospital treatment. A former class-mate said: 'Boys called her names because she was fat. When she got ill, she was a lot thinner but then people used to call her "The Skeleton"'.

Carr battled through her GCSEs, achieving seven passes and aimed to be a teacher . . .

One of her first boyfriends was scaffolder Paul Selby, 25. She met him in 1997; she was 19 at the time but told him she was 23.

At this time her favourite way out of her repressed character was to drink vodka and coke – downing more than a dozen in a night.

Paul said: 'After a couple of drinks, she'd get up on the tables and start dancing and flashing her boobs.' . . .

Her favourite pubs were frequented by young people out to meet a partner for the night.

Carr would happily go home with most men who expressed an interest in her. One of the many who had a fling with Carr said: 'She asked me if I'd take her back to bed. She was drunk and not my type but I'd had a few and I just went along with it'.

Though desperate for a steady partner, she found it impossible to resist one-night-stands . . .

Yet all this physical passion never led to any real feeling. She would just roll over, fall asleep and in the morning say: 'Bye, then, are you off now?'

Given her strange habits, it is perhaps unsurprising that Carr found it difficult to hang on to her men . . .

But Carr remained in desperate need of a man she could at last lean on. Her chance finally came when she and Huntley were flung together at a club during a pub crawl in the summer of 1998. Carr was out for the night with her former boyfriend Paul Selby and a group of his friends. Huntley saw Carr and zeroed in. The attraction was instant. Carr was bowled over by this seemingly charming, yet arrogant man. Before the night was over, they were having sex.

Carr soon jumped at the chance to move in with a man who seemed to provide her with the security she had craved . . .

They eventually sought a new life by moving to East Anglia, where Huntley learned, through his father, of a caretaker's job available at a school in a little village called Soham.

And there, by the summer of 2002, Huntley and Carr had achieved an appearance of normality and stability.

(Yates 2003)

Crime and Punishment: Maxine Carr and Other 'Evil Women'

Maxine Carr is currently the 'most hated woman in Britain'. There's a strong case for saying she's the most hated *person* in Britain, but woman seems to be the favoured word. This tells us a number of things about why there is such strong hatred being expressed for Carr, who as I write has just been released from her prison sentence on parole, into the care of parole officers. Police officers have apparently advised Carr to wear a bullet-proof vest, such is the risk of someone trying to harm her . . .

The media treatment of Maxine Carr is worth considering more closely as part of a feminist awareness of discrimination and prejudice against her as a representative of women associated with, or accused of, violent acts. My view is that Carr is receiving extreme and unusual treatment because she is a woman, and that this has wider implications for all women in Britain in terms of how we are or might be treated as convicted or suspected criminals.

On 13th May, the day before Carr's projected release, GMTV ran a feature on the rights and wrongs of this, with a *Daily Mirror* columnist, Sue Carroll, as the guest of hosts Fiona Phillips and Eamonn Holmes . . .

[At one stage] Eamonn Holmes helpfully chipped in about Carr that 'She's had numerous boyfriends, too'. Aha, I thought, at last we come to that old chestnut: a woman who's had numerous (anyone want to estimate what number is actually intended by 'numerous'? More than one?) boyfriends is obviously what would once have been called a 'person of low moral fibre', evidently capable of all sorts of other unspeakable horrors. Sexual women = evil women, though it's the first time I've seen this used as a excuse to lock someone up indefinitely since I last read a Victorian novel.

This demonization of Carr has been going on since she and Ian Huntley were charged with their respective crimes. What disturbs me about this is the creeping increase of attributed responsibility on Carr's part for things done by Huntley. Fiona Phillips suggested during the GMTV discussion that people's anger over the murders was displaced onto Carr because Huntley will be permanently unreachable, whereas she will be free and, in some people's eyes 'getting away with it' . . .

One of the major issues when considering Carr's guilt during the Soham trial was the unthinkable idea that a woman could be complicit in violence and abuse towards children . . .

The nature of crimes involving children, especially where sexual abuse or murder are concerned, inevitably evoke strong reactions in the public; their perpetrators are probably the most unpopular group of criminals in existence. Huge attention is always focused on women involved in these cases, whether they are the grieving parent (such as Sara Payne, Sarah's mother) or someone deemed to be complicit, such as Marie Therese Kouao, the aunt of murdered Victoria Climbie – or Maxine Carr. Extreme responses result, with one considered a heroine, one, perhaps understandably a monster. These views are derived from underlying beliefs that the worst thing that can happen to a mother is to lose her child, and that the potential for motherhood in all women makes them, or should make them, incapable of abusing a child or even of tolerating abuse. This, at least is the ideal.

These polarized representations of womanhood are a legacy of the Victorian image of the Angel in the House, whose opposite is the demonic Fallen Woman. The logic behind the Fallen Woman is that one sin makes you capable of others, leading on and on to an ever more shocking chain of crimes. Thus little sins add up to big ones . . .

This angel/demon dichotomy may be behind another timely announcement on women and crime. While Sue Carroll and other media columnists were making the cases for Carr being kept in prison indefinitely, or at least for a lot longer, the Prison Reform Trust have stated that the number of women prisoners has now reached a record high, and described the devastating effects of women being imprisoned on their families . . .

I can't help thinking that the constant attention to Carr and the media-fuelled desire to punish her further is likely to hinder the cause of her female fellow prisoners.

(Knowles J., June 2004, www.thefword.org.uk)

▋ QUESTIONS

- How would you describe the portrayal of Carr by Yates? What stereotypes does it uphold?
- Suggest some other examples of the 'angel/demon' dichotomy.

Another example of the way that women (especially) are victimized and demonized within the media is the press coverage of Sonia Sutcliffe, wife to Peter Sutcliffe, the Yorkshire Ripper. Sutcliffe was arrested in 1980; however, years later Sonia Sutcliffe was still being 'blamed' for her husband's crimes. In 1989, Sonia Sutcliffe was awarded damages of £600,000 against the satirical magazine *Private Eye*, after unsubstantiated claims that she had negotiated with the press so as to profit from her fame as the wife of a serial killer and had sold her story to the *Daily Mail* for £250,000. Her lawyers said she had done no such deal and did not want to capitalize on her husband's crimes. At the time, the sum of £600,000 was substantially larger than previous libel awards, and on appeal, and partly due to media-led public outrage over her gaining such a large amount of money, it was reduced to £60,000.

More than a decade later, the barrister John Upton described how the media portrayed Sonia Sutcliffe as a failure as a wife and consequently a direct cause of Peter Sutcliffe's crimes. He referred to newspaper articles put forward at the time of Sutcliffe's arrest that suggested she was a cause of her husband's crimes, and that cited her:

> failings as a wife – her inadequacies as a sexual partner, her wish not to have children, her mental health difficulties – as the direct cause of his butchery. A woman was expected in the eyes of the prurient, disapproving public not to just stand by her serial killer man but to stand in place of him.
>
> (Upton J. cited in Jewkes 2004, p. 115)

It is not only women who are subjected to stereotypes based on social constructed norms. As a final and more recent example of secondary victimization by the media, the case of Chris Jefferies is interesting. Jefferies was the landlord of Joanna Yeates, a 25-year-old architect who was murdered in December 2010 in Bristol and he was arrested on suspicion of her murder. He was 65 years old at the time and lived in the same building as Miss Yeates in Clifton, Bristol; he had previously taught English at the nearby Clifton College public school for nearly 30 years. After his arrest there was intense media coverage of the case, with a focus on Jefferies 'strange' appearance and the fact that he was a bachelor. Indeed he was described by neighbours as 'a little bit eccentric' and the image of him below was widely used. Eventually Jefferies received substantial damages from eight newspapers following the conviction of Vincent Tabak, a Dutch engineer who had lived next door to Jo Yeates, for the murder of Yeates. He had been held in police custody for three days and was only released from police bail in March, three months after his wrongful arrest.

In considering the unbalanced media reporting of the arrest of Chris Jefferies, *The Guardian* commented:

> Unfortunately, her [Joanna Yeates] land-lord, Mr Chris Jefferies, seems to have been the 'ideal suspect'. On his arrest, the media seized upon his background and appearance to make their views about him clear. *The Sun*, the *Daily Mail* and the *Daily Mirror* have described him, respectively, as 'Professor Strange', 'The Strange Mr Jefferies' and a 'suspect peeping Tom' . . . His photograph has appeared on the front page of national newspapers 11 times. He was described as 'weird', 'lewd', 'strange', 'creepy', 'angry', 'odd', 'disturbing', 'eccentric', 'a loner' and 'unusual' in the course of just one article.

(*The Guardian*, 5 January 2011)

THEORIZING SURVEILLANCE: THE ROLE OF CCTV AND SURVEILLANCE IN THE REPRESENTATION OF AND SUPPORT FOR VICTIMS

In this section, we will consider the extent to which the massive expansion of media technologies, in the form of CCTV and other surveillance forms, have affected the portrayal of victims of crime. On one level, it might be argued that everyone is the 'victim' of surveillance. The UK seems to be the market leader in terms of levels of CCTV usage; according to the CCTV User Group (2011), in the last decade the use of CCTV for public space surveillance has developed faster than anywhere else in the world. In 1990 there were only a handful of city systems while well over a thousand UK towns and cities now have systems in their centres. In addition to that are all the systems in schools and universities, shopping malls, hospitals, airports, bus and train stations to give just some examples, all of which cover 'quasi-public open space'. Indeed, we are watched everywhere we go, driving to work, shopping, taking a train and so on; we are under surveillance not just from cameras, but by the chips in our credit, debit and store cards. Our emails and telephone conversations can be monitored and tracked by a range of agencies and private companies. And we expect to be subject to new and more sophisticated means of surveillance, as the following extract from BBC News 24 illustrates:

'Talking' CCTV Scolds Offenders

'Talking' CCTV cameras that tell off people dropping litter or committing anti-social behaviour are to be extended to 20 areas across England. They are already used in Middlesbrough where people seen misbehaving can be told via a loudspeaker, controlled by control centre staff.

(4 April 2007)

On the other hand, CCTV footage showing people being victims of crime can help in providing evidence for court and in police investigations of crime. Indeed, governments have invested heavily in CCTV cameras as part of their crime-prevention programme. During the 1990s, the Home Office spent 78 per cent of its crime-prevention budget on surveillance (Gill and Spriggs 2005). The increased presence of (and awareness of) CCTV cameras, and the fact that their evidence is often irrefutable, is also likely to deter would-be offenders from breaking the law.

Surveillance within society can take varying forms, from DNA databases and identity cards to the use of CCTV cameras. In criminological theory (see the work of Foucault 1977, in particular) and classic twentieth-century texts (such as George Orwell's *1984*), surveillance has been used to describe power dimensions within society and explain a growing trend towards totalitarianism. In his famous study, *Discipline and Punish*, Michel Foucault highlighted the disciplinary potential of surveillance in his discussion of the panoptican:

> The perfect discipline apparatus would make it possible for a single gaze to see everything constantly. A central point would be both the source of light illuminating everything and a locus of convergence for everything that must be known: a perfect eye that nothing would escape and a center towards which all gazes would be turned.
>
> (Foucault 1977, p. 172)

George Orwell wrote what might be considered the first social science reference to a computer-based surveillance society in his book *1984*.

> It was terribly dangerous to let your thoughts wander when you were in any public place or within range of a telescreen. The smallest thing could give you away. A nervous tic, an unconscious look of anxiety, a habit of muttering to yourself – anything that carried with it the suggestion of abnormality, of having something to hide. In any case, to wear an improper expression on your face . . . was itself a punishable offence. There was even a word for it in Newspeak: *facecrime*.
>
> (1989[1949], Chapter 5)

QUESTION BREAK

Surveillance and especially the use of CCTV has surpassed the levels that even Michel Foucault or George Orwell depicted.

Using your own day-to-day life as a blueprint, explain how you are affected by the increased use of CCTV and other surveillance techniques. What are the positive and negative effects on your own life?

Discuss the negative and positive impact of surveillance on criminal justice.

In terms of crime, theorists, politicians and criminal justice agencies have failed to agree on the role of CCTV cameras as a form of crime prevention – but one thing is certain, if your image is caught on camera while committing a crime then you are more likely to be caught and prosecuted. For victims, this has been welcomed as a positive development, whether people are victims of corporate crime or personal crime.

We are all quite used to the grainy images of both victims and offenders caught on camera – for example, Jill Dando's last moments and Rodney King's beating by the police in the USA. Jill Dando was a television presenter who worked for the BBC for 14 years, and co-hosted the popular *Crimewatch* programme. She was murdered outside her London flat in April 1999 and, as part of the investigation into her killing, police examined hundreds of hours of video footage of her movements in the hours before she was killed. In 1991, George Holliday videotaped the brutal beating of Rodney King by the LAPD police in Los Angeles. The video showed four white police men kicking and repeatedly striking the black man while six other stood by and watched the violence. The evidence was shown internationally and King became the face of racism and police brutality. After the four policemen were acquitted, there was outrage throughout the city and this led to the LA riots of 1992.

However, the most famous case to date, because of the nature of the crime itself, is that of the murder of James Bulger in Liverpool in 1993, James Bulger, a three-year-old child, was abducted and killed by two 10-year-old boys. Whatever moral questions the Bulger case posed for late twentieth-century Britain one fact remains – the CCTV footage from the Bootle Strand Shopping Centre allowed the police to air James's initial abduction from that shopping centre to the murder scene, and thereby illustrated the identities of the perpetrators. This allowed the police to get on with the case much quicker than if they had had no information about the offenders – they had clear pictures of two children as the abductors rather than (as might have been suspected otherwise) an older paedophile.

The frustration of CCTV footage

One of the major problems with the use of CCTV in terms of victims is the fact that the image viewed is almost always and inevitably of past events; these events can therefore never be prevented. Indeed, this helps explain why the footage of Jill Dando, Rodney King and Jamie Bulger, amongst other examples, have become some of the most deeply ingrained news images of recent years. Part of this sense of helplessness that is felt when viewing images of horrific crimes that have happened is illustrated by the comments from Jill Dando's cousin, Judith, after viewing video clips of the last few hours of Jill's life, which included showing her shopping in Dixons:

> The worst thing with seeing the film clip of Jill's last moments . . . was the fact that she was just going about the ordinary things that Jill did. And that you

almost want to be able to stop the camera and stop the action and shout at her, 'Jill, don't go home!'

(Judith Dando, quoted in Burn 2001)

While it is a fact that Britain has the highest number of CCTV cameras in the West, this does not always mean that cameras are reliable – many do not work, or are so poor that they fail to capture the crime or criminal image. Even when cameras are working the images they capture may be deleted or disappear. On 15 April 1989 the Hillsborough Stadium was the chosen venue for the FA cup semi-final between Liverpool and Nottingham Forest football clubs. A build-up of fans outside the stadium resulted in a crush that killed 96 Liverpool fans. The Taylor Report into the 'disaster' pointed to a problem with police control. For the families of the victims the intervening years have been one of attempting to acquire justice for the victims – a task made more difficult by the apparent loss of filmed evidence, as indicated by the comments in the *Police Review* journal:

> Hundreds of photographs were taken. A total of 71 hours of video material was recorded. On the night after the disaster, two video tapes were taken from the locked Sheffield Wednesday camera room. Like all the club's tapes, they would have shown scenes outside the ground. They have not been recovered. The tapes from the police CCTV system were preserved. Tape TB1 (after the initials of the operating officer) ran from noon to 3.04 pm. When the tape was full, the disaster was unfolding and, in the heat of the moment, Constable Bichard forgot to replace it until 3.34 pm. The theft of two Sheffield Wednesday tapes, the break in continuity of one of the police recordings and Constable Bichard's evidence that one of the police cameras was not operating properly, may have caused confusion.
>
> (The Freedom of Information Unit, South Yorkshire Police,
Police Review, February 2005)

Of course, the technology of surveillance is developing all the time and, in spite of the concerns and difficulties highlighted above, it is evident that CCTV and other forms of surveillance can and do help capture and convict offenders. However, as a final comment, while CCTV cameras may record the daily routine of millions of people around the world, at present it is only the public world that is captured. Corporate crime and private crime, such as insider dealing and fraud, or domestic violence and child abuse, for instance, are impossible to capture. CCTV cameras do not and cannot capture the plight of those whose victimhood remains invisible.

QUESTION BREAK

Victimization, the Internet and trolling

Another development which has had important implications for the media representation of victims of crime has been the massive advance in communication networks in recent years, particularly with regard to the Internet and social networking sites. While this issue is examined in much greater detail in Chapter 7, a brief comment here is appropriate.

The development of social networks such as Facebook and Twitter has increased the ways in which people express their thoughts and feelings. The 'openness' of these forums in which this communication occurs is now also open to new abuses; so that online stalking, bullying and defamation of character have increased as a consequence.

An example of this new form of abuse is trolling, a phenomenon that has swept across various websites in recent years – in Internet slang a troll is typically someone who posts hurtful, cynical, sarcastic or inflammatory comments online in order to provoke an emotional response. A survey in early 2013 of over 2,000 respondents aged between 13 and 19 carried out for www.knowthenet.org, and entitled 'Trolled Nation', highlighted the extent of trolling. It found that males aged 19 are the group most likely to be affected by trolling or online bullying and that while two in three teenagers have experienced trolling or online bullying few would turn to parents (17%) or teachers (1%) for help and support. The study found that trolling was more extensive than 'real life' bullying and that the bullying tended to be ongoing, often lasting for months.

In many cases the personal and abusive nature of the comments verge on hate speech. And in more extreme forms trolling can be a criminal offence, as the examples of this behaviour below illustrate.

Twitter has now become an arena in which abusive and hurtful text towards individuals and or groups can be viewed almost instantly by millions. Some outrage individuals, others society in general. In 2012 student Liam Stacey pleaded guilty to a racially aggravated public order offence after he tweeted moments after the Bolton footballer Fabrice Muamba suffered a cardiac arrest during a game with Tottenham Hotspurs. The tweet which caused widespread revulsion was forwarded to the police by twitter users within minutes. In 2011, Sean Duffy was jailed for posting offensive material on tribute pages about young people who had recently died.

Facebook has led to similar issues. In 2010, Facebook launched an application to address cyber abuse on its sites – however, this has been widely criticized for being ineffectual. In 2012, Nicola Brookes brought a landmark case to force Facebook to reveal the identities of trolls who had targeted her for nine months, falsely portraying her as a paedophile and drug dealer. In June 2010 a High Court Master granted an order compelling Facebook to disclose material relating to the identity of seven Internet trolls. The Brookes case is unique as it is the first time a disclosure has been granted by the High Court in the case of Internet trolling and the first case in which the disclosure order will be used to prosecute trolls for a criminal act.

The case played a substantive part in Parliament's initial discussions to implement a new Defamation Act, which was passed by Parliament in 2013.

This act reforms English defamation law and legislates that websites, such as Facebook, comply with a procedure that allows victims of Internet abuse to contact the authors concerned directly.

QUESTIONS

- Think about how you (and others) speak to people on the Internet.
- How can this cause offence in a different way to ordinary conversation?
- How far do you think behaviour on the Internet should be controlled and curtailed?

PHONE HACKING AND SECONDARY VICTIMIZATION – THE LEVESON INQUIRY

In concluding this chapter we will look briefly at the recent Leveson Inquiry and subsequent report in 2012. The Leveson Inquiry was a judicial public inquiry into the culture, practices and ethics of the British press. It was established in the wake of the phone-hacking scandal at News International and the demise of the *News of the World* newspaper. Although not focused solely on victims of crime, a major finding of the Inquiry was the secondary victimization of the families and friends of murder victims. The most shocking example of this related to the murder of Amanda Jane 'Milly' Dowler in 2002. Milly Dowler's murder played a significant role in the *News of the World* phone-hacking scandal when *The Guardian* (initially) reported that journalists working for the *News of the World* had hired private investigators to hack into Milly's voicemail inbox while she was missing. Furthermore, it was alleged that some messages had been deleted leading the family and police to believe Milly might still be alive, as well as destroying potentially valuable evidence.

The initial investigations of phone hacking and improper media intrusion involved a number of celebrities including actress Sienna Miller, former cabinet minister Tessa Jowell and sports pundit Andy Gray. However, in July 2011, it was revealed that as well as Milly Dowler, the phones of the relatives of British soldiers killed in action and of victims of the 7/7 London bombings had also been accessed. These revelations led to the establishment of the Leveson Inquiry and the report of 2012 which recommended that a new regulatory and independent body be set up to replace the existing Press Complaints Commission.

During the Inquiry the chairman of News International, Rupert Murdoch, admitted that a cover-up of the phone-hacking activities at the *News of the World* had occurred and it was little surprise when the paper finally folded. In its final edition on 10 July 2011 the headline read 'Thank You and Goodbye' and the editorial in that edition carried an apology and admitted that phones had been hacked and there 'is no justification for this appalling wrongdoing'.

FURTHER READING

Mawby R. and Walklate S. (1994) *Critical Victimology: International Perspectives*, London: Sage. A text that details the rise of victimology and provides a critical account of theoretical debates in the area.

Meyers M. (1997) *News Coverage of Violence Against Women: Engendering Blame*, Thousand Oaks, CA: Sage. Meyers argues that there is a gender bias in the media reporting of male and female victims and that there is a strong tendency to imply that some victims are 'innocent' and others 'guilty'.

Mulley K. (2001) 'Victimized by the Media', *Criminal Justice Matters*, 43:30–31. In this article, Mulley points out how the media harasses and intrudes on victims of crime.

Victim Support (n.d.) Available online at www.victimsupport.org.uk. Victim Support is a national charity which gives free, confidential help to victims of crime and its website is a useful source of general information.

CHAPTER 6

- Media portrayal of the police
- Media portrayal of the courts/legal system
- Media portrayal of prisons

The Media and the Criminal Justice System

In this chapter, we will move away from the media representation of crime and those involved in criminal behaviour, be they offenders, victims or even onlookers affected by the media presentations of crime (as in the cases of moral panics for instance). Here the focus is on the way that the media represent the criminal justice system, and in particular how the major criminal justice agencies are presented in our mass media. The discussion will consider the three major areas or stages of the criminal justice process and the enforcement of the law. First, the police and how they have been represented in the media, then the courts and sentencing and, finally, prisons. In each case, we will look at real-life or factual representations and also at how these different areas of our criminal justice system and process are presented in fictional accounts and presentations. It is not always easy to separate out what is fact from fiction – and fictional programmes such as dramas and soap operas will usually try and make their 'fiction' as realistic as possible. As Mason (2003) puts it: 'Audiences "commuting" between the realms of factual news and entertainment programming has implications for public perceptions of law enforcement agencies, the courts and prisons as well as offenders and victims' (p. 5).

As well as the massive interest the general public have with crime and criminals, there is also a deep fascination with how these crimes and criminals are discovered and dealt with by the criminal justice system – with how the police go about catching and charging offenders, with how the courts and judiciary sentence them and with what happens to those offenders who enter the penal system.

Our criminal justice system is a massive operation. A few years ago, data from a Home Office report in 2001, *Criminal Justice: The Way Ahead*, showed that the police service deal with over 25,000 '999' calls, make over 5,000 arrests and carry out 2,200 stop and searches every day; that over 4,400 people turn up to do jury service,

1,000 people to act as witnesses in our courts, with 5,600 defendants being sentenced each day (Levenson 2001). More recent Home Office data on police powers and procedures showed that in the 12 months from 1 April 2010 to 31 March 2011, the police in England and Wales arrested 1.4 million people, stopped and searched 1.3 million people and/or their vehicles and breath tested 0.7 million people (Home Office 2011). However, in spite of those quite dramatic figures, most people still only have a fairly limited experience of the criminal justice system and its workings. As with our knowledge and understanding of criminal behaviour, so our understanding of the criminal justice system is derived largely from the mass media we consume. As mentioned in previous chapters, crime stories are a staple of many forms of our media; these stories often focus on crimes that have reached the stage of getting to court. There is a tremendous interest in 'who gets what' from within our criminal justice system. And because the media will almost inevitably focus on the more spectacular crimes and those which lead to the most severe punishments, the picture portrayed by the media about law enforcement and punishment is liable to be distorted in a similar way. Therefore, much of the media coverage of punishment focuses on prisons, the most severe form of punishment available in our criminal justice system, even though the great majority of offenders who are sentenced do not receive prison sentences. After all, offenders being fined is not likely to make such interesting reading or viewing as are stories and films about imprisonment.

While it is understandable that the media focuses on solved crimes, through covering the trials and courtroom drama, Leishman and Mason (2003) point out that this coverage can give the wider public the impression that most crime is solved and that the police are pretty effective in detecting crime – impressions which information on the actual clear-up rates of all crimes committed demonstrates to be way off the mark. The crimes covered by the media are the more solvable sort of crimes because, as mentioned above, they are the more serious sorts of crime, such as murder and sexual offences. And these are the crimes which the police will usually solve – because they will spend considerable resources on high-profile and serious crimes and because such crimes are often relatively easy to solve as the offender (in the case of murder) will more often than not have had some previous association (and often a close association through marriage or family ties) with the victim. This sort of media coverage might reassure the public that the police are effective at catching criminals, but can also lead to criticism when they fail to solve crimes. However, Leishman and Mason make the point that, 'the lack of emphasis in the media on unspectacular unrecorded, unsolved property crimes can be seen to let the police "off the hook" for underperformance in such areas'.

QUESTION BREAK

1. What role (if any) has the media played in developing your knowledge and understanding of the police, the court system and prison life?

What part has fictional media (in the form of film, television, magazine, books, etc.) played in this process?

2. Look at a couple of newspapers and watch a TV news broadcast.

    What crimes were covered by them?

    How many of the crimes involved the sentencing of offenders? How many of the sentences were imprisonment?

    Why do you think the media coverage of criminal behaviour often centres on what happens in court to offenders?

    Why might there be less coverage of crimes which do not reach court?

The British Crime Survey (Kershaw *et al.* 2000) found that television or radio news was cited by most people (nearly three-quarters of the population) as their major source of information about the criminal justice system, with newspapers also having a significant impact. So it would seem fair to conclude that how the media portray the police, the courts and judiciary and our penal system will have a major influence on public knowledge and public opinion.

MEDIA PORTRAYAL OF THE POLICE

In introducing his chapter on 'policing and the media' in the fourth edition of *The Oxford Handbook of Criminology* (2007), Robert Reiner, one of the foremost academic writers on the media and policing, highlights the collaborative nature of the relationship between the police and journalists and broadcasters. He cites the comment of Sir Robert Mark, Commissioner of the Metropolitan Police in the early 1970s, that the police and media relationship could be compared to 'an enduring, if not ecstatically happy, marriage'. Reiner describes the relationship between the police and media as one of 'mutual dependence and reciprocal reinforcement'. On the one hand, and as we have highlighted in introducing this chapter, the way that the criminal justice system, including and in particular the police, has dealt with offenders, has always been a significant part of the mass media content, in both factual and entertainment contexts. Also, though, the police are concerned with how they are portrayed by the media and, more specifically, with creating and encouraging a positive police media image, as they are aware that public support and cooperation will help them in enforcing the law.

It is self-evident that in order to solve crimes the police need to collect relevant information; the public are one of the most important sources of information for the police when investigating crime. This is notably the case with regard to some of the more serious crimes, such as murder investigations, when the police make use of the media as part of their investigation strategy – for instance, through using the media to appeal for information that might help them solve the crime. Innes (2001) makes the point that the police can use the media as a means of mass communication for informing the general public that a crime has occurred and witnesses need to be identified. One of the earliest and longest running 'reality TV' programmes, *Crimewatch*, is based on this idea, but appeals to the public from bereaved victims and/or senior police officers can also be made via newspapers. And these communications, whether through television or the press, are presented by the police in a way that they hope will persuade people to come forward with information – either as witnesses or perhaps through suspecting someone of an offence or being an acquaintance of an offender. This form of public appeal is relatively cheap and easy for the police to use as well as having, as Innes puts it, an 'important symbolic function . . . [that is] important in producing a sense of public legitimacy for the institution of policing'. However, police use of the media in this way can cause difficulties – such appeals can generate an enormous amount of information, much of which will be irrelevant to the particular enquiry; they can also lead to an expectation that the particular case should be solved by the police. More seriously, there have been problems with media appeals where relatives of a victim have made a public appeal and later been found to have been involved in the offence itself. An example of this was in the case of Tracey Andrews, who was found guilty, in 1997, of murdering her fiancé after claiming he had been killed in a 'road rage' attack and who had used the media to appeal for witnesses to this supposed road rage attack (see p. 91). Other examples of media appeals by family members who have later been found to be guilty and that have attracted widespread media attention include appeals given by Karen Matthews and Mick and Mairead Philpott. In 2008, Karen Matthews, the mother of missing nine-year-old Shannon, made a tearful appeal for anyone holding her daughter to come forward. She was later found guilty of kidnapping, false imprisonment and perverting the course of justice and sentenced to eight years' imprisonment, along with Shannon's uncle. The case of the Philpotts again attracted massive publicity. In May 2012, Mick and Mairead Philpott appealed at a press conference for anyone with information about a fatal house fire that killed six of their children to contact the police. The couple were later arrested, found guilty and jailed (Mick for life and Mairead for 17 years) for causing the deaths of the children themselves.

As well as the collaborative relationship between police and the media, there are also overlaps and similarities between the job of a police officer (and in particular a detective) and a journalist. Leishman and Mason (2003) provide a number of examples that make this point. Both jobs can involve working odd and long hours, pressure to get 'results' and a need to meet deadlines, and in both cases rules and regulations have to be followed which might get in the way of a 'result' – journalists have to work within laws of libel and contempt and police officers within regulations governing the stopping, searching, arresting and so on of suspects. And while there might be a lot of bureaucratic and routine work for those employed in both areas, they are also faced with quite dramatic events in the course of their work. In addition, informants can and do play an important and useful role for journalists and police officers. Leishman and Mason also look at the crossover that exists between the nature of police work and news gathering. In spite of some antagonism between the two professions, what the police do overlaps with what makes news, which 'drives a sense of dependency between police and members of the media, uneasy though this may be at times' (Leishman and Mason 2003, p. 31). The nature of the police–media relationship has inevitably been affected by recent changes in the media industry, particularly by the technological developments that have enabled a massive increase in media outlets. The 24-hour continuous news programmes on satellite television have increased the demand for news stories and the time available to delve into such stories; as the police are an important source of news stories, this has increased the media demands on them. Technological advances have also impacted on the accountability of the police. Mawby (2001) considers how the use of lightweight cameras, including on mobile phones, has increased the scrutiny which the police are subject to. For instance, amateur filming of the policing of demonstrations or police dealing with incidents can be used on news programmes and through the Internet.

In his examination of media images of policing, Mawby (2003) considers why these images matter. He cites Reiner's categorization of media representations of policing (and law and order more generally) under the headings of either 'hegemonic' or 'subversive'. The first sees the police as being in a dominant position with regard to the media in that they can choose and filter the information they provide and the media treatment of the police can play an important role in fostering a positive and favourable image of the police. By contrast, the 'subversive' position suggests that the media can be a threat to authority and can undermine respect for the police; in the past it has done this by exposing police malpractice and corruption. For instance, in the late 1960s, when exposure of corruption in the Metropolitan Police led to some of the most senior police officers in the country being imprisoned through to the reporting of 'institutional racism' in the police, highlighted by the Macpherson Report into the murder of Stephen Lawrence (1999). Mawby suggests that these quite distinct headings and positions indicate the importance of examining media images.

QUESTION BREAK

Read the extracts from *The Guardian* and the BBC News web page and look at the pictures of different styles of policing and consider the questions below.

Met Suspends Nine Police Officers in Corruption Inquiry

Scotland Yard suspended nine detectives over corruption allegations. The nine are based in the north London borough of Enfield and face allegations concerning stolen flat-screen televisions, computers and other consumer electrical goods. Anti-corruption detectives have been investigating claims that electrical goods were taken from criminal suspects.

(Dodd V., *The Guardian*, 17 February 2009)

Corrupt Officers Jailed for Leaks

Two former Nottinghamshire police officers have been jailed after pleading guilty to corruption charges. Charles Fletcher, 25, and Phillip Parr, 40, admitted at Birmingham Crown Court to separately passing data on serious inquiries to suspected criminals. Fletcher, a trainee detective, was jailed for seven years and Parr, a former PC, was sentenced to 12 months. The 25-year-old leaked details of investigations including the murder of Nottingham jeweller Marian Bates. Fletcher also admitted two charges of conspiracy to pervert the course of justice . . .

The court heard Fletcher trawled police computer data bases to find information that he supplied to criminals over a two-and-a-half-year period between December 2002 and June last year . . . In return for his service, the 25-year-old received discounts on designer suits from a Nottingham fashion store.

(BBC News, 26 October 2006, http://news.bbc.co.uk/2/hi/uk_news/england/nottinghamshire/6088150.stm)

Community policing – policing demonstrations

How would you describe the styles of policing shown/illustrated in the six extracts?

What effect might these images have on the public view of policing?

How do they relate to Reiner's categorization of 'hegemony' and 'subversive' representations of policing?

As we have seen, for many people the media, and particularly television, is how they find out about the police. Policing is popular on television, with police programmes having attracted high viewing figures for many years (Mawby cites *Frost* and *Heartbeat* as being in the top five watched programmes in 1999). Police programmes can also inform the wider public about the nature and future of policing; they can, to quote Mawby: 'fulfil a symbolic role, providing a commentary on policing and on society, and offering interpretations of the police in society' (2003).

In the final part of this section, we will provide a potted history of the way the police have been represented in the media, and particularly in television drama. Leishman and Mason (2003) argue that, since the formation of the 'modern police' in the nineteenth century, the police have always been concerned with presenting a positive image to the general public. In the early days of organized policing, there was by no means universal public support for there even being a centralized, government-run police force. Histories of the origin and development of formal, modern policing in England and Wales illustrate the concerns about and opposition to the police. While there had been institutions of law enforcement going back to medieval times, with watchmen and constables performing community policing-type functions from the thirteenth century, it was not until the late 1700s that more organized forms of local policing, such as foot patrols and horse patrols, developed in London. Emsley (1996), amongst others, suggests that it was concern about crime and disorder, highlighted by the growth of industrial capitalism and the consequent growth of urban industrial cities, that led to a fear amongst 'respectable' society of a new and potentially dangerous urban working class and a demand for better, more coordinated policing of the capital and elsewhere. These concerns and social changes led, then, to Robert Peel introducing legislation in 1822 for the creation of the Metropolitan police force in London. The model of the Metropolitan police was soon copied elsewhere in the country and, following further legislation in 1857, the formation of local police forces was made obligatory for local government throughout the country.

However, while there was support and even affection for the new English 'bobby' (named so after Robert Peel), there was also a good deal of opposition, and often hostile opposition, to the new police. Emsley refers to police officers being regularly assaulted by the public and having to patrol with cutlasses in some of the 'rougher' working-class areas, with certain areas virtually left to themselves and unpoliced. In view of these reactions and worries, it is not surprising that the police were concerned from the start with promoting and maintaining a positive image of themselves and their role in society. And to some extent the police did win the public over and became an accepted and acceptable part of British society; indeed Emsley cites a comment from *The Times* in 1904 talking of the police as 'a great human mechanism, perhaps the greatest of its kind'. The development of a sort of admiration for, and certainly acceptance of, the new police was in part at least due to the portrayal of them in both fiction and newspaper reporting of the time.

From these early days, the new police were represented in two main ways – as an approachable patrol officer helping to prevent crime through his (early police officers were invariably male) presence on the streets or as a skilled detective, working, almost Sherlock Holmes-like, to solve major crime. This combination, or division, of images has been continued through to the present day in media presentations of police and policing – a combination of a soft police service and hard law enforcement (Leishman and Mason 2003). The plots in the comedy series, *Thin Blue Line*, for instance, centre around the different approaches to law enforcement of the morally principled, but often bumbling, everyday policing epitomized by Inspector Fowler and the more devious, 'results at any cost' style of Detective Sergeant Grimshaw.

Indeed, this dual approach in policing – of service against force, of soft against hard policing, has led to a tension that is still apparent in the police service today – the uniformed bobby on the beat against the more hidden work of the plain-clothed detective. In her discussion of the way the role of the police has been portrayed by the media, Jewkes (2004) considers two 'mediated ideals' of the police, representative of these two styles of policing. Here, we will consider these two ideals in a little more detail – on the one hand, illustrated by PC (later Sergeant) George Dixon in the *Dixon of Dock Green* series that ran from 1955 to 1976 on ITV, who exemplified community policing at its best and, on the other, by Detective Inspector Regan and Detective Sergeant Carter, the no-nonsense crime fighters in *The Sweeney* (which ran for four series from 1975 to 1978 on BBC1), whose style of and approach to investigating and arresting major criminals often skirted on the margins of legality.

Of course, there have been many more television and film representations of police and policing which we will not be able to consider in this brief overview. Police detective films, for instance, have been a popular staple of cinema films for years – and many of these films portray police officers kicking out against authority and the constraints placed on them in doing their job (a theme central to *The Sweeney* television drama). Films such as *A Touch of Evil* and *The Big Heat* in the 1950s, through to the glut of police detective films in the 1960s and 1970s, including *Bullit*, *Klute* and *Chinatown*, portrayed the leading police officers as heroic crime fighters. Probably the seminal film of this ilk was *Dirty Harry* (1971), starring Clint Eastwood, which focused on the conflict between crime-solving and following the rules, and was followed by other vigilante cop films such as *Lethal Weapon* and *Die Hard* in the 1980s and 1990s (Leishman and Mason 2003). Here, though, our focus will be on British television representations and in that context *Dixon of Dock Green* and *The Sweeney* provide sort of extreme, almost stereotypical, examples of the role of the police officer and of different styles of policing.

Jewkes and other commentators have highlighted and examined the key role that the *Dixon of Dock Green* series played in setting a benchmark for television portrayals of the police. The series and, particularly the character of Dixon, created a symbolic representation of the 'British bobby'. In his discussion of media images of the police, Mawby (2003) argues that, in the early days of the series, Dixon was viewed as a realistic portrayal of policing but that towards the end of its run it was widely viewed as irrelevant and outdated – with tougher police series such as *Z Cars* (1962–1978), *Softly, Softly* (1966–1976) and, as mentioned, *The Sweeney*, seen as providing a more modern and accurate picture of policing.

During the period when these early police television series were shown, there was a change in the construction of policing, reflecting changes in the police's relationship with the wider public. The last three series mentioned above, and especially *The Sweeney*, were made at a time when there was more questioning of (and dissatisfaction with) the police. Mawby (2003) sees the central characters as 'symbolic of their respective times' – the late 1950s and less settled mid-1970s – with the optimism of Dixon and his pride in his job replaced by the cynicism of Regan.

PC George Dixon originally appeared in a film, *The Blue Lamp* (1950), and although only playing his part for the first 20 minutes of the film (until he was shot) the popularity of his character led to the drama series *Dixon of Dock Green*. As mentioned above, the series was seen as a realistic portrayal of day-to-day policing, a realism that was accentuated by it focusing on the everyday aspects of the job, rather than the spectacular or comic aspects that tended to be highlighted in films. Leishman and Mason (2003) describe the Dixon character as the 'embodiment of all that was good and dependable' and this was reinforced by his final monologue at the end of each episode where he 'would use the night's story as a reminder to his audience to stay on the straight and narrow'. This caring approach sits in stark contrast to the harsher image presented by later series such as *The Sweeney*. In comparing the two styles of police programme, Reiner (1994) sees *Dixon* and *The Sweeney* as thesis and antithesis respectively:

The thesis, represented by *Dixon,* presents the police primarily as carers, lightning rods for the postwar consensual climate. Its antithesis, *The Sweeney,* portrays the police primarily as controllers, heralding the upsurge of a tough law and order politics in the late 1970s.

Before considering *The Sweeney* as illustrative of a harder style of policing, there were other police drama programmes that presented a different view of policing to the *Dixon* model and we will refer to the *Z Cars* series, which overlapped with *Dixon* for a number of years. Leishman and Mason (2003) suggest that Reiner ignores the importance of *Z Cars* by interpreting it as essentially a transition between the two styles of policing represented in his comparison of *Dixon* and *The Sweeney.* Leishman and Mason argue that *Z Cars* was 'a world away from the stately pace of *Dixon*' – it attacked the conventions of the older series and portrayed a different world of policing, set in a fictional estate, Newtown, based on the large new town of Kirkby on the outskirts of Liverpool, which was the first area of the country where Unit Beat policing (with police in panda cars rather than on foot patrols) was practised. Indeed, the success of *Z Cars* was largely due to its perceived realism. The first episode, in 1962, introduced the four PCs who were the patrol officers featured in the series – they were not of the same high moral standards that George Dixon continued to exemplify. To use Leishman and Mason's description of them:

> Lynch is depicted as a 'lady's man and uses the police telephone to check on the odds for his horses, while Steel argues with his wife, Jayne, who has a black eye received in retaliation for throwing a hotpot supper at him . . .' Fancy Smith, an imposing Lancastrian, who explains to two young girls attempting to get into a nightclub, 'Anyone who spoils my patch with trouble gets the back of my hand' . . . dour Scotsman Jock Weir, introduced to the audience on a stretcher semiconscious after a rugby match. Assuring his superiors of Weir's suitability for the job, [Sergeant] Watt tells them 'He can handle himself in a bundle'.
>
> (2003, p. 57)

Both *Z Cars* and *Dixon of Dock Green* attracted high viewing figures; however, *Z Cars* attacked and undermined the 'too good to be true' world of George Dixon and its 'warts and all' portrayal of the police laid the ground for a range of other series, including *Softly, Softly, Barlow at Large* and *Barlow.*

Leishman and Mason (2003) describe *The Sweeney* as 'perhaps the ultimate celebration of the police breaking the rules in order to obtain a conviction'. It was the first police drama to acknowledge police corruption, or at least rule-bending, as part and parcel of everyday policing. As mentioned earlier, it was clearly a product of its times and the late 1960s and early 1970s were a time when public confidence in the police was being undermined in a number of ways and in particular through concerns over police corruption. Robert Mark, Commissioner of the Metropolitan Police from 1972, established a department to investigate complaints against police officers and during his five-year term 500 officers were dismissed or required to resign. Although scandals and corruption were not unique to this period, what was new was the revelation that they were systematic and widespread and went to the very top of the police force. Some of Scotland Yard's most senior officers were found guilty and given lengthy jail sentences in the 1970s, including ex-commanders Ken Drury and Wallace Virgo, the two most senior officers to come before British courts.

The publicity surrounding these and other high-profile cases affected the police's relationship with the wider public. In a similar vein, the publicity surrounding the way the police handled demonstrations and industrial disputes excited concern and widespread criticism. In their handling of political demonstrations, over the Vietnam War and apartheid for instance, the police were criticized for being too heavy-handed and increased media coverage served to sharpen such criticism. Perhaps most dramatic were the television and news pictures of the policing of the miner's strike of 1984/1985. The policing of this strike was very confrontational (indeed one 'event' is popularly referred to as the 'battle of Orgreave') and polarized the police from 'ordinary' working people. And the inner-city riots and disorders of the early 1980s in Brixton, Toxteth, Moss Side and elsewhere reflected an increased alienation between the police and sections of the population.

All of these events were filmed and appeared in our living rooms almost as they occurred and they could be seen as signifying and encouraging a move away from traditional notions of policing, and the image of the local bobby, towards a more militaristic and reactive form of policing. And *The Sweeney* was influenced by and to some extent a product of these socio-political influences and their presentation in the media. After the success of a one-off television film, 13 one-hour programmes were made under the title of *The Sweeney* (cockney slang for 'The Flying Squad').

Although not as heavily violent as films of the time such as *Dirty Harry* or of more recent portrayals, *The Sweeney* presented crime fighting as a battle – taking place in the 'urban jungle of London' (Leishman and Mason 2003). The rule-bending by Regan, Carter and other members of the 'squad' was confined to what was needed to catch villains, with the official procedures seen as red tape getting in the way of the police's attempts to save and shield the public from crime and criminals. As with other commentaries on the importance of *The Sweeney*, Leishman and Mason cite Regan's rant from an episode called *Abduction*:

> Try and protect the public and all they do is call you 'fascist'. You nail a villain and some ponced-up, pinstriped Hampstead barrister screws it up like an old fag packet on a point of procedure and then pops off for a game of squash and a glass of Madeira. He's taking home thirty grand a year, and we can just about afford ten days in Eastbourne and a second-hand car. No, it's all bloody wrong my son.
>
> (2003, p. 75)

The Sweeney certainly broke the mould in terms of television portrayal of the British police. Before moving on to look at media representations of other areas of our criminal justice system, in finishing this section we will mention some more recent examples of police dramas. Any review of police drama on British television would be incomplete without mentioning *The Bill*, which in terms of longevity has been Britain's most successful police programme. First broadcast in 1984, it outstripped *Dixon of Dock Green* in August 2005 and continued until 2010. It has adapted to meet the challenges of the highly competitive world of television drama and by the end of its run it was being shown for two one-hour episodes per week (plus past episodes on UK TV Gold). Each episode attracted over 4 million viewers and it was broadcast in over 50 countries worldwide. The Bill recounted the goings on in and around a fictional Metropolitan police station, Sun Hill, located in the East End of London (based on the 'real' London Borough of Tower Hamlets). It is unusual in police dramas in that it adopted a series, soap opera format and did not focus on one aspect of police work only but rather on the lives and work of officers on one shift of the uniform division and on the work of detectives based there.

In terms of the division between 'soft' and 'hard' policing and the portrayal of these different police styles exemplified by *Dixon of Dock Green* and *The Sweeney* respectively, *The Bill* established a kind of midway position and balance between the two poles, as well as accommodating both the uniformed and detective sides of policing (Leishman and Mason 2003). Indeed, Reiner (2007) argues that *The Bill* can be interpreted as the 'synthesis of the dialectic' that was represented by the police portrayals in *Dixon* and *The Sweeney*. It shows a range of contrasting images of police work, from community constables to rule-bending detectives. Reiner (1994) also comments that *The Bill* represented the 'spectrum of contemporary policing in terms of gender, race, organisational specialism and rank'. This approach was developed and can be found in a number of other, more recent police programmes which we are not able to consider here (programmes such as *Heartbeat*, *Morse*, *Juliet Bravo*, *The Gentle Touch* and *Prime Suspect*).

Taking on Reiner's argument, Leishman and Mason (2003) suggest that as *The Bill* developed in the 1990s and into the 2000s it became a 'new synthesis' of police representations in the media. It began to highlight more disturbingly corrupt police characters, while the 'ordinary' police officers began to be portrayed with serious moral failings and personal flaws. As Leishman and Mason put it:

> Ever the synthesis, *The Bill* has come to define the virtually real territory of a contemporary TV copland, where the moral certainties of *Dixon* are long gone and television cop heroes have become people whose virtue is relative rather than absolute.
>
> (2003, p. 103)

QUESTION BREAK

Consider current portrayals of police officers in television programmes (both police dramas and more general soap operas and dramas).

What examples are there of police officers portrayed as

1. 'carers' and 'soft';
2. 'controllers' and 'hard'?

How are uniformed police officers represented in comparison to detectives?

So far we have focused on fictional representations of the police and in concluding we will refer briefly to the police reality programmes of recent years – what might be termed 'factional representation'. Again, given the confines of space in an introductory overview, we will focus on one major example of this genre – *Crimewatch UK*. *Crimewatch UK* began on BBC in 1984 and is broadcast on a monthly basis; it uses dramatic reconstructions and surveillance film of crimes to try and gain information from the public that will help the police to solve particular crimes. It was developed from a popular German programme *Aktenzeichen XY* which had been running since 1967. Our discussion will be based on the more in-depth analysis of the programme offered by Jewkes (2004), in which she examines some of the myths about crime that she argues it helps to perpetuate.

From its beginning until 2007 *Crimewatch UK* was presented by Nick Ross; however, and tragically, it became the subject of police and media attention in 1999 when Ross's co-presenter, Jill Dando, was the subject of a violent murder. As well as continuity of presenters, the format of the programme has remained virtually the same since 1984. There are reconstructions of a few (usually three or four an episode) serious crimes, plus appeals to the public for information about offenders and suspects from a range of crimes across the country. There are updates on crimes and offenders covered in previous programmes – particularly where some progress has been made in catching offenders. Jewkes comments that this continuity and reference back to previous episodes and crimes serves the purpose of

> congratulating the audience for helping to secure convictions, making them feel absolutely integral to the show, and further giving the (inaccurate) impression that *Crimewatch* is largely responsible for solving serious crime in the UK.
>
> (2004, p. 153)

It is difficult to measure the 'success' of the programme; in 2000 the *Crimewatch* team claimed that since 1984 there had been 582 arrests resulting directly from the programme. However, it is difficult to substantiate such claims as many of those arrests may well have occurred without the programme anyway.

Jewkes goes on to emphasize the inherent tension between information and entertainment which lies at the heart of *Crimewatch* and, indeed, 'reality' television programming in general. While specific items might not be included just for entertainment value, programme editors are aware that there has to be some visual and journalistic impact so as to make 'good television'. This tension between entertainment and 'its public service remit', as Jewkes puts it, is illustrated by the sort of crimes which are represented on the show – basically the most uncommon (statistically) crimes such as murder and rape are those which are most often featured, while the more common but less spectacular property crimes and corporate crimes are rarely shown.

However, it is clear that *Crimewatch* has been important in helping the police improve their public relations through demonstrating the police and public working together to investigate and solve real crimes:

> The benefits to [the police] in terms of the warm feelings induced by watching the police and public working together to solve crimes arguably outweighs all other benefits of the programme.
>
> (Jewkes 2004, p. 163)

Each programme includes up to 30 officers from across the UK making statements and appeals and taking part in interviewers with the presenters. This helps to lend a 'personal touch' to the investigations and presents the human face of the police service, hopefully acting as an encouragement to informants and witnesses to contact the police with information.

While very popular and clearly having some positive impact on the police's relationship with the wider public and on solving particular crimes, *Crimewatch* has been criticized for contributing to the fear of crime through its emphasis on and dramatic reconstructions of violent and sexual crime. Leishman and Mason (2003) acknowledge that it is difficult to establish whether the programme does engender an increased fear of crime, but refer to British Crime Survey information, which suggests that *Crimewatch* has helped to create a climate of fear of crime. *Crimewatch* has also been criticized for its reliance on police information and for the fact that the police largely determine the content of the programme; indeed without police cooperation it would not exist.

MEDIA PORTRAYAL OF THE COURTS/LEGAL SYSTEM

QUESTION BREAK

Before considering how the media present court cases and the sentencing of offenders, it would be useful for you to consider how recent criminal trials have been reported.

Look at the headlines reporting the beginning of the trial of serial killer Dr Harold Shipman in October 1999, the murder trial of Amanda Knox in 2009 and the trial of Michael and Mairead Philpott for the manslaughter of their six children in a house fire in 2012 and consider the questions below.

Harold Shipman trial:

Doctor Enjoyed Killing, Court Told

Jury hears that GP murdered 15 women patients because exercising power of life and death was 'to his taste'

(*The Guardian*, 12 October 1999)

The Family GP Who 'Killed 15 Women Just for Kicks'.

(*Daily Mirror*, 12 October 1999)

Amanda Knox trial:

> American Amanda Knox, 21, and Italian Raffaele Sollecito, 24, appeared in front of an eight-member jury in a courthouse in the university town of Perugia at the opening of the trial, which will start taking evidence early next month.
>
> (*The Guardian*, 17 January 2009)

> Foxy Knoxy Trial: Smirking, Relaxed . . . on Trial for Murder.
>
> With her wide smile and calm demeanour party girl Amanda Knox looks as if she is off to have fun . . . not facing trial for murder
>
> (*Daily Mirror*, 17 January 2009)

Michael and Mairead Philpott trial (and see p. 152):

> Mick and Mairead Philpott Started Fire that Killed Their 6 Children, Court Told
>
> Deaths in Derby house fire were result of 'plan that went horribly wrong and resulted in total tragedy', prosecutor tells jury.
>
> (*The Guardian*, 12 February 2013)

> 'He wanted a house full of kids for the benefit cash': Prosecutor claims 'father started blaze which killed six of his children to frame mother of his other four'. . .
> Court heard Mairead Philpott carried out sex act on third defendant Paul Mosley following the fire.
>
> (*Daily Mail*, 12 February 2013)

QUESTIONS

- How would you describe the media presentation of the different cases in each 'type' of newspaper?
- How might their coverage influence readers' views?
- Find newspaper reports of a current or recent criminal trial from a 'quality' and a 'popular' paper and consider their different styles of reporting on court trials.

Although we have what is termed 'open justice' in the UK, with our courts open to the public, who are able to watch the proceedings in cases at both magistrates and crown courts (apart from in special circumstances – for instance, where national security issues might be present – and in youth courts), television cameras or filming and photographing are not allowed in our courts. Indeed, the issue of whether to allow the televised recording of court proceedings has been widely debated for many years and raises the question as to what exactly does the phrase 'justice must be seen to be done' mean.

In his overview of the issues around this debate on public viewing of British justice, Stepniak (2003) considers the rationale for why cameras were initially banned from English courtrooms and why this ban has remained in force. It was the Criminal Justice Act of 1925 which banned the taking and publishing of photographs in courts in England and Wales, in part due to the publication of a photograph in the *Daily Mirror* in 1912 of Judge Bucknill passing the death sentence on Frederick Seddon. This photograph, which was taken secretively without the court's consent, caused a public outcry and was widely referred to in Parliament in the years up to the 1925 Act. Although passed before television broadcasting had begun, the Act's provisions have been extended to include television. More generally, the growing level of public interest in gruesome crimes and criminal trials helped persuade the authorities to ban cameras and keep them banned.

However, that was over 80 years ago, before the massive technological developments which enable filming and photographing to be done in a much more discreet manner and before the enormous increase in news and information, including films and pictures available through the Internet as well as traditional media sources. There have been committees and working parties set up to revisit this issue and we will refer to some of the recent discussion on the issue.

The Caplan Report in 1989, entitled *Televising the Courts,* was based on a study of overseas experiences of televising court cases undertaken by a working party of the Public Affairs Committee of the General Council of the Bar and led by Jonathan Caplan, a practising barrister. Their overall conclusion was in favour of televising court proceedings and they recommended a two-year trial period to allow such televising but under strict controls. These proposals led to a Private Members Bill being introduced in Parliament but, after vigorous debate, the Bill failed and the recommendations were not acted on. Stepniak points out that the Caplan Report's conclusions were in line with all other studies and evaluations of this issue – none of which have indicated there would be a detrimental impact on what happens in our courtrooms as a result of televising. Stepniak then asks whether the continued courtroom ban is incompatible with the principle of open justice. Open justice should not just mean courts being open to the public but should refer to publicity in a wider context. Many, in fact most, people are unable to attend court proceedings in person and depend on the media for their information. As Stepniak puts it 'as open justice clearly no longer depends on public attendance of proceedings, public scrutiny and informed debate relies almost entirely on the media'. And while courts no doubt recognize the role played by the media, they have been very reluctant to welcome in audio and visual media; rather they have confined reporting to the press, in spite of the role played by television in contemporary society as the most relied upon source of public information.

Although the 1925 law and the ban on televising in courts does not apply to Scotland, up until 1992 the courts had effectively barred cameras there too. However, after much perseverance the BBC persuaded the Lord President of Scotland to allow a trial filming at Edinburgh Sheriff Court. This resulted in a five-part documentary on BBC2 in 1994, called *The Trial*, that used footage from Scottish courts. The feedback from those involved was essentially positive – as the producer, Nick Catliff, said in 1999:

The reviews were very kind. It was good telly, it got a huge amount of press coverage and was watched by healthy audiences . . . The courts were pleased too . . . Our presence hadn't caused chaos, there were no complaints that the administration of justice had been interrupted.

(cited in Stepniak 2003, p. 265)

Indeed, those in favour of filming and photographing in courts can refer to a range of research that suggests cameras have virtually no effect on proceedings (Stepniak (2003) refers to studies by Kassin (1984), Borgida *et al.* (1990) and Johnson (1993)). A more recent review by Mason (2001) looks at the filming of the International Criminal Tribunal for the former Yugoslavia in The Hague, which is an English-speaking court that has been using audio-visual equipment since 1996. There are six remote-controlled cameras in each of the three courtrooms, with the footage filmed live but broadcast after a 30-minute delay (in case participants mistakenly identify other protected parties). In research that involved interviewing judges, prosecutors, defence counsel and court staff, Mason found that the vast majority of respondents (92%) said they were only 'occasionally' or 'rarely' aware of the cameras in court. Very few (4%) felt that the judges were affected by the cameras, although a large majority (80%) felt that counsel would be much more likely to be affected, and may tend to 'play acting' and 'dramatics'. As with other studies, this research offered strong support for cameras in court, on the grounds that they enabled justice to be seen to be done, that filming would enable the international community to have faith in the trials and that cameras might well enable relatives of those who died to see a trial that they would otherwise have been unable to see.

It was in the 1990s that viewers in England and Wales were also able to see televised trials from other countries, largely due to the spread of satellite television. However, two trials from the United States that gained massive publicity in Britain had a major effect in turning public and political opinion against the idea of routinely allowing cameras in British courts – the O. J. Simpson case and the Louise Woodward case. The media coverage of these and other high-profile court cases in the United States, while being viewed by some commentators as showing justice being done, has also led to accusations of 'justice being reduced to voyeuristic entertainment' (Stepniak 2003). Brief details of these cases are included in the question break below.

QUESTION BREAK

Courts on TV?

Although the courtroom drama has long been a regular and popular element of films, TV dramas and soap operas, as we have seen in our discussion above, there has been a long-running debate as to whether television cameras should be allowed in British courts. Televised trials from the USA have been shown on satellite TV in Britain and have had a major impact on this debate – examples of some of these cases are highlighted below.

Nanny murder trial

Teenage British nanny, Louise Woodward, was accused of first-degree murder for allegedly shaking to death 8-month-old Mathew Eappen in Massachusetts. In a trial in 1997 that attracted international interest, the jury verdict (guilty of second degree murder) was followed by a surprise judge's ruling whereby the charge was reduced to involuntary manslaughter and Woodward was given a custodial sentence that amounted to the time she had already spent in prison awaiting trial and was then sent home to England. Louise Woodward was subject to massive and detailed media scrutiny throughout her trial, subsequent appeal and final ruling. Every aspect of her expression and what she was wearing was commented on, her parents and friends were featured as they sat in courts and her anguished response to being found guilty at the first hearing were broadcast live and to millions watching worldwide.

O. J. Simpson murder trial

American football star O. J. Simpson was tried for the 1994 murders of his ex-wife Nicole and her friend Ronald Goldman. Weekly reviews broadcast on the BBC were watched by an average of 1 million viewers and the live weekday coverage on Sky by an estimated 7 million viewers. Eventually Simpson was acquitted of the double murders. The televising of this high-profile and lengthy trial (from November 1994 to October 1995) raised the issue of cameras in court in the United States and elsewhere as well as highlighting issues around racism and prejudice in the criminal justice system. Early on in the trial, the Sunday newspaper The Sunday People *reported that O. J. Simpson would be spared the death penalty even if found guilty of double murder (and even though in California murderers guilty of more than one murder are sent to the gas chamber). They quoted a Los Angeles lawyer as saying, 'this guy is such a hero that no jury would convict if he faced the gas chamber' (The Sunday People, 20 November 1994). And in reflecting on the coverage given this trial,* The Mail on Sunday *described the damage the case had done to the American criminal justice system – 'We have watched an astonishing display of irrelevance for months on end, invented defence strategies, personal jury dramas, and a judge fighting back tears. It has been long, preposterous entertainment . . . Part of the fault lies in the continuous television coverage, which has turned what used to be a solemn duty into a frivolous spectacle . . . The root of the problem is the American appetite for publicity' (The Mail on Sunday, 1 October 1995).*

The Menendez brothers

Lyle and Erik Menendez, sons of a successful Cuban businessman, were convicted in March 1996 of first-degree murder of their parents, allegedly due to greed. They are both serving life sentences without the possibility of parole. The defence counsel argued that the boys had been subject to years of sexual abuse at the hands of their parents. These convictions were at the end of the second trial – the first had run for six months up to January 1994 and ended with the juries (one for each brother/defendant) deadlocked. Ironically, at the second trial of the Menendez brothers, the judge ruled against live broadcasting due to what he termed 'the carnival atmosphere' that overtook the O. J. Simpson trial.

List what you consider to be the main advantages of and potential difficulties and problems with the televising of criminal trials.

Moving on from the 1990s, the debate over live broadcasting from court has continued into the twenty-first century. Although the issues are not exactly the same, for many years there was no televised broadcasting of the UK Parliament, partly due to a concern it would encourage politicians to play up to the cameras and would bring Parliament into disrepute. This ban was ended in November 1989 and television cameras in Parliament are seen as part of the landscape. However, any recording of proceedings in a court in England and Wales is still seen as contempt of court. And it is also contempt to produce a drawing inside the court – the artists' pictures of trials that we do see are done from notes made in court but drawn from memory outside the courtroom itself.

In August 2004, the Lord Chancellor, Lord Falconer, announced that there would be 'wide-ranging consultation on the contentious issue' (of cameras being used in courts) and that judges had agreed to a pilot scheme whereby appeal court cases would be filmed in the next few months. As he put it: 'Technology and public attitudes have moved on since the legislation controlling the broadcasting of courts was passed in 1925' (BBC News 24, 15 November 2004).

Lord Falconer saw one of the key issues or problems as the danger that witnesses might be put off coming to court if they knew they were to be filmed; which is partly why the pilot was kept to appeal cases, where witnesses rarely appear in person. The broadcasters were delighted with this move, which at least opened up the possibility of partial televising of trials in the UK. However, the resulting footage from the pilot scheme was never broadcast and there has been relatively slow progress since then; in November 2006, Lord Falconer is quoted as saying that he aimed to set out a 'way forward before the end of the year', but that he believed witnesses, defendants and jurors should not be shown (BBC News 24, 13 November 2006).

More recently, in January 2013, the government announced that broadcasters would be allowed into the Court of Appeal from October 2013 and that this is likely to be extended to crown courts in due course. As before, this move has not been widely approved by the judiciary. The Lord Chief Justice, Lord Judge, commented that the government plans to extend filming to crown courts would 'provoke disruption and deter witnesses from giving evidence'. Speaking before the House of Lords' constitution committee in January 2013 he commented: 'I'm perfectly happy with cameras coming into court, provided their presence doesn't increase the risk that justice won't be done . . . (but) I'm very troubled about having cameras just swanning around the court' (cited in *The Guardian*, 30 January 2013). He also referred to problems that had occurred in New Zealand where cameras have been allowed and where cheers and booing had accompanied sentences.

MEDIA PORTRAYAL OF PRISONS

The notion and practice of using imprisonment as a penal sanction, a specific form of punishment, dates back perhaps two hundred or so years. Although prisons of one type or another had existed for many years before this time, such prisons were used mainly for holding people before trial, or indeed without trial. The sentencing of offenders to an actual period of imprisonment as a punishment was not typical; imposed punishments tended to be visible, quick and harsh, symbolized by the gallows and guillotine, for instance.

A key theorist in describing and explaining this change in the nature of punishment was Michel Foucault. Foucault's work focused on issues to do with knowledge, power and the human body, and was not confined to the area of crime and punishment. However, as regards our interest here, he examined the emergence of crime and the changes in the form of punishment in the late eighteenth and early nineteenth centuries. This was the time of the industrial revolution and of hectic and dramatic social change that led to a widespread concern over the threat to social order that might result from a new, industrial working class. In his classic text, *Discipline and Punish*, subtitled *The Birth of the Prison* (1977), Foucault examined and analysed the changes brought about by the emergence of modern industrial society and applied them to the area of crime and punishment. In this detailed study of the prison system that emerged in the early nineteenth century, he emphasized that the methods of dealing with criminals in the modern prisons were part of a wider process of control and regimentation in society.

His work examines and explains the disappearance of punishment as a public spectacle of violence and the emergence of the prison – he saw the target of punishment as changing, it focused on the soul of the offender rather than just the body, on transforming the offender rather than just avenging the particular crime. Foucault saw these developments as illustrating how power operated in modern society, with open, physical force and the ceremonies around it replaced by a more detailed regulation of offenders – troublesome individuals were removed from society and, hopefully, re-socialized, rather than being broken and destroyed.

So the 'modern' prison was established in the later eighteenth and, particularly, the early parts of the nineteenth century – and imprisonment became a normal form of punishment. Indeed, with the decline in public, physical punishments and the end of transportation to America (in the later eighteenth century) and, eventually, to Australia (in mid-nineteenth century) imprisonment soon became the main area for the disposal of offenders who had been found guilty of the more serious forms of criminal behaviour. The development of the prison was accompanied by debate and argument as to the best method of organizing and managing imprisonment as a form of punishment, and over the running of prisons in terms of organizational structure.

This debate centred around the pros and cons of different systems of prison discipline – and in particular the separate system and the silent or solitary system. In the separate system, prisoners spent all their times in single cells where they would eat, work and sleep – this, it was believed, would stop prisoners being contaminated by fellow prisoners and would allow them to contemplate their offending and emerge reformed characters. The silent system allowed prisoners to associate with and work with other prisoners but to be silent at all times. Both systems were influenced by the religiously motivated reformers of the time:

> Both systems were based on the idea that first offenders or young offenders could be contaminated by more experienced criminals, and that prisoners should be silent, or separate from others, to allow reflection and repentance for their criminal behaviour.
>
> (Johnston 2006, p. 106)

Contemporary writers and commentators examined and discussed these two systems; one such writer who was hugely influential at this time was Charles Dickens. Dickens was strongly critical of the separate system and, given his importance as an author and writer who was read widely in his day (and remains, of course, one of the great figures of English literature), we will look briefly at his ideas here. Dickens argued that the separate system was 'cruel and wrong', and even if devised with the best of philanthropic intentions, those who were behind its introduction did not know what they were doing. Johnston (2006) points out that Dickens was particularly concerned about the psychological effects this system had on prisoners. She quotes from Dickens's *American Notes* of 1842:

> Very few men were capable of estimating the immense amount of torture and agony which this dreadful punishment, prolonged for years, inflicts upon the sufferers . . . there is a depth of terrible endurance to it which none but its sufferers can fathom, and which no man has a right to inflict upon his fellow creature . . . I hold this slow and daily tampering with the mysteries of the brain to be immeasurably worse than any torture of the body.
>
> (p. 107)

As an aside, it is not surprising that the prison and prison life feature regularly in Dickens's writing, given his family's first-hand experience of imprisonment. Dickens's father was a naval clerk who got into financial troubles and debt when Charles was a young lad, in the early 1820s. Eventually arrested for unpaid debt, Charles's father, John, was sent to a debtor's prison in South London and all the family belongings were sold to the pawnbroker. The whole Dickens family moved into the debtor's prison for a while as it gave them a better standard of living than their previous difficult circumstances. Charles moved out to separate accommodation but remained living close to his father in prison; after leaving prison, Dickens's father and family lived together in Camden, London with Charles joining them. It was these first-hand experiences of prison life which Dickens used in many of his famous works, including *Pickwick*, *David Copperfield* and *Little Dorrit*.

Of course, Dickens's views were not the only literary or media representations of the separate system. As well as the concern for the mental health of prisoners articulated by Dickens, there was an alternative viewpoint which did not want this system to be seen as too soft.

To return to more general issues concerning the emergence of the modern prison, the moving of punishment away from the public arena to behind the walls of the prison has given this form of punishment a secrecy that means the wider public are pretty poorly informed as to what prisons are like and how they function. It has meant that most people rely on the media for their information and understanding of prison and prison life. Mason (2003) points out that media representations of prison do not only affect the wider public but can and do influence those working in the criminal justice system. He refers to two director generals of the Prison Service acknowledging the role the media played in their own experience of prisons:

> In 1992, Derek Lewis confessed that prior to taking the post as head of the prison service, 'his knowledge of prison life came from the media and the BBC comedy programme *Porridge* . . .' [and] More recently, the current Director General, Martin Narey, said that the BBC documentary *Strangeways* 'played a big role in my deciding to join the prison service'.
>
> (Mason 2003, pp. 279, 280)

We have seen throughout this book that crime is a natural and major subject for the media to cover and that the most serious crimes receive the greatest coverage. This means that the media inevitably presents a distorted picture of crime and punishment (as the more serious crimes naturally receive the most severe punishments). So much of the media coverage of punishment focuses on prisons (the most severe punishment available within our criminal justice system). However, in spite of prison being the form of punishment that most usually springs to mind when punishment is considered, our knowledge of prisons is limited. As Levenson (2001) puts it

> Despite this familiarity [with prisons], few people are aware of even the basic facts about imprisonment, such as the number of prisoners or the number of prisons, let alone the realities and routines of prison life. Rather, the familiarity is based on the symbolism of the prison and is fed by media images and portrayals of the prison in television and film, from *Porridge* to *Prisoner Cell Block H*, *Escape From Alcatraz* to *Shawshank Redemption*.
>
> (p. 14)

There are obvious dangers with this reliance on media portrayals. Rather than emphasizing punishment, prisons can be portrayed as easy-going and even privileged places. And the media coverage will almost inevitably highlight the more extreme aspects of prison life, such as riots or deaths in prison – the events they see as newsworthy. Indeed, these two contrasting aspects of the media representation of prisons – as easy-going 'holiday camps', as the popular press regularly put it, or as dangerous and violent places – are highlighted by Coyle (2005). On the one hand, prisons are portrayed as dangerous, where there is an ever-present threat of violence and brutality (either from other prisoners or the prison staff). On the other hand, the holiday camp portrayal suggests prisoners lie in bed all day if they choose to, eat well and have amenities and leisure activities that most people on the outside do not have access to (these two media pictures are explored in the question break below). In reality, Coyle points out, daily life in prison is 'far removed from either of these extremes'. In similar vein, Levenson makes the point that giving people accurate information about the criminal justice system is vital to secure public confidence in it; as the public relies so heavily on the media any misrepresentation is very damaging.

In contrast to these media representations and images of prison life, the most overwhelming feature of prison life would seem to be the routine and boring nature of it. Large institutions necessarily follow a fairly strict timetable and routine, and the features that are common in institutions of many kinds are liable to be more important in custodial institutions that have to be focused on security. The prison day is dominated by routine – cells are unlocked and locked at given times, meals are served at the same time and the activities of the day follow a tightly scheduled pattern. Not surprisingly, perhaps the major feature of day-to-day prison life is the monotony of it.

QUESTION BREAK

Consider the extracts below, illustrating the contrasting extremes of the media picture of prison life – the holiday camp and the brutal and violent environment. They are taken from a number of different newspapers, national and local, and the BBC News website.

'13 Yrs Inside . . . What a Laugh'

A former armed robber has penned a crime book – about the FUNNY side of prison life. James Crosbie was a career criminal for over 40 years – spending more than half behind bars. He worked for the Krays and rubbed shoulders with Glasgow Godfather Arthur Thompson . . . But instead of detailing his hardman encounters, and police stand-offs, James's tome Peterhead Porridge *reveals the laughs he enjoyed during 13 years inside one of the country's toughest nicks. James, now 70, said: 'So many crime books paint a picture of how tough prison life is and how hard it is to survive . . . but the truth is they can be a laugh too'.*

(*The Sun*, 4 August 2007)

Now Prisoners Get to Watch TV to Save Distress

Prison bosses were criticized yesterday for spending thousands of pounds on an information service designed to stop inmates suffering 'emotional distress'. Rapists, murderers and paedophiles waiting to be locked up at Pentonville jail will be comforted by a state-of-the-art TV providing information on prison life. The Ministry of Justice said it wanted to stop 'boredom' and 'emotional distress', as well as lessening the risk of self-harm.

The decision to install the flat screen TV . . . was slammed as a waste of taxpayers' money and an insult to crime victims. Blair Gibbs, spokesman for the Taxpayers' Alliance, said: 'If they can spend money on this, why can't they build prisons'. A Spokeswoman for the Ministry of Justice said: 'The last report by the chief inspector of prisons criticized Pentonville for holding prisoners in the reception area for long periods of time with no distractions which led to boredom and emotional distress . . . This will be paid for out of the prison's annual budget.'

(*Daily Express*, 2 July 2007)

Huntley's Happy to Die in Jail: Child Killer's Cushy Life

Ian Huntley is happy Britain's law chief wants him to die behind bars – because he has got such a cushy life in jail. Huntley, 33, stunned jail staff with his reaction to the declaration by the Lord Chancellor Lord Falconer that he should never go free. The double child killer is so comfortable being a con he does not want to be let out.

Huntley is monitored round the clock in Wakefield Prison's healthcare wing – so he does not get vigilante attacks. He gets three meals a day in the West Yorkshire jail – plus extra dishes in cookery classes . . . He also gets regular letters from smitten sweetheart Maxine Carr, who was also jailed for giving him a false alibi for the 2002 murders of 10-year-old Soham schoolgirls Holly Wells and Jessica Chapman . . . and unlike other inmates he is allowed to see visitors in a private room. According to insiders, the monster, who was ordered to serve at least 40 years, 'struts round as if he owns the place'.

(*The Daily Star*, 26 March 2007)

Prison? It's Just Like a Holiday Camp: Animal Rights Terrorists Gloat on Website about 'Fantastically Easy, Blissful' Life Behind Bars

Animal rights extremists jailed for a campaign of terrorism have mocked their punishment, describing prison as a 'holiday camp'. Seven fanatics were sentenced to a total of 50 years for their ruthless intimidation of workers connected to a laboratory which used animals in experiments . . .

But on a website for supporters of the group called Stop Huntingdon Animal Cruelty, they gloat that life in jail is 'fantastically easy'. They boast of living in 'en suite' pads, enjoying delicious vegan cuisine and spending their days painting and studying literature. One thug calls his jail 'Butlins' while another describes scoffing dairy-free chocolate as she watches the US sitcom Friends.

(*Daily Mail*, 24 December 2010)

Prison Doesn't Work. It's Like a Holiday Camp

Tommy Knight has been in prison 12 times, taking up a total of nine years of his life. Honest citizens and victims of crime in particular would hope this punishment would have worked . . . But, sadly, this is not the case.

To put it in Tommy's words: 'Prison doesn't work. It is actually not that far removed from a holiday camp. It is just like you are in another little world for a while' . . . He describes the British criminal justice system as a 'soft touch' . . . 'When you come in here you get exactly the same as what you get on the outside. You can have more of a laugh in here as everyone has something in common. I would say that some people actually have a better life in here compared to the life they have outside of prison.'

(*Liverpool Echo*, 23 October 2003)

Prison Wing 'Unfit for Animals' Closed Down

A damning report from environmental health inspectors has led to the closure of a prison wing after inmates threatened the Prison Service with a high court action. The last of 80 prisoners from Gurney wing at Norwich prison were moved to other jails this week as the 81,333 prison population in England and Wales was expected to reach record levels today . . .

The wing was originally scheduled for closure in January after the Independent Monitoring Board declared it was 'unfit for animals', but it was reopened after three days because of overcrowding. The Prison Service only put inmates in cells certified as fit for habitation, but prisoners complained they were living next door to uncertified cells which had broken soil stacks, mould on walls, nesting pigeons, rodent infestation and a terrible stench. Environmental health inspectors found that cells on Gurney wing were between 50 and 75 times more hazardous to inmates' health than normal housing conditions.

(*The Guardian*, 5 October 2007)

Concerns Over Prison Conditions

Conditions at Dartmoor Prison are putting staff, visitors and the public in 'real danger', a report has claimed. The Independent Monitoring Board says the jail has too many prisoners and that some cells are 'barely habitable' . . .

Margaret Blake, vice chairman of the Independent Monitoring Board, formerly the Jail's Board of Visitors, said: 'We have been concerned for some time . . . that the condition of the prison is deteriorating . . . Shortages and resources mean that prisoners are left longer in their cells. Tensions can increase and frustrations can lead to a greater risk of attacks between prisoners or attacks on staff.'

(*BBC News*, 5 November 2009)

Chief Inspector of Prisons Says Conditions in Young Offender Institutions Are Deteriorating

The chief inspector of prisons, Nick Hardwick, says young people aged 15 to 18 are being held in deteriorating conditions in the YOI {Youth Offenders Institutions} network, with fewer feeling safe while they are locked up.

The inspection showed that fewer young inmates felt they could tell someone they were being victimised or believed a member of staff would take them seriously.

(*The Guardian*, 26 October 2011)

European Watchdog Criticises UK Prison Overcrowding

European prison watchdogs have strongly criticised the acutely overcrowded conditions in jails in England and Wales, saying a fresh approach is needed to eradicate the problem.

The Council of Europe's committee on the prevention of torture and inhuman and degrading punishment said too many inmates continued to spend too much time locked in their cells with little access to meaningful activities . . .

The committee raised concerns about the number of incidents of violence between inmates at Huntercombe young offenders' institutions, and criticised the use of restraint techniques that involved inflicting pain. It said that at the time of its visit a technique known as the nose grip was being used 40 times a month by staff . . . This involved the nose being pulled back and a finger rubbed hard across the base of the nostrils. The delegation said this technique should be banned.

(*The Guardian*, 8 December 2009)

QUESTIONS

- How would you describe the portrayal of prison life from the different newspapers?
- What reaction might these images produce from the wider public?
- What explanations can you offer for such different representations?
- How might politicians and policy-makers use these images?

As was suggested earlier, the images of prison from the media are a, if not the, major source of information on prison and prison life for the vast majority of the population. As we have seen, the media representation of prisons can be both fictional as well as factual and can be found in written form and in film and television. Before looking at fictional representations of prison it is important to acknowledge the role of television documentaries in providing the public with information about prison life. In this context, a number of the largest and most well-known of English prisons have featured in recent documentaries. Strangeways prison in Manchester, Britain's largest high-security prison, has been the subject of a series of fly-on-the-wall documentaries, first an eight-part series in 1980, then a follow-up to the infamous riots there in 1990 and then a three-part series in 2011. In commenting on the later of those series, the governor of Strangeways, Richard Vince, said that he hoped the documentary would dispel some of the myths surrounding the Manchester jail. He commented, 'We are pleased to be able to show the high quality, important and at times difficult work that prison staff do' (*Manchester Evening News*, 10 May 2011). Other prisons which have been the focus of prime time television documentaries have been Wormwood Scrubs (a two-part documentary in 2009), Holloway, Europe's largest female prison (a three-part documentary in 2009) and, most recently, Aylesbury prison, which houses some of the most dangerous young offenders in the country (a two-episode documentary in 2013).

As we have indicated, much of the public's knowledge of prison and prison life comes from fictional representations of prison in literature, film and television. We will touch on some examples of this fictional representation in concluding this section.

Mason (2003), in an overview of cinematic representation of the prison, describes how prison has been a feature in films from the early days of the cinema. He categorizes the main different approaches and themes of the 300 plus prison films that have been made. Some highlight the sheer brutality of prison life (*Midnight Express* (1978), *McVicar* (1980) and *Scum* (1979), for example). Others focus on prisoners battling with the authorities and jailers (such as *Cool Hand Luke* (1967) and *Papillon* (1973)). In spite of the number and range of prison films, Mason points out that there is a lack of literature on the media representation of imprisonment, and the prison film is not a recognized genre, in that 'prison film' is not used in the same way as 'western' or 'gangster film'. Also, and in a similar way in which a prison scene or example might be part of a piece of literature, as in the case of many of Dickens's books, a major problem with the term prison film is deciding what proportion of a film should be made inside a prison to 'earn' that categorization. Scenes of imprisonment can be found in many different types of film, and in a wide range of television programmes.

In suggesting different themes of the prison film, Mason (2003) argues that 'cinematic representations of prison are not easily classified . . . due partly . . . to the variation in the number of prison films that have been made across the decades'. He does, though, attempt to suggest some main themes. These include, the representation of the prison as a machine that grinds people down with its rules and regulations and the emphasis on the effect of imprisonment on the newly imprisoned offender – in particular, the dehumanizing process of becoming a prison statistic.

Although perhaps not as much a feature of day-to-day television as the police, prison and prisoners are a common feature on a range of television programmes. In her review of this aspect of media coverage Jewkes (2006) provides a number of examples:

the world of prison and prisoners has now permeated most television genres: sitcom (*Porridge*), 'serious' drama (*Buried*, *Oz*), light entertainment drama (*Within these Walls*, *Bad Girls*, *The Governor*, *Prisoner*), documentary (*Strangeways*, *Life: Living with Murder*, *Jailbirds*, *Prison Weekly*, *Feltham Sings*) and reality TV (*The Experiment*, *Real Bad Girls*), to name but a few.

(p. 137)

Here we will look at a television programme that is most generally cited as influencing people's views on and knowledge of prison – *Porridge*. This was a BBC television sitcom broadcast between 1974 and 1977, written by Dick Clement and Ian La Frenais and starring Ronnie Barker and Richard Beckinsale. It was set in a fictional prison 'HMP Slade' and led to various spin-offs, including a film and a follow-up series *Going Straight*. While dramas and comedies are not always seen as bona fide sources of information, it is interesting that *Porridge* was popular with British prisoners, who recognized it had a high degree of authenticity. As ex-prisoner and, more recently, *The Guardian* columnist Erwin James put it:

What fans could never know, however, unless they had been subject to a stint of Her Majesty's Pleasure, was that the conflict between Fletcher and Officer Mackay was about the most authentic depiction ever of the true relationship that exists between prisoners and prison officers in British jails up and down the country . . . When I was inside, *Porridge* was a staple of our TV diet. In one high-security prison a video orderly would be dispatched to tape the programme each week. If they missed it, they were in trouble.

(James 2005)

In her examination of popular media and prisons, Jewkes (2006) considers the impact and importance of *Porridge*. A key element of this programme was its depiction of human relationships and particularly that between the old-time, persistent criminal, Norman Fletcher, and the naïve, young first-time offender, Lennie Godber. The relationship between a street-wise, cunning mentor figure and an innocent, gullible friend is common to many British sitcoms (Jewkes cites *Only Fools and Horses*, *Steptoe and Son* and *Blackadder*, amongst others, as examples). This element is not necessarily dependent on the prison setting; however, other aspects of the programme are. The series illustrates a period in British prison history when the 'justice' model was coming to the fore and the welfare/rehabilitation emphasis of the previous decade was being undermined. Jewkes sees this 'dynamic . . . [as being] represented in the form of a "soft" screw and a "hard" screw; the benign and well-meaning Mr Barrowclough, who always saw in his charges the potential for reform, and officious disciplinarian, Mr MacKay, who ruled his wing with an iron will and military disposition'.

From a more critical angle, *Porridge* can also be interpreted as working against prisoners' interests and against penal reform by the rather cosy picture of prison life which might make the wider public less concerned about prison conditions and the reality of a prison system facing dangerous levels of overcrowding. From this perspective, *Porridge*, while giving the public some sense of what prison is like, could be seen as having ignored the humdrum, boring but often tense reality of prison life by showing it to be, basically, a 'bit of a laugh'. It does not encourage the viewing public to think critically about prisons. Jewkes (2006) compares it with *Bad Girls*, in that it is essentially character-driven and only explores imprisonment at a relatively superficial level. Summarizing Wilson and O'Sullivan's study of the representation of prison in film and television drama (2004), Jewkes comments:

> Their recurrent theme is that *Porridge* has failed because it presents a sanitized, comic version of confinement, which allows the public to sidestep the reality of incarceration and absolves them from concerning themselves with the grim reality of confinement at Her Majesty's Pleasure.
>
> (Jewkes 2006, p. 148)

QUESTION BREAK

Do a brief content analysis of two newspapers. How many articles refer to prison and imprisonment?

Consider a number of different television 'soap operas'. How many of the characters have been in prison or have contacts with prisoners (members of their family, friends and so on)?

How would you describe the representation of prison and prison life in television dramas/soaps?

FURTHER READING

Leishman F. and Mason P. (2003) *Policing and the Media: Facts, Fictions and Factions*, Cullompton, UK: Willan Publishing. An examination of the nature and effects of media images of crime and policing. It looks at how the police promote themselves in the media and considers both fictional and documentary representations of police and policing.

Mason P. (ed.) (2006) *Captured by the Media: Prison Discourse in Popular Culture*, Cullompton, UK: Willan Publishing. This book explores media representations of and discourses on prison, again considering both fictional and factual representations. It includes articles looking at press, television and cinematic portrayals of prison and prison life.

New Media Technology and Crime – Cybercrime

So far we have focused our attention on how the mass media represents crime, criminals and victims of crime. In this chapter, we look at recent developments in the media and the impact they have had on crime and the reporting of it. In particular, we will consider how new forms of electronic media have altered the relationship between the media, crime and justice. As regards this last comment, it is clear that the Internet has become an integral part of social and business activity over the last two decades. The educational, financial and social benefits of the Internet cannot be underestimated; however, its proliferation has also raised concerns about the potential for criminal opportunities.

Crime via the Internet has become known as cybercrime. This type of crime is particularly nasty as the perpetrators for the most part remain 'faceless'; the 'virtual offender' is able to enter the victim's personal space, unintentionally invited into living rooms, bedrooms and so on. The victims of such crimes range from governments and businesses to individuals and many tend to be from particularly vulnerable groups – for example, children in the case of paedophilia. This crime has none of the conventional boundaries that we associate with criminal behaviour – victim and perpetrator can be in different cities, countries or continents. The crime is unbounded by 'real-time', crimes can occur at any time, the victim may well be asleep or away from their computer when the crime occurs. Cybercrime is also unique in the fact that it only exists because of the Internet/World Wide Web; in other words this chapter would not be written if it were not for the recent development and spread of new forms of mass media of communication, and particularly the Internet.

Cybercrime is not a minor or minority area of criminal behaviour; its costs as well as its extent in human and economic terms is enormous and growing. Writing in *The Guardian*, David Batty highlighted the massive growth in Internet child pornography offences in recent years, citing Home Office figures he found that the number of people cautioned for possessing child abuse images rose from 13 in 1994 to 363 in 2004 (a rise of 2,692%), the vast majority of these cautions being for downloading child porn images from the web. The number convicted for these offences rose from 63 in 1994 to 1,162 in 2004 (*The Guardian*, 16 January 2006). In 2004, card fraud over the Internet cost the UK £117 million (Association for Payment Clearing Services) and it seems to be a booming business – research from Garlick, a personal data management service, claimed that identity fraud alone could cost the UK £4 billion by 2011 (*The Guardian*, 23 February 2007). Also in 2004, 77 per cent of medium to large businesses reported virus attacks costing £27.8 million, while 17 per cent suffered financial fraud costing £121 million (Home Office 2005).

This chapter will explore the extent and impact of cybercrime in today's society. We will discuss the variety of forms of cybercrime with which society is faced. Most cybercrimes, for example, are old crimes but in new guises. The Internet facilitates the commission of what might be termed 'traditional' criminal behaviour. The criminal or criminally minded are faced with the opportunity to commit illegal behaviours on a whole new level. The potential for the targeting of different individuals and groups is vast. Owing to the sheer expanse of the Internet, the following crimes, to name a few of the most obvious, have flourished – online fraud from banks and other accounts (given the name 'phishing'), identity theft and a range of sexual crimes. With regard to that last group, there has been a proliferation of sexual crimes through the use of the Internet by paedophiles and the exploitation of children through child pornography and the increased opportunities for online stalking due to social networks such as Facebook. Furthermore, crimes often related to the traditional use of the term subculture have also flourished, for example, the coordination of football hooligans, which at one time were organized through local gangs. And terrorism now poses a different threat through the fear of cyber terrorism (see pp. 193–197). As we have pointed out, all these activities existed, even if to a lesser extent, before criminologists and journalists referred to cybercrime. Finally, we will look briefly at the difficulty of policing such crime and the problems of finding laws and regulations that achieve a balance between freedom and control.

CHAPTER 7

THE MEDIA REVOLUTION – THE PROLIFERATION OF THE INTERNET

The massive technological developments and changes of recent years have widened access to technology; the use of the Internet has risen sharply over the last decade and does so year by year. We will not go into any great detailed statistical review here, but it is obvious from our daily lives, at home, in work and during our leisure, that computers and the Internet play a major part in contemporary twenty-first century life. In terms of computer use, the average person can now use the web to further their social activity. Free websites such as Myspace.com and more recently Facebook.com and Twitter (sometimes referred to as interfacing networks) allow online communication and correspondence with other groups and or individuals through an interactive network of user photos, profiles and web logs. According to research conducted by Socialbakers, Facebook had 31,174,580 monthly active users in 2013 (www.socialbakers.com).

In terms of leisure, online shopping has also increased over the last few years, BCG (Boston Consulting Group) stated that the UK carries out more retail online than any other major economy, 13.5 per cent in 2010, with a projected rise of 23 per cent by 2016 – a total of £220 billion (www.bbc.co.uk/news/business-17405016, 19 March 2012). The most popular products bought online are now holidays, music and films; and the growth of online fraud mentioned in the introduction to this chapter has not stopped people spending increasingly more online. And of course, much financial business is also conducted online. IMRG (Interactive Media and Retail Group) reported that consumers spent an estimated £78 billion on online retail stores in 2012 and that the online retail market is projected to grow by 12 per cent in 2013.

QUESTION BREAK

Think about your everyday lives – at work and home.

How often and for what purpose do you use the World Wide Web?

How and in what ways might your use of the Internet leave you vulnerable to crime/criminals?

As an example of the impact of the Internet, we will consider the global panic that arose over the 'millennium bug'. During the 1990s, the approach of the new millennium saw a gradual rise in panic over what might happen on the actual turn of the millennium – concerns about potential incidents of apocalyptic mayhem were induced by millenarian doomsday cults, predicting the end of civilization as we know it. For example, in 1997 the mass suicide of the Heaven's Gate cult in California was an event that illustrated both the panic over the new millennium and the power of the Internet. The leader of the group, Marshall Applewhite, persuaded 38 group members to commit suicide so that their souls could be taken to a higher place of existence by riding on a spacecraft that was travelling behind the comet Hale-Bopp. The group believed that the comet Hale-Bopp was a sign that they were meant to leave Earth before it was destroyed, or 'recycled' as the cult put it. In terms of the role of the Internet, the following comment was made by the CNN news network a year after the mass suicide:

> It was perhaps the strongest sign yet that the Internet was coming of age: it was implicated in a tragedy that shocked the nation. The 39 members of the Heaven's Gate cult who took their own lives one year ago were professional Web page designers who used the Internet to attempt to win converts and spread their message.
>
> (CNN Interactive, 25 March 1998, http://edition.cnn.com/ US/9803/25/heavens.gate/)

However, the greatest panic that was excited by the approach of the new millennium came through the realization of just how much modern society relied on technology and the consequent fear of the effects of the impending 'millennium bug'. With regard to the millennium bug, which was given the name of Y2K (for Year 2000), the argument was put forward that the date-related processing system would break down when the numbering assumption became invalid with the change from 99 to 00 on 1 January 2000. Therefore, computers would fail to recognize the year 2000. It was argued that, at the stroke of midnight, all computer networks would break down and critical industries and services would be severely and catastrophically affected. Governments put forward contingency plans – Britain spent over 100 million pounds on a project called Package 2000 and the USA spent over 300 billion dollars.

At a speech in March 1998, Tony Blair went as far as to argue,

> So the problem starts now, but will gather pace up until the year 2000. And it is serious because there are few, if any, areas of modern life that are not touched by IT. If we don't tackle this problem, the economy will slow as many companies divert resources to cope with computer failures and some even go bust.
>
> (www.number10.gov.uk)

Tabloid newspapers on the run up to the year 2000 added to the moral panic around the millennium bug. The following two headlines from a British tabloid newspaper demonstrate the panic involved:

Millennium Bug to Hit 999 Calls

POLICE forces and fire brigades across Britain could be plunged into chaos because of the millennium bug, it was revealed last night.

(Sunday Mirror, 17 May 1999)

Army Calls in Reserves for Millennium Chaos

OFFICERS from Britain's Army reserves have been put on alert to deal with the chaos of New Year's Eve 1999. They have been asked to help cope with possible civil unrest and communications disasters as the year 2000 begins. Whitehall fears the huge celebrations, plus widespread computer failures due to the 'Millennium Bug', will leave the country facing a 'Doomsday' scenario.

(Sunday Mirror, 15 November 1998)

The tabloid newspapers were not the only media source to detail and discuss the millennium bug and its perceived consequences. The end of the 1990s saw hundreds of books published that marketed the 'crisis' in often disturbing and unique ways. The content of these books ranged from the practical preparation for the crisis (stockpiling of foods and the like) to religious and spiritual interpretations of the millennium bug meltdown to political conspiracy theories and to the simply weird and wacky. Below is an example of the kind of texts that were being written and the publicity blurb that appeared on the covers.

What Will Become of Us? Counting Down to Y2K

The average American depends wholly on computers to provide food, water, fuel, light, money and health. What would it be like to find ourselves without the things we take for granted? Imagine total vulnerability. This is the essence of the Y2K crisis.

(Gregori 1998; an Electronic Commerce Expert in Washington, DC)

Millennium Bomb: The Y2K New World Order Conspiracy

Is the predicted Y2K bug all a clever hoax or a real global disaster in the making? Who is behind this disturbing turn of events . . . and why?

(Schwartz 1999)

The millennium bug also heightened awareness of the infallibility of computers and the risk of attack through cyber terrorism (something we will discuss later in the chapter, p. 193).

Everyday lives and the Internet

Of course, the millennium passed without any major catastrophes occurring, but the concerns surrounding 1 January 2000 demonstrate societies', and especially Western societies', reliance on the computer and information technology for all aspects of life – from the delivery of food items and clean running water to the functioning of nuclear power plants and world economies. Indeed, we seem to have become dependent on the Internet in a relatively short period of time.

THE EMERGENCE OF CYBERCRIME

In recent years, the development of information communication technologies (ICTs) have allowed the growth of networks which connect world economies, political groups, academic and scientific communities, and diverse populations. The Internet has become an integral part of social activity. One of the most prominent writers associated with research into information technology communications is Manuel Castells. Arguably his most eminent work is *The Information Age*, in which he analyses contemporary capitalism (this work is divided into three volumes with the first, titled *The Rise of the Network Society: The Information Age*, published in 1996). As indicated by the title of this study, Castells's theory is based on the premise that at present society is in transition from the industrial age to the information age through our use of information technologies. This transition Castells called the 'morphology of society'. According to Castells capitalism remains but its driving force has changed from energy to information. These processes have created, according to Castells, the 'network society'. A wide range of networks, then, pervade and transform all domains of contemporary life.

Accordingly, the form of power has also changed and, 'is no longer concentrated in institutions (the state), organizations (capitalist firms), or symbolic controllers (corporate media, churches). It is diffused in global networks of wealth, power, information and images, which circulate and transmute in a system of variable geometry and dematerialized geography. Yet it does not disappear' (Castells 1997, vol. II, p. 359).

In terms of cybercrime, Castells focused primarily on the role of technology and organized criminal groups. In volumes two and three of *The Information Age* he identified what he termed the 'Global Criminal Economy' as a feature of the new network society. In other words, the Internet has allowed criminal groups to communicate and interact on a global scale. The use of the Internet by diverse populations has meant that the scope for potential victims is almost limitless. Castells argues that these criminal organizations are new phenomena that have been empowered through networks to advance their goals, which in turn affects national and international economies, security and politics.

Defining cybercrime

Defining cybercrime is not easy and there continues to be debate over what it is that actually constitutes cybercrime. For example, international jurisdictions render some cybercrime legal in one country but illegal in another. As of yet there does not exist any internationally agreed-upon definition of cybercrime. The European Union, for example, has created a forum on cybercrime and many countries have signed The Council of Europe's Convention on Cybercrime Treaty 2001 in order to aid in the standardization of European law. As of 2010, thirty states had signed and ratified the treaty and acceded to the convention. In 2007, the United States passed two Bills regarding cybercrime – the Cybercrime Act and later that year the Identity Theft Enforcement and Restitution Act, the latter of which has toughened cyber security standards.

While the UK does not have a coherent set of laws that deal with cybercrime it has expanded existing laws in order to deal with certain aspects of cybercrime, especially within the area of child protection (for example, the Computer Misuse Act of 1990). The Criminal Justice and Immigration Act 2008 created the new offence of possessing an extreme pornographic image.

In spite of the difficulties, and the complex nature of cybercrime, theorists within the area have been, and still are, striving to achieve a workable definition. According to David Wall (2005), the following statements suggest three different ways in which the Internet impacts on criminal opportunity.

1. *The Internet has become an advanced vehicle for communications that sustains existing patterns of harmful activity through the circulation of information.* By this Wall is

referring to the ways in which individuals, groups and websites circulate harmful information. Examples of this kind of activities would be chipping (the bypassing security devices within mobile phones, games consoles and the like) or the trading of sexual materials.

2. *The Internet has created a transnational environment that provides entirely new opportunities for harmful activities currently the subject of existing criminal or civil law.* Under this definition harmful activities would include, for example, viruses, large-scale fraud, online sex trade, child abuse (organized paedophilia) and organized football hooliganism.

3. *The Internet has engendered entirely new forms of (unbounded) harmful activity.* Here might be included unauthorized appropriation of images, software and music products through downloading, virtual rape, targeted hate speech or cybersex.

Wall has been one of the foremost criminologists who have investigated cybercrime and in trying to grapple with the definitional difficulties suggested above he has developed a fourfold categorization of computer-related crime (1999). These four categories refer to types of behaviour that encompass a range of activities and are worth considering briefly:

Cyber violence

This does not refer to physical violence but instead describes the impact of certain cybercrimes on the individual or group. For example, cyberstalking, which refers to the continued harassment of a victim via the Internet and through emails – this can and does include paedophilia. Additionally, hate speech which can affect ethnic or social groups – this can be done via the spread of racist/homophobic images and/or doctrines via websites such as those belonging to the British National Party or the Ku Klux Klan. Cyber violence also covers terrorism and the use of the Internet to facilitate terrorist activities.

Cyber obscenity

Refers to the production and trading of sexually explicit material. This type of cybercrime is difficult to police as there are different political and moral beliefs regarding pornographic material. And these differences are particularly apparent across countries and cultures – so in the UK we accept images which would be seen as obscene in other parts of the world, such as Middle Eastern countries. In our discussion below we look at paedophilia and child abuse under the heading of cyber obscenity, although such behaviour clearly overlaps with the category of cyber violence as well.

Cyber trespass

Can be described as gaining unauthorized access to computer systems for the purpose of either corrupting or stealing data. It includes the invasion of private spaces on the Internet by hackers.

Cyber theft

This includes traditional types of theft that are carried out through computers; for example, credit card fraud and theft from online bank accounts. It also includes the downloading of material that does not necessarily deprive the owner (music downloads for instance), and, more generally, what Wall refers to as 'cyberpiracy', the appropriation of intellectual properties.

Although we will not be able to explore all of these different categories of cybercrime in great detail, we will refer to and consider examples of cyber obscenity and cyber violence to illustrate the extent and spread of cybercrime.

CYBER OBSCENITY – PAEDOPHILIA AND THE INTERNET

Paedophilia is an area of crime that has gained much media attention over the past two decades. Indeed, concern over this type of crime has at times reached fever pitch. As we saw in our discussion of moral panics (Chapter 3), the use of the Internet to engage in paedophilia has been an important aspect of the panic that has surrounded this area in recent years.

It is difficult to measure the extent of paedophilia on the Internet for obvious reasons, such as the secrecy and anonymity that such behaviour encourages. This difficulty is exacerbated by the lack of clarity in defining this behaviour. This lack of clarity is reflected in the Home Office's description of Internet paedophilia as:

> A course of conduct enacted by a suspected paedophile, which would give a reasonable person cause for concern that any meeting with a child arising from the conduct would be for unlawful purposes
>
> (Home Office 2002)

The Internet has created an environment where children and teenagers can be educated and be socially interactive with each other. However, these 'spaces' for children can also be accessed by adults who wish to harm children, either as a way of making money or by way of sexual exploitation (and often both together). Internet paedophilia leaves children particularly vulnerable to such exploitation due to the invisibility and secrecy of paedophile networks.

Essentially, Internet paedophilia can be displayed on two levels. First, information sharing – through the Internet paedophiles are able, very easily to share and swap child pornography, disclose/access information about individual children, or work in tandem with one another to bring about paedophilic activities. Second, it might actually involve taking part in paedophilic activities – through, for example, viewing illicit material involving children, grooming children, especially through chat rooms, or the involvement may be for forms of passive sexual gratification.

There is also a growing concern that the proliferation of and easy access to the Internet will mean that ordinary and generally law-abiding citizens could be lured towards child pornography. The following extracts from *The Daily Telegraph* illustrate this concern:

> Access to paedophilia was very limited in the past . . . restricted to a small group of people operating in the darkness. Now the internet is pumping this stuff straight into your home, anyone can see it. The danger is that the internet is going to convert people to things that have traditionally been suppressed.
>
> (*The Daily Telegraph*, 18 February 2002)

> Ministers believe the anonymity afforded by computers to users is tempting ordinary people, who would never buy illegal magazines, to look at child pornography out of curiosity. This then leads to them becoming hooked on more extreme material and to come into contact with paedophile rings.
>
> (*The Daily Telegraph*, 18 June 2000)

Two murders of young girls in sexually motivated murders in 2012 highlighted the issue of online child abuse and paedophilia. Mark Bridger was found guilty in 2013 of murdering April Jones in October 2012 and Stuart Hazell was found guilty in 2013 of murdering Tia Sharp in August 2012. In each case the killers had accessed online images of child sex abuse – Bridger had a library of between 100 and 150 graphic images and Hazell had sought out indecent images of prepubescent girls. The Child Exploitation and Online Protection Centre (CEOP) said the proliferation of indecent images online and the spread of high-speed Internet connections were putting more children at risk. Jim Gamble, the founding head of CEOP, commented, 'there is this spiral of abuse theory: they begin to want more, they want access not to still images but to video images, and then they want to get more real experience' (*The Guardian*, 30 May 2013). However, while the spiral of abuse theory might sound plausible there are difficulties in proving any causal links between Internet activity and child abuse:

> It is very difficult to be able to say that viewing indecent images can lead to sexual abuse. But what we can definitely say is that, in the great majority of cases, when someone has indecently assaulted a child they are then found with indecent images on their computers as well.
>
> (Elena Martellozo, quoted in *The Guardian*, 30 May 2013)

At present there is little significant research into the profiling of Internet paedophile offenders. However, there is some research regarding those who download and view child pornography. In the USA, Wolak and colleagues (2005) conducted an intensive online victimization study entitled *Child Pornography Possessors Arrested in Internet-Related Crimes*. They examined 1,713 arrested people who possessed child pornography; the key findings from the data they gathered suggested that those arrested for child pornography generally fitted into the following categories:

1. those sexually interested in prepubescent children (paedophiles) or young adolescents (hebephiles), who use child pornography images for sexual fantasy and gratification;
2. sexually 'indiscriminate' users, meaning they are constantly looking for new and different sexual stimuli;

3. sexually curious users, downloading a few images to satisfy that curiosity;
4. those interested in profiting financially by selling images or setting up websites requiring payment for access.

As regards the demographic characteristics of those arrested, Wolak and colleagues found that virtually all of those arrested were male, white (91%) and over the age of 25 (86%); the majority where unmarried yet had access to minor children, for example, 42 per cent had biological children and 46 per cent had access to children through jobs and/or through organized youth activities which they were involved in.

However, it must be remembered that this research was based on those who were eventually arrested and therefore is not totally reliable or valid as it cannot give an accurate picture of all of those people who view child pornography. Indeed, we can only guess at the extent of such viewing, but it is highly likely to be undertaken covertly by the vast majority of those who do download child pornography images.

QUESTION BREAK

Read the following report from the trial and conviction of an Internet paedophile and consider the questions that follow.

Jail for Paedophile Who Terrorized via Internet

A paedophile who admitted terrorizing teenage girls into sending him explicit photographs of themselves via the internet was jailed for 10 years yesterday.

Adrian Ringland, 36, used his hi-tech knowledge to remotely seize control of his victims' computers in order to force them to strip and strike humiliating poses.

The jobless father of two even boasted to one 14-year-old who threatened suicide unless he left her alone: 'Call the cops . . . they won't trace me'.

Ringland, from Derbyshire, adopted the alias of Ant Jones, an 'attractive' 14-year-old boy, to use internet chatrooms, where he lured young girls into correspondence before brainwashing them with technological trickery. Victims believed they were opening a photo of their new online friend, but when they clicked on the bogus picture the attached file contained a Trojan virus which infected their computers, allowing the sexual predator to establish remote control.

Ringland took over the computers, terrifying the girls into complying with depraved demands.

Lisa Wilding, prosecuting at Inner London crown court, said: 'This is about manipulation, exploitation and ultimately sexual gratification, and reveals the horrors that lurk within the internet and the minds of some individuals that use it'.

Ringland's computer expertise allowed him to move cursors around the girls' screens; text would appear, their printers would go into action, and their CD-ROM trays would fly open and snap shut.

He even forwarded naked photographs of them to their email buddies – all from the safe anonymity of a special study room in his own home. One girl said it was like a scene from the film *The Matrix* when Ringland blanked out her screen.

But he was caught when a 14-year-old girl from Manitoba complained to her parents. They told the Royal Canadian Mounted Police, sparking an international manhunt. The teenager emailed: 'Dude, you're scaring me . . . please don't do this. I'm freaked' when Ringland demanded a nude photo of her, but eventually sent him intimate poses, despite protesting that this was 'internet rape'.

The investigation, which involved Canadian, US and British police, led to Ringland's address at Ilkeston, Derbyshire, where he lived with his partner, their two children, and her 14-year-old son. Even then, he tried to blame his partner's son. But detectives who interviewed the boy quickly realized he did not have the expertise to carry out the crimes.

After Ringland's first court appearance he was released on bail and banned from having computers in his home while his case was prepared. But when police called to check on him they found a 14-year-old girl in his bed. He had groomed her from an internet chatroom and had been having regular sex with her while on bail.

Ringland pleaded guilty to 20 charges relating to internet abuse, two of indecency with a child, four of hacking, four of blackmail, and 10 of making indecent photographs of a child. They involved three girls in the UK and in Canada. Thirteen similar charges concerning several girls on both sides of the Atlantic were ordered to remain on file. Ringland also admitted six charges of unlawful intercourse with a child and one of internet grooming.

(Cowan R., *The Guardian*, 10 November 2006)

QUESTIONS

- To what extent does Adrian Ringland fit the characteristics of the 'typical Internet paedophile' suggested by Wolak and colleagues' research?
- Suggest the characteristics that distinguish Internet paedophiles such as Ringland from 'conventional criminals'.

However, one of the UK's most recent high-profile paedophile cases in recent years has demonstrated the problems inherent in attempting to profile paedophiles. What was to become known as the Plymouth Child Abuse case of 2009 centred upon five adults (four of whom were women) who formed an Internet paedophile ring. The case focused mainly on indecent pictures of children but also sexual assault of a child under 13 and a baby. The case involved Vanessa George, Colin Blanchard, Angela Allen, Tracy Lyons and Tracy Dawber. It was the involvement of the four females that caused most controversy and the majority of the media attention focused on Vanessa George due to the fact that she was female, a mother and had used her position of trust as a nursery nurse to commit her crimes.

In the next section, we look at cyber violence; however, this division between cyber obscenity and cyber violence is to some extent artificial as certain types of criminal behaviour, such as child abuse, straddle both aspects of cybercrime. Child abuse is, of course, a crime that has existed throughout history, with the new forms of media perhaps merely offering different and wider opportunities for people to engage in such behaviour. The extract from *The Observer* newspaper in the question break below considers how child abusers and paedophiles exploit the Internet to pursue their criminal behaviour. It also raises some of the difficulties involved in policing cybercrime (an issue we look at later in the chapter, pp. 207–209).

QUESTION BREAK

Child abuse shown live on Internet

Children are being sexually abused to order by paedophiles who charge other members of their virtual sex-rings a fee to watch over the Internet as it takes place.

Abusers promise other members of their secret online societies that they will use a live webcam to film a particular child on a specified day, provided enough money has been deposited in their bank account beforehand.

Police have known for some time that real-time sexual abuse of children takes place over the Internet and that images of abuse are bartered between paedophiles who are keen to increase their collections.

But this is the first time that real-time images of Internet abuse have been sold for cash, raising concerns that criminal entrepreneurs have moved into the world of online child abuse. In a further twist, paedophiles watching the abuse take place are increasingly being allowed by the abuser to direct what is done to the child. There are even cases of the abuser and the paedophile voyeur working together to groom the child before the abuse begins.

'This is an online version of what has been happening for years', said Tink Palmer, a specialist in child abuse on the Internet for Barnardos, who has identified the new tactic by paedophiles. 'Children have long been sold by paedophiles to other abusers in their ring. This is the obvious next step'.

'In these paedophile societies, having access to a child makes you enormously important and it seems abusers have realised they can use that status to profit financially', she said.

Palmer has come across situations where paedophiles direct the abuse over the webcam as it takes place. 'The final step is that the paedophile forms a relationship with the child through the camcorder, so they can encourage them to do certain things', she said.

It is the perfect scenario for paedophiles: not only can they orchestrate situations that make it look like the child is proactively taking part but, because the child is left believing they were responsible for the situation, they will never tell anyone what took place.

Peter Robbins, chief executive of the Internet Watch Foundation, has established arrangements with Visa and Mastercard to help to track paedophiles using their credit cards to purchase images over the Net.

'It was inevitable that this form of pay-per-view abuse would develop given the possibilities of the Internet', he said. 'We already have live, pay-per-view, adult pornography webcams where you can pay a woman to carry out specific requests; this is the paedophiles' version'.

So far, police have failed to break the encryption codes created by online paedophile societies to block access into the group in time to prevent the abuse taking place and before the closure of bank accounts that could lead them to the abusers.

Jackie Bennett, from the National Crime Squad's Paedophile Online Investigation Team, admitted that the police were finding it difficult to keep up with the new ways paedophiles were finding to exploit the Internet.

A spokeswoman for Greater Manchester Police also confirmed that they were familiar with such cases, but added: 'We can't talk about this without compromising cases we're working with' (Hill A, *The Observer*, 9 November 2003).

QUESTIONS

- To what extent do you think that Internet paedophilia is more dangerous than offline paedophilia?
- What psychological and sociological explanations can you suggest for the child abuse described above?

■ CYBER VIOLENCE – HATE SPEECH

As we have seen, the Internet is rapidly transforming the way that messages and ideas are disseminated. With regard to hate speech, it can be argued that the web is now a new frontier for the spread of extremist ideas and views which can and do prey on particular minority groups. Hate websites contain bias or prejudice based on a range of areas and characteristics, including race, religion, ethnicity, gender, disability and sexual orientation.

The Internet is a vehicle that enables extremist groups and their views to flourish. Whereas such extremists and hate mongers once had to spread their views via leaflets and clandestine networks and meetings, they are now able to promote their views via websites and chat rooms which potentially reach millions of people, including and especially impressionable youth. Furthermore they are also able to promote and recruit for their cause cheaply, effectively, anonymously, 24 hours a day, reaching people in an instant.

In this context and with regard to hate speech and the encouraging of violence against vulnerable minority groups, the rise of the Far Right is of particular concern. The use of the Internet by far-right groups has led many of them to develop and promote their own cyber cultures. Far-right groups such as the BNP (British National Party), Combat 18, National Alliance, KKK (Ku Klux Klan) and Stormfront are continually involved in creating and making use of website technologies such as internal hyperlinks, email links, Realplayer audio and video extracts.

In an examination of cyber culture, Back (2002) asks why it is that society is seeing a proliferation of far-right groups on the Internet and what draws people to them. He looks at the relationship between cyber culture and the spread of racism in contemporary society. In pointing to the problems with defining and classifying ultra right-wing groups he makes the following point 'For the sake of conceptual clarity I shall be deploying the notion of "cyber racism" to speak about a range of subcultural movements in Europe, North America and beyond'. While these movements are diverse, according to Back, they exhibit the following common features:

- a rhetoric of racial and/or national uniqueness and common destiny;
- ideas of racial supremacy, superiority and separation;
- a repertoire of conceptions of racial Otherness;
- a utopian revolutionary world-view that aims to overthrow the existing order.

(Back 2002, p. 632)

Back then suggests five ways in which the net assists racist activities:

1. It enables the celebration of real instances of racial violence with photographs and dehumanizing comments.
2. It enhances racial narcissism, promoting indifference towards victims by using images and cartoon caricatures.
3. It enables the merchandizing of white power music and Nazi paraphernalia – building an economic power base.
4. It enables the archiving and downloading of collections of racist materials in one place – such as racist speeches and debates.

5. It enables people to experience and yet remain geographically distant from racist culture.

In relation to recruitment to their causes, it is very difficult to tell what impact these far-right websites have. Back argues that

> the number of white racists regularly involved in the Internet globally is somewhere in the region of 5,000 to 10,000, divided into 10–20 clusters. Once again, it is impossible to offer anything other than an educated guess. The number of 'hits' on a web page, for example, need not indicate 'sympathetic inquiries', rather they could include opponents, monitoring agencies and researchers. The key point is that the relatively small numbers of people can have a significant presence.
>
> (2002, p. 639).

Recent research has also concluded that accessing far-right and white supremacist web pages is relatively easy. In examining how and why white racialist groups use such websites, and the impact of them on community safety, Sutton and Wright (2009) make the point that while the Internet could be seen as just an extension of the traditional mass media, and that much journalism has been racist in the past, the material published on far-right websites is generally much more vitriolic and extreme. They make the point that

> Internet website addresses, provided by anti-racist groups are currently picked up by immensely popular search engines such as Google when searching on racist terms of abuse. This means that curious web surfers are currently aided in finding the websites of white racist movements – free of any, objective anti-racist educational or social commentary regarding their content.
>
> (Sutton and Wright 2009, p. 17)

Sutton and Wright ask if it is 'socially responsible' for search engines such as Google to offer such easy and unmoderated access to white racialist websites.

QUESTION BREAK

View the examples of the web pages of far-right organizations such as:

British National Party
Combat 18
National Alliance
Stormfront
Ku Klux Klan

Choose a far-right web page from the list above. Find and consider evidence of how the Internet has assisted it in pursuing racist activities.

Use Back's (2002) five criteria to examine your chosen website. How do they apply to the site you are considering?

How do you think that hate speech encourages hate crime?

CYBER VIOLENCE – TERRORISM

Another area where cyber violence can be seen is with regard to terrorism and the use of the Internet to aid terrorists in their particular campaigns. One part of this which has been of particular concern has been the use of the Internet by terrorist groups to recruit followers; especially followers prepared to fight and, if necessary, die for the cause.

The al-Qaeda terrorist network has made use of the Internet in this context. For instance, Syed Talha Ahsan was arrested in 2004 for operating websites across the world (including the USA, the UK, Ireland and Malaysia) which incited murder and urged Muslims to fight the holy war (Jihad), as well as encouraging people to donate money. There has also been a concern that, to quote Coll and Glasser (2005):

> Al-Qaeda and its offshoots are building a massive and dynamic online library of training materials – some supported by experts who answer questions on message boards or in chat rooms – covering such varied subjects as how to mix ricin poison, how to make a bomb from commercial chemicals, how to pose as a fisherman and sneak through Syria into Iraq, how to shoot at a US soldier, and how to navigate by the stars while running through a night-shrouded desert. These materials are cascading across the Web in Arabic, Urdu, Pashto and other first languages of jihadist volunteers.
>
> (*The Washington Post*, 7 August 2005)

Coll and Glasser (2005), writing in *The Washington Post*, make the point that as al-Qaeda has gradually lost its sanctuary in Afghanistan, the movement has scattered into hiding and exile and has relied increasingly on the Internet. They suggest al-Qaeda has become:

> the first guerrilla movement in history to migrate from physical space to cyberspace. With laptops and DVDs, in secret hideouts and at neighbourhood Internet cafes, young code-writing jihadists have sought to replicate the training, communication, planning and preaching facilities they lost in Afghanistan with countless new locations on the Internet.
>
> (7 August 2005)

In his examination of Jihadi and far-right websites, Whine (2006) highlights the extent to which the Internet has been used by far-right and terrorist groups as a means to communicate and publish material in a way which seems to have credibility and authority but which, if published in a hard copy form, would be deemed illegal. And the Internet can be used to communicate around the world at a very low cost.

Whine (2006) goes on to consider how the al-Qaeda group has become a much more 'de-centralized and diffused network of the Global Jihad Movement (GJM), in which the Internet plays a crucial and developmental role'. The Internet serves as a sort of meeting place for terrorists to discuss and exchange plans and ideas. He refers to Weimann's study, *Terror on the Internet*, which quotes from a website that was linked to al-Qaeda which emphasized the ease of using the Internet for such activities:

> We strongly urge Muslim internet professionals to spread and disseminate news and information about the Jihad through e-mail lists, discussion groups and their own websites.
>
> (www.azzam.com)

In an online article accompanying his book *Terror on the Internet*, Weimann (2006) identifies eight different ways in which terrorists use the Internet. In the adapted extract from Weimann below, this list is summarized in some detail as it provides a very useful, and worrying, illustration of just how widely cyber violence can be and is aided by new forms of media and the Internet in particular.

> Psychological warfare – There are several ways for terrorists to do this. For instance, they can use the Internet to spread disinformation, to deliver threats intended to distil fear and helplessness and to disseminate horrific images of recent actions, such as the brutal murder of the American journalist Daniel Pearl by his captors, a videotape of which was replayed on several terrorist websites . . .
>
> Publicity and propaganda – Until the advent of the Internet, terrorists' hopes of winning publicity for their causes and activities depended on attracting the attention of television, radio or print media. These traditional media have 'selection thresholds' (editorial selection) that terrorists often cannot reach. No such thresholds, of course, exist on the terrorists' own websites . . .
>
> Data mining – The World Wide Web alone offers about a billion pages of information, much of it free – and much of it of interest to terrorist organizations . . .
>
> Fund-raising – Like many other political organizations, terrorist groups use the Internet to raise funds. Al-Qaeda, for instance, have always depended heavily on donations, and its global fund-raising network is built upon a foundation of charities, non-governmental organizations and other financial institutions that use websites and Internet-based chat rooms and forums . . .
>
> Recruitment and mobilization – The Internet can be used to recruit and mobilize supporters to play a more active role in support of terrorist activities or causes. Most terrorist websites stop short of enlisting recruits for violent action but they do encourage supporters to show their commitment to the cause in other tangible ways . . .

Networking – Through the use of the Internet loosely connected groups are able to maintain contact with one another – and with members of other terrorist groups. The Internet connects not only members of the same terrorist organization but also members of different groups. For instance, dozens of sites exist that express support for terrorism conducted in the name of jihad. These sites and related forums permit terrorists in places such as Chechnya, Palestine, Indonesia, Afghanistan, Turkey, Iraq, Malaysia, the Philippines and Lebanon to exchange not only ideas and suggestions but also practical information about how to build bombs, establish terror cells and carry out attacks . . .

Sharing information – The World Wide Web is home to dozens of sites that provide information on how to build chemical and explosive weapons. This kind of information is sought not only by sophisticated terrorist organizations but also by disaffected individuals prepared to use terrorist tactics . . .

Planning and coordination – Terrorists use the Internet not only to learn how to build bombs but also to plan and coordinate attacks. Al-Qaeda operatives relied heavily on the Internet in planning and coordinating the September 11 attacks.

(Adapted from Weimann 2006)

There have been other, similar attempts to categorize and typologize the different ways in which terrorists can make use of the Internet to further their interests. Conway (2006) highlights what she terms are the core uses of the Internet by terrorists. First, financing, referring to the raising of funds and how 'the immediacy and interactive nature of Internet communication, combined with its high-reach properties, opens up a huge potential for increased financial donations'. Second, networking, allowing terrorist groups to act in a more decentralized manner and 'to communicate quickly and coordinate effectively at low cost'. Third, the recruitment and mobilization of sympathizers to 'more actively support terrorist causes or activities'. Fourth, and finally, information gathering, referring to the Internet's capacity to access huge amounts of information which would previously have been very difficult to retrieve and use.

Conway concludes her discussion of the Internet and terrorism by commenting that research findings are still inconclusive as to whether the spread of the Internet has led to an increase in terrorist violence. However, it is clear that online communications have improved the ability of terrorist groups to raise funds, attract recruits and reach a mass audience. As Conway puts it:

Obviously, the Internet is not the only tool that a terrorist group needs to 'succeed'. However, the Net can add new dimensions to existing assets that groups can utilize to achieve their goals as well as providing new and innovative avenues for expression, fund raising and recruitment.

(2006, p. 14)

We will conclude this brief review of terrorism and the Internet by referring to a particular case study (in the question break below). This example is of a young male recruit who became involved with al-Qaeda and became the 'world's most wanted cyber-jihadist'.

QUESTION BREAK

Al-Qaeda's 007

Younes Tsouli arrived in London in 2001 . . . He studies IT at a small college in central London. With few friends, he soon immersed himself in the world of the internet. Online images of the war in Iraq radicalized him. In his mind it was evidence of a war against Muslims. Soon he was in the darker areas of the net, and graduated from viewing images to publishing them. He used variations of the username Irhabi 007 – *irhabi* meaning terrorist in Arabic, and 007 being reference to Britain's most famous fictional spy . . .

By 2004 he was posting extremist videos and propaganda. That was when he came to the attention of al-Qaeda leaders in Iraq, who spotted his potential. They were making videos but struggling to get them to a wider audience because of the size of the file and the difficulties of finding websites that could host them. Tsouli solved this problem, making him invaluable . . . He converted the material into various formats, including one that allowed the videos to be watched on mobile phones . . .

In August 2005 Tsouli became administrator of al Ansar, a password-protected web forum where extremists communicated with each other . . . Among the discussion were details of how to get to Iraq to be a suicide bomber . . . When London was bombed in July 2005, Tsouli wrote: 'Brother, I am very happy. From the moment the infidels cry, I laugh'. He grew enamoured of his reputation . . . In a message dated June 5, 2005, he wrote: 'I am still the terrorist 007, one of the most wanted terrorists on the internet. I have the Feds and the CIA, both would love to catch me, I have MI6 on my back' . . .

What makes Irhabi 007's case so chilling is the evolution from simply setting up websites to becoming involved in terrorism itself . . .

It was Tsouli's links to a planned attack that brought the police to his door in October 2005 . . . After Tsouli's arrest, police spent five days searching the flat . . . But it was only when they started to pick apart the files on Tsouli's computer that they realised what they had . . . as the team dug deeper, scouring through two million files, they realized that there was much, much more . . . Tsouli was a major player . . .

In December, Tsouli's sentence was increased from 10 to 16 years. His conviction was the first for incitement to commit an act of terrorism through the internet, and a sign of what terrorists are capable of . . . Peter Clarke, the head of the Metropolitan Police Counter-Terrorism Command, told me: 'It was the first virtual conspiracy to murder that we had seen'.

The power of the internet is its ability to put like-minded people in touch from every corner of the world. But the benefits for terrorists can also be an advantage for detectives when they catch a suspect, because they can quickly trace the people with whom the suspect was in contact.

(Corera G. 'Al-Qaeda's 007', *The Times*, 16 January 2008)

QUESTIONS

- To what extent would Tsouli be able to act as he did without the new mass media forms he used?
- Suggest the advantages and disadvantages for the terrorist of using the Internet rather than conventional forms of mass media.

CYBER VIOLENCE – CYBER STALKING

We cannot cover the whole range of cybercrime and the media coverage of it in a single chapter. However, in considering different forms of cyber violence, a brief comment on cyber stalking would be appropriate. Cyber stalking involves the use of the electronic media, particularly the Internet but also mobile phones, to pursue and harass other people. Given the ability of the Internet to communicate across great distances, cyber stalking will often never manifest itself in the physical sense, although as Williams (2005) puts it, 'this does not mean that the pursuit is any less distressing'. The Internet allows the stalker to communicate with another person or persons without the usual social constraints of 'reality'. This can, according to Williams, encourage the stalker, or potential stalker, to become disinhibited, enabling him (usually) to express his desires (however disturbed or bizarre) more easily than in more direct forms of communication.

The extent of cyber stalking is difficult to measure accurately. However, it is clear that stalking in general is a widespread offence, The CSEW (Crime Survey for England and Wales) of 2011/2012, previously known as The British Crime Survey, found that *under the heading of 'prevalence of intimate violence', since the age of 16, 10.4 per cent of males and 18.3 per cent of females had experienced stalking.* These percentages add up to massively large numbers of people and it is reasonably self-evident that the spread of media technology has enabled stalking to be carried out more easily. Cyber stalking of victims has increased sharply in recent years. Many of the offenders are men who are angry at being rejected by their partners and use the Internet to put details of their victim on websites. Examples of this type of cyber stalking were illustrated in an article by Julie Bindel (2007) in *The Guardian* newspaper, entitled 'The rise of the cyber stalker':

When sexually explicit emails are sent to a victim's workplace, they risk humiliation and even losing their jobs. Jane Thompson split from her boyfriend of only three weeks, 'because I felt smothered by him'. One morning soon after, when she arrived at work, a colleague asked her if she had emailed her from home over the weekend. It turned out that her ex-boyfriend had sent Thompson's colleague 'a folder with about 10 photos of us both having sex,' she says, 'and at that moment I wanted to die'.

Thompson's ex had used a method common to cyber-stalkers – tracing their victim's email address and sending messages from that address containing offensive, pornographic and even libelous material.

(*The Guardian*, 10 January 2007)

The article goes on to look at research into stalking by Lorraine Sheridan of Leicester University, which found that half of all stalking victims are harassed via the Internet. Sheridan highlights the growing online support networks which can help cyber stalkers, with so-called 'revenge' websites, such as 'Avengers Den' and 'Get Revenge on Your Ex'. It quotes Sheridan saying:

I spent an hour surfing such sites and what I found was profoundly disturbing. One site advertised itself as being able to assist those wishing to experience 'the pure, unadulterated satisfaction you get from totally crushing your ex's self-esteem and annihilating their reputation'. Another offered a service called 'fake SMS', where a message can be sent 'to your ex' which appears to come from somewhere else.

(*The Guardian*, 10 January 2007)

However, because cyber stalkers have to leave a trail of evidence from computers and/or mobile phone, the 'good news' is that they are probably more likely to be caught than other, more conventional stalkers; or at least there is 'hard' evidence to assist in any convictions of such cybercriminals.

CYBERCRIMINALS

Cybercrime is a new form of criminal behaviour and it is unique for a number of reasons. One of the most important features of the Internet is its anonymous and borderless nature and indeed it is probably this which attracts the cybercriminal. The popular image of computer criminals, and perhaps especially hackers, is of a lonely disaffected adult or teenage male who has excellent computer skills but is less adept socially. However, although there are examples which fit this stereotype, like most such stereotypes, such a picture does not tell the whole story. It is clear that computer-based crime lacks a structured environment. As Clough and Mongo put it: 'There is no organized structure in the computer underworld, no mysterious chairman of the board to run things. The underground is anarchic, a confederation of phreakers/ hackers and virus writers from all over the world whose common interest transcend culture or language' (1992, p. 18).

However, there are now subcultures which have built up around paedophilia and other forms of cybercrime, including terrorism. And because of the nature of the crimes, cyber subcultures are unique – these crimes involve secrecy, invisibility and are typically egalitarian in nature. Although the focus of this study is on the media and crime, we will look briefly at these characteristics of cybercriminal subcultures.

Secrecy and anonymity

Cybercriminal subcultures are based to a large degree on the secrecy of their members. The Internet does not require the physical presence of the user, and identity is protected by the use of pseudonyms when in communication, a process which Paul Taylor (1999) terms 'disembodied anonymity'. The anonymity of cyberspace makes identity tracing a significant problem and this is an important factor (and attraction) for those engaged in illicit behaviour; so, for example, it is easy for a criminal to create a fictitious identity to perpetuate fraud or child pornography or other offences which can be committed entirely online. The use of 'handles' that individuals give to themselves or their group so they can identify themselves, yet keep their offline identity secret, helps to explain why paedophiles can pretend to be (and get away with it) something completely different to what they are – in terms of age, background and so on.

Egalitarian criminality

Because of the anonymity of the cybercriminal there does not appear to be a traditional hierarchy based on inequalities of status, wealth and so on – members of cyber subcultures can and do remain faceless. Therefore, physical appearance and social characteristics, such as gender, race, class and wealth do not become a key feature in the organization of subcultures. In 'normal' offline life and face-to-face interaction we are able to gain what social psychologists, such as Erving Goffman (whose work is discussed later), have termed non-verbal clues – intentionally and unintentionally, based on expressions, non-verbal communications, signals and other social clues. These characteristics are absent when communicating online, which makes judgements and, in turn, feelings of inequality of a different nature to those we might feel during 'normal' communication. Any such 'judgement' has to occur through the media's communication of messages rather than social characteristics of the sender. For instance, consider the non-verbal messages that you get when you read an email from someone you have not met face-to-face. Most likely you would answer, none.

As with conventional crime, offender profiling is becoming increasingly important as regards the cybercriminal. However, it is debatable as to whether a criminal committing crime in cyberspace could be easily fitted into any such profile. It would seem doubtful as we have virtually no information about the individual to work with. However, there is evidence which suggests that distinguishing characteristics do regularly present themselves. In considering cyber obscenity (p. 186) we looked at the work of Wolak and colleagues (2005), which listed the demographic characteristics of people arrested for child pornography offences related to the Internet. Here we will consider a study of 80 young hackers in the USA by Donn Parker (1998) which found that, although it was difficult to describe the typical cyber-deviant (his term), there where common psychological and behavioural traits that he believed where held by hackers (remembering that hackers are only one type of cybercriminal). These were:

- precociousness, curiosity and persistence;
- habitual lying, cheating, stealing and exaggeration;
- juvenile idealism;
- hyperactivity;
- drug and alcohol abuse.

Parker argued that these behaviours can manifest themselves in a number of ways, including what he termed differential association and the Robin Hood syndrome. We will look at Parker's definition of these two 'theoretical positions'.

Differential association syndrome

This is where the individual is so socialized into the computer underworld that he (usually) enjoys the recognition and respect that comes with being able to use the computer for more and more difficult examples of illicit activity – indeed the offender can be motivated to try ever more daring forms of computer-based crime, so as to then be able to show off about it.

Most of the cybercriminals I have encountered could not engage in a person-to-person crime if their lives depended on it. They could not look victims in the eye and rob them or attack them, but [they] have no problem attacking or robbing a computer because a computer does not look back or exhibit anguish. Cybercriminals often distinguish between the unacceptable practice of doing harm to people and the impersonal acts of doing harm to or through computers. Yet, many receive a measure of satisfaction in their crimes by personifying the computers they hack, viewing them as adversaries and deriving some enjoyment from ripping them off.

(Parker 1998)

Robin Hood syndrome

According to Parker, intense personal problems with the individual cyberdeviant are typically the key. In these cases, offenders take on the notion that the victims of cybercrime are often big businesses and organizations that can, in the offender's mind at least, afford to suffer relatively small losses. As Parker puts it:

Despite the common view that greed usually motivates individuals to commit business crime, I have found that most cybercriminals are attempting to solve intense personal problems. At the time that a criminal perpetrates the crime, he is indeed attempting to achieve some type of gain. Law enforcement and the news media usually interpret this as greed or the desire for high living, but my interviews with criminals indicate that intense need, rather than greed, causes them to commit crimes. The problems that they are attempting to resolve run the usual gamut of human difficulties: problems with a marriage or love relationship, failure to progress as fast as others in a career path, a need for money to settle outstanding debts . . .

In today's hacker culture, malicious hackers regularly engage in fabrications, exaggerations, thievery, and fantasy. They delight in presenting themselves to the media . . . as idealistic do-gooders, champions of the underdog. . . . Juvenile hackers often fantasize their roles as Clark Kents who become Supermen of cyberspace. Unfortunately, their public persona is far from the truth. Although malicious hackers range in age from preteen to senior citizens, they are characterized by an immature excessively idealistic attitude.

(Parker 1998)

QUESTION BREAK

Parker's research focused on hackers. Look at the different categories of cybercrime provided earlier in the chapter (pp. 183–184).

What sort of cybercrimes would be most satisfactorily explained by differential association and which by the Robin Hood syndrome?

Motivations and explanations for cybercriminality – Hirschi and control theory

This chapter is not aiming to look at social theories of cybercrime, but rather to focus on the role of the media, and new media technology in particular, in relation to cybercrime. However, the control theory developed by Trevor Hirschi (1969) does offer an interesting approach to helping us to understand the cybercriminal and will be considered briefly here.

The central focus of control theory is that individuals commit criminal and deviant acts when their bond to society is lacking in some way. The classic theoretical approaches (such as Durkheim's) to explaining crime have emphasized the relationship between the individual and society; with a strong feeling of social solidarity encouraging individuals to conform to society's rules and regulations. Hirschi, on the other hand, suggests that law-breaking, rather than law-abiding, behaviour is natural and the key issue he addressed was that of why most people choose to follow the laws.

Williams (2004) highlights four elements that Hirschi associates with law-abiding people as 'their attachments with other people; the commitments and responsibilities they develop; their involvement in conventional activity; and their beliefs'. We will elaborate on these elements and try to apply them to cybercriminals.

Attachments – with other people and institutions in the community. Strong social and psychological attachments make criminal behaviour less likely as they make individuals more aware of and sensitive to the opinions of other people and to the norms and values of society (Hirschi is aware that strong attachments to criminal groups would have the opposite effect and encourage criminal behaviour). The weaker the attachments the more likely are individuals to engage in cybercrime; and it could be that cybercriminals, and perhaps particularly hackers and online paedophiles, will tend to be less attached to the norms and values of their society.

Commitment – the more an individual has 'invested' in partners, children, education, occupation, property ownership and so on the less likely will she or he risk losing it through law-breaking behaviour. Individuals who do not consider such commitments important or who have less of them are seen as relatively more free to commit criminal acts. As with attachment, those individuals with less commitment to their wider society are more likely to engage in cybercrime.

Involvement – refers to the extent that the individual is involved in a legitimate lifestyle and activity. Crime is less likely if being involved in conventional activities is an important part of the individual's life. Partly this is because the individual's involvement with a range of activities leaves them with less time to engage in other activities – and cybercriminals often spend long hours on the Internet (for example, cyber thieves and online pornography viewers), which would suggest a lack of involvement in conventional social activities.

Beliefs – in this context Hirschi is referring to things an individual chooses to accept, rather than deeply held convictions. As these beliefs can be changed (by the individual accepting different arguments, for instance) they need constant social reinforcement. If individuals have relatively strongly held beliefs in conventional norms and values, they are less likely to engage in the individualistic, antisocial behaviours typical of the cybercriminal.

SOCIAL NETWORKS AND CRIME

In recent years the growth of social networks such as Facebook, Twitter and Myspace.com has been phenomenal. Facebook alone has a global audience of over 800 million users worldwide which equates to one in every 13 people using the medium. According to www.digitalbuzz.com 48 per cent of 18–34 year olds check their Facebook account on waking, 200 million users access Facebook via their phone and 48 per cent of users get their news through Facebook. It is not surprising then that Facebook has become another medium used in pursuit of criminal activities.

As of yet data on social networks and crime is very limited and 'unreliable'. In terms of the police, most statistics relating to the use social networks and crime is withheld information available only through freedom of information requests. However, it is fair to say that social networks facilitate a number of crimes including scamming, bullying, sexual predation, stalking and malicious content, trolling and even the instigation of societal disturbances (such as the use of Facebook during the UK riots in 2011). It would seem that due to the disembodied anonymity of the Internet, criminals are attracted to the relative privacy that it evokes.

In 1959 Ervin Goffman published a now classic text *The Presentation of the Self in Everyday Life* – an exploration into the creation and maintenance of our identity in social situations. This work, although written before the social media revolution, is now being used to understand the presentation of identity 'online' and especially within social networking sites.

Goffman used what he termed the 'dramaturgical approach' to explain everyday interaction and self-presentation. In other words, in everyday circumstances we all perform roles to various 'audiences' who are in our 'front stage'. Within our day-to-day lives we present the identity that we wish to portray to others and we do this through 'impression management' to control or guide a specific impression in the minds of others (the audience). As actors, we must, like a chameleon, change our behaviour and our identity in different social settings. Each new role that we play involves a new drama in which we perform to the specific audience – we are only truly ourselves when we return to the non-performing backstage area of our lives. So Goffman's dramaturgical approach relates to our interaction and identity management and how this can be compared to and understood in relation to a theatrical performance.

When we go through a performance we make an effort to create a specific impression in the minds of others (or the audience). In order to manage the impression others have of us we may use what Goffman refers to as 'sign vehicles' (for instance, props, costume, tone of voice, gestures or body language) which all serve to convey an impression that we want to give. The aim is to get the desired reception and response from the 'audience'. The audience on the one hand can see the managed impression – but those performing the role may also spill real or true emotions indirectly through involuntary expressive behaviour. In effect, then, our impressions are false as we are likely to present ourselves in a light that is desirable and within the expected cultural standards. 'Spillage' can shatter the illusion we have created.

QUESTION BREAK

Goffman and the dramaturgical approach

Consider the different roles you have to play during the course of a day then answer the following questions.

What are these roles and how might they conflict with one another?

What aspects of your own behaviour might you want to keep hidden or 'backstage' from others?

What might happen if such behaviour is exposed to others – and becomes 'front stage'?

Before we look at how Goffman's work might be relevant to communication through new media technologies, how do you think people could manage the impression others get of them through social network sites?

How might people gain impressions of others without face-to-face contact?

In a context in which we increasingly use the virtual world to communicate, it becomes much more difficult to 'gauge' the definition of the situation. It is this aspect of Goffman's work that can help us understand how being the victim of crime and deviant behaviour can occur on social networks such as Facebook.

One of the greatest problems relating to criminal and deviant behaviour on the Internet is the absence of body language and cues that in 'real life' we measure in order to judge a person's intent, and so on. In 'real life' we gather information about individuals through 'sign vehicles'. These also help us to gauge the 'definition of the situation' – is the situation hostile, friendly, formal, informal and so on. So in the absence of face-to-face interaction online, how do we make sense of others' behaviour.

Although we remain disembodied 'online', we are still in the process of managing our identity and impression others have of us. We can do this through status updates, through listing our likes and dislikes, our biography, profile messaging or on our wall (which could be considered as front-stage areas in Goffman's model) and through our private online chat (our back stage).

Lieve Gies (2008) in his description of identity deception on the Internet states that it 'severely impairs users' ability to rely on physical cues in verifying each other's identity' (what Goffman referred to as 'vocabularies or bodily idiom'). The anonymity of the Internet was also captured in Peter Steiner's famous cartoon which first appeared in *The New Yorker* in 1993. The cartoon features two dogs – one on a chair in front of a computer screen the other on the floor. The caption reads 'on the Internet nobody knows you're a dog'. The cartoon can be seen at www.unc.edu/depts/jomc/academics/dri/idog.html. Its meaning is taken to be a comment on how the Internet can liberate us from social characteristics such as age, gender or class, but also how it allows for the fabrication of identity whether it is for illegal or legal purposes.

Therefore the disembodied anonymity involved in social networking sites allows individuals (and groups) to manage false impressions as in the case of predators and paedophiles online.

The dangers of social networks have been highlighted in a number of recent cases involving fabricated identity. In 2010 Peter Chapman was jailed for life after pleading guilty to the abduction rape and murder of a 17-year-old girl he had met on the networking site Facebook. Chapman fabricated a profile complete with pictures of a bare chested 19-year-old boy he called Peter. Chapman used this to lure his victim to her death. In 2012 Gary Cooper aged 47 years was jailed for the rape and abduction of a 12-year-old girl. Cooper began his deception when he joined tagged.com – an open access social networking site and began communication under a fabricated profile in which he called himself Chantelle – a teenage girl. He was able to groom his victim in this way for nine months before abducting and raping her twice.

Victimization and social networks

In trying to make sense of victimization in cyberspace, scholars (including Holt and Bossler 2009; Marcum, Ricketts and Higgins 2010; Reyns, Henson and Fisher 2011) have adapted and applied one of the most influential theories within victimology – routine activity theory. This theory is particularly useful for examining victimization through social networks. Cohen and Felson (1979) put forward the idea that routine activity was the answer to understanding why some people become victimized. According to their theory there are important components necessary for a crime to be committed; there must be a suitable target, the lack of a guardian, and a motivated offender. As stated above, the targets, in terms of social networks, are invariably younger people who, due to their age and maturity, are likely to take risks on the Internet. It is also clear that monitoring, filtering and blocking software are largely ineffectual on the Internet and so there is a lack of informal and formal guardianship where social networks are concerned. And where there is opportunity there is a motivated offender. Cohen and Felson's argument is based on the idea that being a suitable target or victim is based on a person's availability, and the absence of proper guards. It is clearly the case that young people, especially, spend many hours on social network sites and this will inevitably highlight their 'availability'.

Childwise are research specialists on aspects of children's lives including their habits. The 'childwise monitor report' is a comprehensive report produced annually which measures the media consumption of children between the ages of 5 and 16 years. Trends for the year 2012 reveal the extent of young people's Internet and computer use. According to the report three-quarters of 15- to 16-year-olds now have their own computer, two-thirds of all 7- to 16-year-olds can access the Internet on their own and do so on average for two hours a day five days a week. And despite the fact that attachment to Facebook is falling it still remains the most popular social network with over a third (36%) of 7- to 10-year-olds visiting Facebook in the week before the survey was conducted. For 11- and 12-year-olds this rose to 71 per cent and 85 per cent for 13- to 16-year-olds. The success and spread of Facebook is further evidenced by the fact that its founder, Mark Zuckerberg, became the youngest billionaire in the USA. According to this, then, the routine activity of young people's Internet behaviour between the ages of 5 and 16 is making them 'available' for victimization.

In terms of guardianship it has been documented elsewhere (Wall 2007) that policing the Internet is extremely difficult. Facebook in particular has come under increasing criticism for its problematic privacy rules. A difficulty in policing social networks is the fact that they are communities in which information is shared willingly and therefore they are not governed by the same rules and regulatory demands that may apply to a newspaper or a broadcaster, for instance. Facebook is in effect a self-regulating community, so offensive material can be removed only when it is highlighted by a user.

The extent of young people's use of Facebook and the problems with policing has an impact on victimization. Crimes that occur on Facebook can be twofold, either individually focused, including crimes directed at individuals such as cyber stalking, cyber bullying, trolling (with many of these cases leading to physical or sexual assault and even murder), or more publicly focused crimes such as incitement to riot or the uploading and sharing of illegal material. We look at examples of some of these activities and crimes later in the chapter but will refer here to an example of the way in which social networking sites (such as Facebook) were used to spread information about the riots in London and elsewhere in the UK in August 2011. An example of how cybercriminals engaged with the riots 'online' rather than on the streets was the case of Jordan Blackshaw and Perry Sutcliffe-Keenan. They were charged and found guilty of using Facebook to try to fuel riot-related incidents in their home town of Warrington, Cheshire and were sentenced to four years' imprisonment. Those sentences were considered by some to be harsh but their actions were said by the judge to be 'disgraceful' and to have 'caused significant public panic and revulsion in local communities as rumours of anticipated violence spread' (Bowcott, Carter and Clifton 2011).

In relation to the use of social networks to incite riots, it is clear that such technologies were not only used by rioters, but by those who were opposed to such activities and by those in charge of policing the riots. And it has been argued, that it was smartphone activity through mediums such as Blackberry Messenger (BBM) that played a much bigger role than Facebook. Speaking on BBC News about the use of BBM during the riots, Iain McKenzie commented:

> There clearly is a lot of texting and even word of mouth going on here, but there is real credible evidence that lots of people have been using BBM, Blackberry Messenger. That is the system you run on Smartphones . . . Essentially it is a closed system not like Facebook or Twitter where the message you post would be visible to all sorts of people including the authorities.
>
> (BBC News, 2011)

As a final comment, Facebook and instant access social networks in general can also be a threat to the criminal justice system. An instance of this has been their use by jury members to research the background of cases they have been trying. There has been a series of prosecutions of jurors who have gone online, a situation which has led the Lord Chief Justice, Lord Judge, to call for a greater awareness of the technological dangers threatening the justice system. An example of this was the case of Joanne Fraill, a juror in a Manchester case, who was sentenced to eight months' imprisonment for contempt of court after using Facebook to exchange messages with a defendant in that case. Another example was of university lecturer, Theodora Dallas, who looked up information about a defendant at a case she was hearing at Luton Crown Court in July 2011. Lord Judge warned that jurors using the Internet might come across false information or uncover allegations that defendants had no chance to challenge (cited in *The Guardian*, 9 December 2011).

POLICING CYBERCRIME

The focus of this chapter is on the spread of cybercrime as a consequence of the massive technological developments in the mass media of communication in recent years. This development and expansion has led to concerns about how to regulate the mass of information that exists in 'cyberspace' and how to police crimes which arise as a result of the new developments. The issue of regulation is particularly problematic due to the fact that cybercrime crosses national and international boundaries more easily than most other forms of criminal behaviour; and therefore is subject to the different legal and moral rules and jurisdictions of many different societies. Although this issue is not of central importance to our general discussion, we will conclude the chapter by commenting briefly on the problems of regulation and policing of cybercrime.

At the beginning of the chapter, we highlighted the enormous impact of the Internet on a range of human activities, and in considering cybercrime we referred to Wall's categorization of different types of cybercrime. Wall has become a recognized expert in the study of cybercrime and we will refer here to his discussion of the policing of cyberspace and cybercrime (Wall 1998). He argues that there are four main levels at which policing takes place within cyberspace. First, Internet users themselves have formed user groups around specific issues 'in order to police websites that offend them'; for instance, the CyberAngels are a 1,000-strong group of net users who are based along the guardian angel model and who have a mission statement stating they are dedicated to fighting crime on the Internet. Second, the Internet service providers who, in spite of the difficulties of acting across national boundaries, have a formal, legal status, and who are aware of and fearful of 'negative publicity which might arise from their not being seen to act responsibly'. Third, state-funded non-public police organizations, which are state agencies that are not normally seen as or called 'police'. For instance, Germany has a regulatory agency, the Internet Content Task Force, which requires Internet service providers to allow security forces to read users' emails if necessary. Fourth, state-funded public police organizations, who tend to be organized either locally or nationally, depending on which country they are based in; so in the UK the police are mainly organized locally but there are also national police organizations that deal with certain types of crime. The Metropolitan police force, for example, has a specialist computer crime unit.

Wall concludes his overview by suggesting that a multi-tiered system of policing is already well established and that it is largely based upon self-regulation by users and by Internet service providers. He also points out that it may be that 'developments in technology will simply eradicate the problem, either by deliberate design, for example, through more secure communications, encryptions and firewalling, or as a by-product or knock-on effect'. He argues that there is probably no need for a completely new approach to or type of policing and that building on and adapting what is already in place is the most practical way forward.

As we have seen when considering cybercrimes, criminals who use the Internet and other forms of new media and technology inevitably leave a trail of 'electronic evidence' of some kind. As Conway (2006), in discussing terrorists, puts it: 'Use of the Internet is a double-edged sword for terrorists. They are not the only groups utilizing the Net to forward their goals, which can act as a valuable instrumental power source for anti-terrorist forces also. The more terrorist groups use the Internet . . . the more data that is available to trail them.'

So, use of the Internet can backfire on terrorist groups as it may unwittingly provide information to law enforcement agencies that leads straight to their door; more generally websites can and do provide information for governments' intelligence agencies, and for the wider spying business. Conway cites MI5 posting an appeal for information about potential terrorists on dissident Arab websites in the wake of the 9/11 attacks in New York. Also, as well as official law enforcement agencies, a number of web-based organizations have been established to monitor terrorist activities. And in the UK, Conway refers to Niall Doyle (author of a book titled *Terror Tracker*), who claims to have used the Internet to track suspected Islamist militants based in this country.

More recently, *The Guardian* newspaper reported on a US Justice Department document which described now FBI agents in the USA were taught how to extract information from social networking sites:

> US federal law enforcement agents have been using social networking sites – including Facebook, LinkedIn, MySpace and Twitter – to search for evidence and witnesses in criminal cases, and in some instances, track suspects, according to a newly released justice department memo. FBI agents have created fake personalities . . . In order to befriend suspects and lure them into revealing clues or confessing, access private information and map social networks.
>
> (*The Guardian*, 16 March 2010)

Law enforcement agencies have regularly used Internet chat rooms to lure child pornography traffickers and paedophiles. As an example of policing a specific cybercrime, the 'crisis' of Internet paedophilia has led to new ways of policing that particular crime. Jenkins (2001) points out that the development of police powers in the USA include wiretapping and entrapment to aid in the apprehension and charge of Internet paedophiles. There is also a television series in America, *To Catch a Predator*, which is based on a series of hidden camera investigations by the news magazine programme *Dateline MBC*. The central feature is to identify and expose potential child sex abusers who use the Internet to contact children. The show engages volunteers from Perverted-Justice (a controversial citizen's organization which focuses on online predators). These adult volunteers act as decoys who get involved in sexual discussions with men. The men are then told that the decoys are at home alone and encouraged to go to their home for sex. Once the men turn up they are confronted by Chris Hanson, the show's presenter. During the third series, law enforcement also played a part in the show and many 'potential paedophiles' were arrested. This does come close to entrapment, which the show has been accused of engaging in, in that it clearly encourages people (particularly men) to break the law and then catches them for doing that.

What are the particular problems associated with policing cybercrime?

What factors might make policing such crime easier than policing more conventional crime?

Suggest the pros and cons of programmes like *To Catch a Predator* as a means of policing cybercrime.

The extent of the monitoring and surveillance of Internet activity by law enforcement agencies was revealed by a former CIA worker, Ed Snowden, who, in 2013, leaked documents of a US national security electronic surveillance programme called PRISM. Snowden said he had revealed this information because he was 'horrified' at the extent of US surveillance whereby the US National Security Agency (NSA) had access on a massive scale to individual chat logs, voice traffic, stored data and social networking data of individuals. PRISM has operated since 2007 and the recent revelations about its activities led to questions about the extent to which the British government surveillance department, GCHQ, has had access to information via PRISM, with UK Foreign Secretary, William Hague commenting 'that law-abiding citizens have nothing to worry about, and there is no legal way of "opting out" of monitoring activity carried out in the name of national or security' (www.bbc.co.uk/news/technology-22839609, 10 June 2013).

FURTHER READING

International Journal of Cyber Criminology (n.d.) Available online at www.cybercrime journal.com. It is an open access online journal that is published twice a year and which is devoted to the study of cybercrime. It includes articles that focus on all aspects of cyber and computer crime.

Jewkes Y. (ed.) (2007) *Crime Online*, Cullompton, UK: Willan Publishing. This edited collection includes accounts and analyses of the key issues within the rapidly developing field of cybercrime.

Wall D. S. (ed.) (2001) *Crime and the Internet*, London: Routledge. Starting with an overview of the general problem of crime and the Internet, later chapters explore different types of cybercrime and the problems faced by the criminal justice system in dealing with it.

Williams M. (2006) *Virtually Criminal: Crime, Deviance and Regulation Online*, London: Routledge. This study aims to help us understand the causes of cybercrime through focusing on the role of the Internet and online communications in the origins and control of such crime.

CHAPTER 8

- Public opinion, crime and the media – 'penal populism'
- Media and (mis)representation of crime and justice
- The media and fear of crime

The Media, Punishment and Public Opinion

In this final and fairly brief chapter, we will look at the relationship between the news media's representation of crime and justice and the public perceptions of and reaction to these issues.

It is well established that public knowledge of crime and justice is largely derived from the media and that the media play a key role in the public's perception of criminals, victims and those who work within the criminal justice system. And it is widely accepted that the general public have a distorted and exaggerated view of the extent and the nature of crime. For instance, Hough and Roberts (1998) reported that data from the British Crime Survey showed that the majority of respondents (78%) felt that at least 30 per cent of crimes involved violence (while official statistics showed the figure to be only 6%). The findings from more recent British Crime Surveys have continued to show that the public perceptions of crime are quite at odds with official crime statistics. The 2009 British Crime Survey found that although the overall crime rate had gone down by 5 per cent and the number of murders, manslaughters and child killings had dropped by 17 per cent, the public perception was still that crime was much more widespread and out of control than it really was (Flatley *et al.* 2010). Such findings are supported by evidence from the Office for National Statistics, which in 2011, in its annual report on social trends, published data that showed most people believed crime had gone up when it had actually gone down (Social Trends 2011).

In discussing public opinion and the sentencing of offenders, Hough and Roberts (1999) pointed out that research on public opinion over the previous three decades, and particularly the findings of the various British Crime Surveys, had consistently shown the public to be critical of those who sentence offenders for being overly lenient. However, they found that, although the public systematically underestimate the severity of sentences passed by the courts, when asked to suggest appropriate sentences for specific crimes they tended to be more lenient than the current sentencing practices. In terms of sentencing, then, it would seem that there is a discrepancy between what the actual situation is and what the public believes to be happening. In reviewing public surveys conducted over the past 30 years, Gelb (2006 and 2008) found that most people think sentences imposed by courts are too lenient and that public opinion on sentencing is based on widely held misconceptions about crime and sentencing. However, she also found that when people are provided with more information on particular cases they tend to suggest sentences very similar to those imposed by judges (Gelb 2006). In a similar vein, in a study in Victoria, Australia, Lovegrove (2007) gave over 450 people the same information about a particular crime and defendant that the sentencing judge had. He found that in half the cases, the sentence given by the member of the public was lower than that given by the judge and in the other cases the sentences were much the same. In fact, in no case was the sentence given by the judge lenient compared to the average sentence of the public.

Of course, we are making large generalizations here about the public and their response to the news media. In referring to recent British Crime Survey data, Green (2006) found that readers of tabloid newspapers were almost twice as likely as readers of broadsheet or 'quality' newspapers to believe that crime had 'increased a lot' over recent years – even though there was no statistical evidence of any increase. This apparent link between the choice of newspaper and perceptions of crime provides further evidence of the media's ability to influence people's views of social trends, certainly as far as crime is concerned.

PUBLIC OPINION, CRIME AND THE MEDIA – 'PENAL POPULISM'

In introducing their book, *Understanding Public Attitudes to Criminal Justice*, Roberts and Hough (2005) start with the statement that 'Public opinion has always played a significant role in the administration of criminal justice, and information about public attitudes is clearly important to politicians and criminal justice professionals.' So it is not surprising that governments spend a good deal of effort conducting surveys and opinion polls and trying to find out the public's attitudes to crime and criminal justice. And, given the arguments and findings we have put forward in this book, it is fairly clear that public opinions are strongly affected by the media representation of crime, criminals and criminal justice.

The attempt by governments to measure the public's attitude to the criminal justice system, so as to promote greater confidence in it, leads to what has been termed 'penal populism' – whereby politicians promote and support policies that they feel will appeal to the public. Roberts and Hough suggest that this concern with public opinion can help explain the emergence of hard-line and punitive policies in the criminal justice arena. However, they emphasize that it is important not to be overly critical of this approach, as 'it is perfectly proper for politicians to ensure that the justice system does not fall totally out of step with public opinion'. As well as the general benefits in terms of social cohesion from the public having faith in the system, criminal justice agencies, such as the police, can gain practical benefits from having the help and support of the wider public. For instance, the police rely on the public for information about crimes and for help in solving them.

We have seen throughout our discussion of crime, justice and the media that the public interest in criminal justice is very high, but also that the knowledge the public have of crime and justice is low. Roberts and Hough refer to a survey of Scottish respondents (Hutton 2005) which found that well over half the sample acknowledged that they had little knowledge of the courts or prisons, even though 88 per cent had said they were fairly or very interested in the subject. It is obvious from our own use of the media and our involvement with the wider public on an everyday basis, that most people follow major criminal cases covered in the media and that most people have their own views of the guilt or innocence of people involved in such cases.

Indeed, it could be argued that the courts have a higher media profile than other areas of the criminal justice system – court cases are of great interest to the media, particularly with high-profile crimes and/or criminals; witness the massive public interest when celebrities, such as Jeffrey Archer in the UK, or Michael Jackson in the USA, are on trial, or over cases involving serial killers, such as Harold Shipman, or child killers, such as Ian Huntley and Mick Philpott.

We have noted the tendency for the media to cover crime and criminal justice issues in a sensationalist style. This promotes a skewed view of the area – certainly studies in various countries show that the public think there is far more crime and that it is rising, even though statistical trends might not support this (Roberts and Hough 2005). And, in considering this discrepancy, Roberts and Hough argue that 'the consistent pattern of findings across diverse publics suggests that the source of the public's perception of ever-rising crime rates is the media . . . [and] the public acknowledges the importance of the media as a source of information about crime' (2005).

Linked to the sensationalist style of crime reporting in the media is the tendency for the media to adopt different approaches to reporting different types of crime – both in terms of the extent and the style of their reporting. Media reports are often full of the more gruesome and violent crimes, presumably because they are felt to be more gripping than stories about business crime and credit card fraud. Even within the category of fraud and white-collar crime, different media reporting is liable to influence public opinion about such crimes. Benefit fraud is typically reported as a 'scandal' and as a major drain on national resources, as the following headlines from the *Daily Mail* illustrate:

Are we finally winning the battle against benefit cheats? Convictions soar 40% in two years after fraud investigators are given access to Sky TV bills
(*Daily Mail*, 17 October 2012)

Mother-of-two who posed as struggling single parent to claim £30,000 exposed as benefits cheat when she posted picture of Cyprus wedding on Facebook
(*Daily Mail*, 19 January 2013)

Ugandan family created 100 children and claimed to suffer from HIV as part of £4 million benefit fraud

(*Daily Mail*, 26 October 2012)

The common theme of this sort of reporting of benefit fraud is to highlight how the people claiming benefits do not deserve them because they are much better off than they have indicated and are able to afford satellite TV, weddings abroad or other such 'luxuries'. Indeed there is even a dedicated website which focuses on the 'scandal of benefit fraud' (www.benefitfraud.org.uk). On its home page, this site comments that benefit fraud is rife in the UK and that while the 'government pretends it costs £1.2 billion annually the real figure is probably at least £5.5 billion a year'. It also informs its visitors about how to report a case of suspected benefit fraud, suggesting that 'too often light sentences do not reflect the crime, and offer no deterrent'.

While benefit fraud is clearly a significant cost to the country, other forms of 'white-collar crime', and particularly corporate crime, are far more costly yet are reported by the media in a less sensationalist style. In 2012, the BBC News reported on data provided by the National Fraud Authority which revealed that fraud is costing the country around £73 billion a year, equivalent to each adult in the UK being £1,441 a year worse off (BBC News, 20 March 2012, www.bbc.co.uk).

Of course, we all have opinions on things without having detailed knowledge about them and there are lots of areas of criminal justice where the public's opinions are based on, at best, flimsy evidence. Roberts and Hough (2005) provide an example of this with regard to the Criminal Justice Act of 2003, which allowed for the retrial of a person who had previously been acquitted on that charge. They refer to an opinion poll conducted by *The Observer* which found that four out of five respondents supported this change, even though it was highly unlikely they had ever even considered the issue until responding to the survey – in other words, their response could not be seen as based on evidence or on any deep commitment. Similarly, even though the sentencing of criminals in the UK and the USA has got tougher in recent years (and more people are sent to prison), there is still a public perception that the system is lenient – 'public reaction appears to be based on preconception rather than a reasoned evaluation of the evidence' (Roberts and Hough 2005).

The danger of this discrepancy is that governments and politicians court popularity in chasing votes, which encourage them to focus on the popularity of their policies rather than their ability to promote justice or reduce crime. The message from research on public opinion, crime and sentencing would seem to be that the public needs better information about criminal justice policies and sentencing, rather than simplistic calls for harsher sentencing which politicians feel will appeal to their public.

MEDIA AND (MIS)REPRESENTATION OF CRIME AND JUSTICE

Given our reliance on the media for information about crime and criminals and events we have no first-hand knowledge or experience of, it is fairly self-evident that the media play a key role in promoting such misunderstandings. For instance, Allen (2001) lists a number of serious public misconceptions about crime and sentencing – people overestimate the amount of violent crime and the proportion of offenders who are juvenile and underestimate the severity of sentencing and the range of alternative sentences available to our courts. He argues that, 'all too often (the media) paint a picture of crime out of control, a system failing to cope, criminals as evil monsters and alternatives or reforms as doomed to failure'. Given this, he suggests that it is, 'little wonder . . . that in headline terms, a harsher criminal justice system is attractive to most people'.

QUESTION BREAK

Look at the following extracts of crime reporting from different news media – including the BBC News, the national press and a local newspaper – and then consider the questions below.

Child Killer's Term 'Too Lenient'

The parents of murdered schoolboy Joe Geeling have said his killer's 12-year jail sentence is 'too lenient'. Cystic fibrosis sufferer Joe, 11, was hit with a frying pan and stabbed before his body was dumped in a park in Bury, Greater Manchester, on 1 March. Michael Hamer, 15, was jailed for life for murder last month, but he will be considered for parole after 12 years.

(BBC News, Thursday 9 November 2006, http://news.bbc.co.uk/
2/hi/uk_news/england/manchester/6130566.stm)

Almost 100 Sentences Were Lenient, Says Attorney General

Almost 100 sentences handed down by judges last year were later deemed too lenient, official figures show. The Attorney General's Office said it received complaints about the jail terms or community punishments received by nearly 400 criminals in 2011. Law officers looked in detail at 117 cases and after they were considered by the Court of Appeal, 97 were deemed too soft and all but three were increased . . .

Among the sentences judged too soft last year was one handed down by Cherie Booth, Tony Blair's wife. She spared a drug dealer jail after he was caught with a kilogram of cocaine worth £145,600 in what was described as a 'startling result'. He was given three and a half years behind bars after the case was considered again.

(*The Daily Telegraph*, 5 July 2012)

Public Backs Tougher Jail Terms for Criminals . . .

The public overwhelmingly supports tougher sentences for convicted criminals, a major poll has revealed. More than eight out of ten of those surveyed said sentencing is too soft and seven in ten called for life in prison to be much harder for inmates ... They also rejected proposals to increase the use of community sentences. Eight out of ten see these as a 'soft punishment'.

(*Daily Mail*, 6 April 2011)

Are Magistrates in Southport Too Lenient on Crime?

A have-a-go hero who chased a burglar from his Hoghton Street business has hit out at the 'feeble' punishment dished out. The juvenile – who the *Visiter* is not allowed to name due to his age – was sentenced at North Sefton Magistrates Court on Tuesday after burgling Tyndall's restaurant in April. He received a punishment of just 10 hours community service and was told to pay costs of £90.

Magistrates heard that the youth and an accomplice kicked down the door of the four-star bistro to steal spirits, champagne and cash. Owner Mark Tyndall, 52, gave chase with on-duty policeman DI Ged Seddon. And at the time, Mr Tyndall exclusively told the *Southport Visiter*: 'I just want to see justice done'.

But he believes the culprit has got away extremely lightly. He said: 'This lad has committed burglary, caused £750 damage, and has escaped almost scot-free. The punishment does not fit the crime. Let's get it right; they were out to burgle. To put it into comparison, the last time I was in court I received a £120 fine for a minor parking offence. It's one rule for normal society, and one for the down-and-outs'. Blame does not lie at the feet of the police, according to Mr Tyndall, but in the courts. He believes local policemen are themselves becoming agitated with such alleged soft sentencing.

(*Southport Visiter*, 19 October 2007)

QUESTIONS

- Why do you think there is a strong tendency to believe that sentencing is more lenient than it actually is?
- Can you suggest any ways by which this misconception might be corrected?

The media coverage of crime, justice and punishment can be very frustrating for those with professional involvement in the areas of crime and justice. There is a tendency for those who work in the criminal justice system, or who have academic and research interests in the area, to criticize and blame the media coverage for presenting an inaccurate, or perhaps to put it more generously, a simplistic picture of crime and criminal justice. Here it is useful to consider the work of Enver Solomon, a journalist who worked for the press and the BBC before joining the Prison Reform Trust.

In looking at the role of the press in encouraging a climate of punitiveness, he starts his discussion by suggesting that journalists are one of the professions (along with estate agents!) that are most disliked and distrusted by the wider public. And he found that this lack of trust and dislike was even more noticeable and virulent amongst those working in the criminal justice system. People he came across within the criminal justice system tended to see the media as not reporting facts correctly and as being 'hell bent on whipping up fear with sensationalist reporting' (Solomon 2005). As well as being sensationalist and misinforming the wider public, the media are criticized for oversimplifying issues and ignoring positive and ground-breaking developments and projects from criminal justice agencies.

Of course, the media does not exist in a vacuum and what is presented as news in the media will be influenced by and reflect the agenda of governments and politicians; as Solomon puts it, 'the balance of power ultimately rests with politicians, who have the levers of state control in their hands, and not with the media'. However, a major reason why the media reporting of crime is sensationalist is simply that the media is big business – newspapers at all levels depend on circulation figures and profits to survive and editors and journalists believe that sensationalism sells. As well as sensationalism, Solomon points out that it is controversy which also makes news – for instance, a good story might be when a judge or senior public figure is critical of an aspect of government policy. Furthermore, as a result of the supposed public demand for news, reflected in the round the clock dedicated news programmes, there is increased pressure on the news media to 'churn out stories without having the time or space to sit back and make considered editorial judgements', which will lead inevitably to oversimplification and misrepresentation.

A recent example of how the pressure on the news media for up-to-the-minute news reporting can lead to errors was the appeal of Amanda Knox in October 2011 against her conviction for the murder of Meredith Kercher four years previously. In their rush to be first with the story, a number of news organizations reported the wrong verdict. When the judge began his ruling confusion over the use of the word 'guilty' led the *Daily Mail*, *The Sun* and *The Guardian*, along with Sky News, to report that Knox had lost her appeal. The *Daily Mail*, for example, put the following headline on its web page on 3 October 2011, 'Guilty: Amanda Knox looks stunned as appeal against murder conviction is rejected'. In reality the judge had started by saying that Knox was guilty of slander but that she (and her boyfriend Raffaele Sollecito) had been cleared of the murder and sexual assault convictions.

Solomon then goes on to consider ways in which the criminal justice system and those working in it should deal with and use the media to support their efforts and initiatives. For instance, criminal justice agencies opening up more information channels would ensure journalists were better informed, as would working in a closer and more supportive relationship with journalists so as to provide them with solid and accurate background information. As he puts it in concluding his argument:

> If those who work in the criminal justice sector want to use the media to convey their messages more effectively they must begin to understand why it is prone to

distort the facts and exaggerate. It is also vital to recognize the social and political environment that the media operates in. Only then will organizations be able to realize the limitations of using the media, that it is naïve to expect newspapers and broadcasters to be responsible conduits of information, and to develop more effective communication strategies.

(Solomon 2005, p. 35)

QUESTION BREAK

Look at the two extracts. The first is from *The Daily Telegraph*'s reporting of a murder case; the second from the *Daily Mail*, commenting on a survey that was carried out for them on public perceptions of the criminal justice system.

The Murderer Who Should Have Been in Jail

Laila Rezk, 53, was beaten to death by a burglar as she prepared dinner for her family at their home on Kingston Vale . . . [The murderer] had been in prison but was released two months early. Of course, he was not going to be in jail for ever . . . [but] had he not been freed early, he would not have been where he was on November 29 last year – carrying out an opportunistic burglary after a day's drinking. We can be virtually certain of this: Edwards would not have killed Mrs Rezk if he had been kept behind bars for the duration of his sentence.

(Johnston P., *The Daily Telegraph*, 3 December 2007)

The Judiciary Is Out of Touch with the Public, Says Poll

Deep public unhappiness with a judiciary which is out of touch with the lives of ordinary people and places the interests of convicts and terror suspects first is revealed in a *Daily Mail* poll today. The ICM survey also found that three out of four Britons say the sentences given to criminals are 'too lenient' . . .

The poll suggests a lack of public trust in the judiciary. Most strikingly, only 18 per cent have faith that the sentences they want passed against criminals will be imposed by the courts. Only 36 per cent said judges could be trusted to put the interests of ordinary people first, compared with those of minority groups. The lack of trust stems from a belief judges have no understanding of mainstream public attitudes . . .

The survey of 1,019 men and women for the *Daily Mail*, which was carried out last week . . . [found that] seventy-five per cent said sentences were 'too lenient'. Only 3 per cent said punishments were 'too harsh', while 18 per cent considered them about right.

(Slack J., *Daily Mail*, 8 March 2007)

QUESTIONS

- Find some recent newspaper articles on crimes and sentencing.
- Can you find any evidence of criminal justice practitioners (e.g. police officers, probation officers, youth justice workers, judges) being criticized for how they dealt with those crimes and/or criminals?

It has been well established throughout this book that the news media are very preoccupied with stories and issues around crime, justice and punishment. Also, that the amount of coverage and the range of different crimes and issues reported on is massive. In reflecting on the populist representations of crime and disorder in the media, Sparks (2001) points out that this vast, seemingly insatiable interest can be a source of puzzlement for those researching and/or working in the criminal justice field. He comments:

Why this endless concentration on the bad news about crime? . . . Why are errors, failings and scandals so much more newsworthy than successes and dogged hard work? Must every progressive initiative be undermined by unsympathetic news coverage or every challenging research finding reduced to sound bites?

(Sparks 2001, p. 6)

As we mentioned earlier, the news media does not just exist independently, but both reflects and is influenced by political practices and processes. Sparks refers to the work of Ericson and colleagues (1991) and their argument that it is the general concern with the question of order in society which helps to explain the media's appetite for crime news, and why so much attention is given to 'what is out of place: the deviant, equivocal and unpredictable'. Sparks also suggests that a preoccupation with blame is another key feature of the news media discourse. This blame can be attached to offenders themselves but also to people in criminal justice contexts not doing their job properly, illustrated by comments such as 'over-stretched' police forces or 'inexperienced' social workers. While this might seem to present a rather discouraging picture, Sparks does point out that the media interest in blame can also at times have a positive effect by calling those with positions of power and authority to account. This can be seen in the role the media can play in highlighting miscarriages of justice and in helping such miscarriages to be remedied. The media played a major role in uncovering a number of (in)famous miscarriages of justice in the 1970s and 1980s, including the release of the Birmingham Six in 1991. The BBC television documentary *Rough Justice* played an important role in investigating alleged miscarriages of justice. It ran from 1982 until 2007 when it was cancelled as a cost-cutting measure, although it helped lead to the release of 18 people involved in 13 cases.

THE MEDIA AND FEAR OF CRIME

Another aspect of the media's influence on public opinion is with regard to fear of crime, in particular whether media coverage of crime, and its sensationalist reporting of crime, creates fear amongst the general public. Newburn (2013) makes the point that fear of crime has become a widely discussed and important notion within criminology. However, it was not until the 1960s and 1970s that criminologists and others started to talk about 'fear of crime'. He suggests that this relatively recent academic interest came about as a result of the development of victim surveys as a way of trying to measure the actual amount of crime (rather than the amount of crime known about by the authorities – the official crime statistics). Finding out about people's fear of crime has always been a part of victimization surveys, such as the British Crime Surveys; indeed Newburn refers to the early British Crime Surveys (which started in 1984) as asking questions about how safe people felt 'being out alone after dark'.

QUESTION BREAK

Newburn (2013) cites a question asked by the British Crime Survey: How safe do you feel walking alone in this area after dark?

- very safe
- fairly safe
- a bit unsafe
- very unsafe

What problems can you suggest with this question as a way of finding out about crime and fear of crime?

Fear of crime is a broad notion and it should perhaps be distinguished from worry and concern about crime – for instance, there is a clear distinction between the personal fear of being a crime victim to a more general concern about levels of crime in particular areas. More recent British Crime Surveys have asked about 'worry of crime' and have found that there are high levels of worry about certain crimes, such as burglary and rape. Also, that these worries differed with different groups of the population, with women, for instance, expressing far greater worry over violent crime and burglary than men, but not over car crime.

Although fear of crime has become an important area of criminological consideration, Jewkes (2004) points out that some of the early theorizing in this area came from left-wing, critical criminologists who tended to argue that the powerful in society used crime as a means of social control – crime was viewed by some left-wing theorists as 'an ideological construct; it protects the powerful and further marginalizes the powerless'. Jewkes argues that this sort of theoretical approach assumes that fear of crime is irrational and unreasonable, and is a sort of false consciousness produced by those in authority. However, this view has been attacked by realist approaches in criminology, which argue that the images of crime portrayed in the media and elsewhere are not illusions and that the media coverage of crime reflects what people already know – that, while it may be exaggerated, crime does occur and can be devastating for victims of it. Indeed, a good deal of crime, especially hidden crime such as domestic violence, is not prevalent in the news media or in crime statistics – yet, as Jewkes points out, the British Crime Survey of 2000 finding that over a third of women do not go out alone at night 'is not that surprising and cannot be explained away as an irrational response'.

In terms of the relationship between fear of crime and the media, a central question is whether people fear crime because so much crime is presented in the media or does the media provide such massive coverage of crime because people fear crime and like to see what is happening? The idea that the media have created unwanted levels of fear of crime is by no means new and it is fair to say that if there is a link then the explosion in the forms and extent of media in recent years will have exacerbated these fears of crime.

In considering the extent to which the media affects levels of fear of crime, Newburn (2013) refers to the work of Gerbner and colleagues in the USA, who found that 'heavy' users of television (more than four hours a day) exhibited higher levels of fear of crime. He also highlights a study by Schlesinger and Tumber (1992) in the UK which found that readers of tabloid newspapers and heavy watchers of television were more likely to be worried about becoming a victim of crime, particularly being assaulted. However, the link between use of the media and fear of crime cannot be assumed, as Newburn puts it: 'it is, for example, perfectly possible that people who are especially fearful are attracted to particular types of media'. Of course, the media will clearly have an effect on people's attitudes and views, including their fears; what is debatable is how these effects work. So the relationship between fear and the media is clearly a subtle one. It is apparent, though, that the public view of the extent of crime is strongly influenced by the picture painted by much of the news media – that the crime rate is spiralling and the criminal justice system is too lenient (as the extracts in the question breaks on pages 214 and 217 indicate).

One response to the fear of crime is the regular demand by the wider public for more community policing, in particular for more 'bobbies on the beat'. Jewkes (2004) makes the point that this demand is unflagging even though there is no research evidence that more police on the beat will reduce crime. She suggests that the desire for bobbies on the beat is linked to fears of 'others', such as immigrants, youth gangs, travellers and so on. It may also reflect a lack of public confidence in the police and a feeling that increased bureaucratization in the police, and an emphasis on efficiency at all costs, has pulled the police away from local, community policing which, as Jewkes says, is seen as inefficient in hard economic terms.

It is worth making the point that fear of crime does not necessarily have to be harmful and can sometimes have a positive effect. In a recent research study, Jackson and Gray (2010) found that the fear of crime can spur some people into taking precautions that make them feel safer. They asked almost 3,000 Londoners how worried they were by crime and whether it affected their quality of life and also whether they took precautions (such as avoiding public transport) and if these precautions made them feel any safer. They found that some people who did feel worried about being victims of crime tried to do something about it through practical actions, such as installing alarms or answering the front door with greater caution. In cases where people's fear of crime, and the actions they took to deal with the fear, did not affect their quality of life, Jackson and Gray suggested that the fear has a partly beneficial effect – they classified such fear as 'functional fear'.

In concluding his discussion of the relationship between the media and public attitudes to crime and criminals, Allen (2001) argues that there would be a number of positive outcomes from more informed and objective media reporting of crime; in particular it would lead to a more informed and aware public, as the following comment suggests:

> While eight out of ten people say they think sentencing is too lenient, when confronted with real cases, public sentencing preferences are, if anything, more lenient than sentencing guidelines. It is clear that the public is not nearly so pro-prison as reports in the media would sometimes suggest. Polls have consistently shown that more people disagree than agree with the notion that 'prison works: the more prisons the better'.
>
> (Allen 2001, p. 41)

FURTHER READING

Allen R. (2001) 'Informing the Public', *Criminal Justice Matters*, 43:40–41. This article considers how the media can help to correct public misconceptions about crime.

Roberts J. V. and Hough M. (2005) *Understanding Public Attitudes to Criminal Justice*, Milton Keynes, UK: Open University Press. This book looks at public attitudes to criminal justice and the role of the media in informing these attitudes; it considers, in particular, the lack of confidence the public has in criminal justice processes.

Solomon E. (2005) 'Is the Press the Real Power Behind Punitivism?' *Criminal Justice Matters*, 59:34–35. Starting with a consideration of why there seems to be an endless concentration on bad news and sensationalist reporting in the media representation of crime, Solomon suggests that change of approach is needed.

REFERENCES

Age UK (2011) *Supporting Older People in Prison: Ideas for Practice*, London: Age UK.

Ainley P. (2005) 'Open Your Arms', *The Guardian*, 14 June.

Allen R. (2001) 'Informing the Public', *Criminal Justice Matters*, 43:40–41.

Althusser L. (1969) *For Marx*, London: Allen Lane.

Back L. (2002) 'Aryans Reading Adorno: Cyber-Culture and Twenty-First Century Racism', *Ethnic and Racial Studies*, 25(4):628–651.

Bandura A. (1963) *Social Learning and Personality Development*, New York: Holt, Rinehart and Winston.

Bandura A. (1977) *Social Learning Theory*, Englewood Cliffs, NJ: Prentice Hall.

Banks M. (2005) 'Spaces of (In)security: Media and Fear of Crime in a Local Context', *Crime, Media and Culture*, 1(2):169–187.

Barkham P. (2005) 'How a Top Can Turn a Teen into a Hoodlum', *The Guardian*, 14 May.

Benedict H. (1992) *Virgin or Vamp: How the Press Covers Sex Crimes*, Oxford: Oxford University Press.

Bilton M. (2003) *Wicked Beyond Belief*, London: Harper Collins.

Bindel J. (2007) 'The Rise of the Cyber-Stalker', *The Guardian*, 10 January.

Binks G. (2005) 'Pretty Girls Get the Best', CBC News, 10 June.

Bowcott O., Carter H. and Clifton H. (2011) 'Facebook Riot Calls Earn Men Four-Year Jail Terms Amid Sentencing Outcry', *The Guardian*, 16 August.

Brown J. (2006) 'Your Task: Selling the Real Liverpool', *The Independent*, 27 November.

Brown S. (2005) *Understanding Youth and Crime*, 2nd edn, Milton Keynes: Open University Press.

Burn G. (1984) *Somebody's Husband, Somebody's Son*, London: Heinemann.

Burn G. (2001) 'Watching Jill', *The Guardian*, 3 July.

Cameron D. and Fraser E. (1987) *The Lust to Kill: A Feminist Investigation of Sexual Murder*, Oxford: Polity Press.

Castells M. (1996) *The Information Age: The Rise of the Network Society*, Oxford: Blackwell.

Castells M. (1997) *The Information Age: The Power of Identity*, Oxford: Blackwell.

Cavanagh A. (2007) 'Taxonomies of Anxiety: Risk, Panics, Paedophilia and the Internet', *Electronic Journal of Sociology*.

CCTV User Group (2011) 'New Statistics on CCTV Cameras'. Available online at www.cctvusergroup.com (accessed 10 July 2013).

Chaney D. (1972) *Processes of Mass Communication*, London: MacMillan.

Chaplin R., Flatley J. and Smith K. (eds) (2011) *Crime in England and Wales 2010/11: Findings from the British Crime Survey 2011*, London: HMSO.

Chomsky N. (1989) *Necessary Illusions: Thought Control in Democratic Societies*, Boston: South End Press.

Clough B. and Mungo P. (1992) *Approaching Zero: Data Crime and the Computer Underworld*, London: Faber and Faber.

Cohen L. E. and Felson M. (1979) 'Social Change and Crime Rate Trends: A Routine Activity Approach', *American Sociological Review*, 44:588–608.

Cohen P. C. (1998) *The Murder of Helen Jewett: The Life and Death of a Prostitute in Nineteenth-Century New York*, New York: Alfred A. Knopf.

Cohen S. (1972) *Folk Devils and Moral Panics*, London: MacGibbon and Kee.

Cohen S. (1980) *Folk Devils and Moral Panics*, 2nd edn, London: Routledge.

Cohen S. (1985) *Visions of Social Control*, Cambridge: Polity Press.

Cohen S. (2002) *Folk Devils and Moral Panics*, 3rd edn, London: Routledge.

Cohen S. and Young J. (eds) (1981) *The Manufacture of News*, London: Constable.

Coleman L. (2004) *The Copycat Effect: How the Media and Popular Culture Trigger the Mayhem in Tomorrow's Headlines*, New York: Simon and Schuster.

Coll S. and Glasser S. B. (2005) 'Terrorists Turn to the Web as Base of Operations', *Washington Post*, 7 August.

Collins R. D. and Bird R. (2006) 'The Penitentiary Visit – A New Role for Geriatricians?' *Age and Ageing*, 36(1):11–13.

Conway M. (2006) 'Terrorism and the Internet: New Media – New Threat?', *Parliamentary Affairs*, Oxford University Press.

Coward R. (2012) 'Jimmy Savile was Protected by the Media's Defence of the Status Quo', *The Guardian*, 18 October.

Coyle A. (2005) *Understanding Prisons*, Milton Keynes: Open University Press.

Crain C. (2002) 'In Search of Lost Crime', *Legal Affairs*, August (www.legalaffairs.org).

Creaton H. (2003) 'Recent Scholarship on Jack the Ripper and the Victorian Media', *Institute of Historical Research* (www.history.ac.uk).

Critcher C. (2003) *Moral Panics and the Media*, Milton Keynes: Open University Press.

Crutchfield R. D. and Kubrin C. E. (2007) 'Urban Crime: Are Crime Rates Higher in Urban Areas, Explaining Urban Crime' (http://law.jrank.org).

Curran J. (1977) 'Capitalism and Control of the Press 1800–1975', in Curran J., Gurevitch M. and Woolacott J. (eds), *Mass Communication and Society*, London: Edward Arnold.

Curtis L. P. (2001) *Jack the Ripper and the London Press*, New Haven: Yale University Press.

Donovan P. (2007) 'British Justice's Shaky History', *New Statesman*, 15 November.

Dorfman L. (2001) 'Off Balance: Youth, Race and Crime in the News', Building Blocks for Youth (www.buildingblocksforyouth.org).

Doyle N. (2005) *Terror Tracker: An Odyssey into Pure Fear*, Edinburgh: Mainstream Publishing.

Durkheim E. (1964, [1895]). *The Rules of Sociological Method*, New York: Free Press.

Ellis H. (1937) 'Sexual Selection of Man' in *The Psychological Study of Sex*, New York: Garden City.

Emsley C. (1996) *Crime and Society in England 1750–1900*, 2nd edn, Harlow: Longman.

Ericson R., Baranek P. and Chan J. (1991) *Representing Order*, Milton Keynes: Open University Press.

Eysenck H. J. and Nias D. K. B. (1978) *Sex, Violence and the Media*, London: Paladin.

Ferrell J. (1999) 'Cultural Criminology', *Annual Review of Criminology*, 25(1):395–418.

Ferrell J. (2001) 'Cultural Criminology', in McLaughlin E. and Muncie J. (eds), *Sage Dictionary of Criminology*, London: Sage.

Flatley J., Kershaw C., Smith K., Chaplin R. and Moon D. (2010) *British Crime Survey 2009*, London: Home Office.

Foucault M. (1977) *Discipline and Punish: The Birth of the Prison*, London: Allen Lane.

Foucault M. (1978) *The History of Sexuality*, London: Penguin.

Frigon S. (1995) 'A Genealogy of Women's Madness', in Dobash R. E., Dobash R. P. and Noaks L. (eds), *Gender and Crime*, Cardiff: University of Wales Press.

Gauntlett D. (2007) 'Ten Things Wrong with the Media "Effects" Model' (www.theory.org.uk).

Gelb K. (2006) *Myths and Misconceptions: Public Opinion versus Public Judgement about Sentencing*, Melbourne: Sentencing Advisory Council.

Gelb K. (2008) *More Myths and Misconceptions*, Melbourne: Sentencing Advisory Council.

Giddens A. (1984) *The Constitution of Society*, Cambridge: Polity Press.

Gies L. (2008) *Law and the Media: The Future of an Uneasy Relationship*, London: Routledge.

Gill M. and Spriggs A. (2005) 'Assessing the Impact of CCTV', Home Office Research, Development and Statistics Directorate 43, London: Home Office.

Glasgow University Media Group (1976) *Bad News*, London: Routledge & Kegan Paul.

Glasgow University Media Group (1980) *More Bad News*, London: Routledge & Kegan Paul.

Glasgow University Media Group (1982) *Really Bad News*, London: Writers & Readers.

Glasgow University Media Group (1985) *War and Peace News*, London: Open University Press.

Glasgow University Media Group (1993) *Getting the Message: News, Truth and Power*, London: Routledge.

Goffman E. (1959) *The Presentation of Self in Everyday Life*, New York: Doubleday.

Goffman E. (1969) *The Presentation of Self in Everyday Life*, Harmondsworth, UK: Penguin.

Goode E. and Ben-Yehuda N. (1994) *Moral Panics: The Social Construction of Deviance*, Oxford: Blackwell.

Gramsci A. (1971) *Selections from the Prison Notebooks*, London: Lawrence and Wishart.

Gray D. and Watt P. (2013) *Giving Victims a Voice: Joint Report into Sexual Allegations Made Against Jimmy Savile*, NSPCC/Metropolitan Police.

Green D. A. (2006) 'Public Opinion versus Public Judgment about Crime', *British Journal of Criminology*, 46:131–154.

Greer C. (2007) 'News Media, Victims and Crime', in Davies P., Francis P. and Greer C. (eds.), *Victims, Crime and Society,* London: Sage.

Greer C. and Reiner R. (2012) 'Mediated Mayhem: Media, Crime, Criminal Justice', in Maguire M., Morgan R. and Reiner R. (eds), *The Oxford Handbook of Criminology*, Oxford: Oxford University Press.

Gregori J. (ed.) (1998) *What Will Become of Us? Counting Down to Y2K*, Gerradstown, WV: Academic Freedom Foundation.

Hagell A. and Newburn T. (1994) *Young Offenders and the Media: Viewing Habits and Preferences*, London: Policy Studies Institute.

Hall S., Critcher C., Jefferson T., Clarke J. and Roberts B. (1978) *Policing the Crisis: Mugging, the State and Law and Order*, London: MacMillan.

Haralambos M. and Holborn M. (2004) *Sociology: Themes and Perspectives*, London: Collins.

Hart L. (1994) *Fatal Women: Lesbian Sexuality and the Mark of Aggression*, London: Routledge.

Hirschi T. (1969) *Causes of Delinquency*, Berkeley: University of California Press.

Holmlund C. (2002) *Impossible Bodies: Femininity and Masculinity at the Movies*, London: Routledge.

Holt T. J. and Bossler A. M. (2009) 'Examining the Applicability of Lifestyle-Routine Activities Theory for Cybercrime Victimization', *Deviant Behavior*, 30:1–25.

Home Office (2002) *Protecting the Public: Strengthening Protection Against Sex Offenders and Reforming the Law on Sexual Offences*, London: HMSO.

Home Office (2005) *Hi-Tech Crime: The Impact on UK Business*, London: HMSO.

Home Office (2011) *Police Powers and Procedures England and Wales 2010/11*, 2nd edn, London: Home Office.

Hough M. and Roberts J. V. (1998) 'Attitudes to Punishment: Findings from the British Crime Survey', Home Office Research Study 179, London: Home Office.

Hough M. and Roberts J. V. (1999) 'Sentencing Trends in Britain', *Punishment and Society*, 1(1):11–26.

Human Rights Watch Report (2012) *Old Behind Bars: The Ageing Prison Population in the United States*, Human Rights Watch.

Hutton N. (2005) 'Beyond Populist Punitiveness', *Punishment and Society*, 7:243–248.

Hyland J. (2000) 'British Media Incites Lynch-Mob Atmosphere over Child Sex Abuse', World Socialist Web Site, 12 August (www.wsws.org).

Innes M. (2001) ' "Crimewatching": Homicide Investigations in the Age of Innocence', *Criminal Justice Matters*, 43:42–43.

Innes M. (2003) 'Signal Crimes: Detective Work, Mass Media and Constructing Collective Memory', in Mason P. (ed.), *Criminal Visions: Media Representations of Crime and Justice*, Cullompton, UK: Willan Publishing.

Jackson J. and Gray E. (2010) 'Functional Fear and Public Insecurities about Crime', *British Journal of Criminology*, 50(1):1–21.

James E. (2005) 'Doing Time with Porridge', *The Guardian*, 5 October.

James E. (2007) 'Lost Lifers', *The Guardian*, 17 October.

Jenkins P. (2001) *Beyond Tolerance: Child Pornography on the Internet*, New York: New York University Press.

Jewkes Y. (2004) *Media and Crime*, London: Sage.

Jewkes Y. (2006) 'Creating a Stir? Prisons, Popular Media and the Power to Reform', in Mason P. (ed.), *Captured by the Media: Prison Discourse in Popular Culture*, Cullompton, UK: Willan Publishing.

Jewkes Y. (ed.) (2007) *Crime Online*, Cullompton, UK: Willan Publishing.

Jewkes Y. (2011) *Media and Crime*, 2nd edn, London: Sage.

Johnston H. (2006) ' "Buried Alive": Representations of the Separate System in Victorian England', in Mason P. (ed.), *Captured by the Media: Prison Discourse in Popular Culture*, Cullompton, UK: Willan Publishing.

Jordison S. and Kieran D. (eds) (2003) *The Idler Book of Crap Towns*, London: Boxtree.

Katz E. and Lazarsfeld P. (1955) *Personal Influence*, New York: The Free Press.

Kershaw C., Budd T., Kinshott G., Mattinson J., Mayhew P. and Myhill A. (2000) *The British Crime Survey*, London: HMSO.

Leishman F. and Mason P. (2003) *Policing and the Media: Facts, Fictions and Factions*, Cullompton, UK: Willan Publishing.

Levenson J. (2001) 'Inside Information: Prisons and the Media', *Criminal Justice Matters*, 43:14–15.

Levi M. (2006) 'The Media Construction of Financial White-Collar Crimes', *British Journal of Criminology*, 46(6):1037–1057.

Liebert R. M. and Baron R. A. (1972) 'Some Immediate Effects of Televised Violence on Children's Behaviour', *Developmental Psychology*, 6:469–475.

Lombroso C. (1876) *L'uomo Delinquente*, Milan: Hoepli.

Lovegrove A. (2007) 'Public Opinion, Sentencing and Lenience: An Empirical Study Involving Judges Consulting the Community', *Criminal Law Review*, 769–781.

Macpherson W. (1999) *The Stephen Lawrence Inquiry. Report of an Inquiry by Sir William Macpherson of Cluny*, London: HMSO.

Marcum D., Ricketts M. and Higgins G. (2010) 'Assessing Sex Experiences of Online Victimization: An Examination of Adolescent Online Behaviors Utilizing Routine Activities Theory', *Criminal Justice Review*, 35(4):412–437.

Marsh I., Melville G., Morgan K., Norris G. and Walkington Z. (2006) *Theories of Crime*, London: Routledge.

Mason P. (2001) 'Courts, Cameras and Genocide', *Criminal Justice Matters*, 43:36–37.

Mason P. (ed.) (2003) *Criminal Visions: Media Representations of Crime and Justice*, Cullompton, UK: Willan Publishing.

Mason P. (ed.) (2006) *Captured by the Media: Prison Discourse in Popular Culture*, Cullompton, UK: Willan Publishing.

Mawby R. (2001) 'Promoting the Police? The Rise of Police Image Work', *Criminal Justice Matters*, 43:44–45.

Mawby R. (2003) 'Completing the "Half-Formed Picture"? Media Images of Policing', in Mason P. (ed.), *Criminal Visions: Media Representations of Crime and Justice*, Cullompton, UK: Willan Publishing.

Mawby R. and Walklate S. (1994) *Critical Victimology: International Perspectives*, London: Sage.

McLean G. (2005) 'In the Hood', *The Guardian*, 13 May.

McQuail D. (2005) *Mass Communication Theory: An Introduction*, 5th edn, London: Sage.

Mendelsohn B. (1963) 'The Origin and Doctrine of Victimology', in Rock P. (ed.), *Victimology*, Aldershot, UK: Dartmouth.

Meyers M. (1997) *News Coverage of Violence Against Women: Engendering Blame*, Thousand Oaks, CA: Sage.

Miers D. (1989) 'Positivist Victimology', *International Review of Victimology*, 2:29–59.

Miliband R. (1973) *The State in Capitalist Society*, Harmondsworth, UK: Penguin.

Ministry of Justice (2011) *Statistics on Race and the Criminal Justice System, 2010*, London: Ministry of Justice.

Ministry of Justice (2013) *Prison Population Figures 2013*, London: Ministry of Justice.

Mulley K. (2001) 'Victimized by the Media', *Criminal Justice Matters*, 43:30–31.

Mulvey L. (1975) 'Visual Pleasure and Narrative Cinema', *Screen*, 16(3):6–18.

Naylor B. (2001) 'Reporting Violence in the British Print Media: Gendered Stories', *Howard Journal of Criminal Justice*, 40(2):180–194.

Nelken D. (2007) 'White Collar and Corporate Crime', in Maguire M., Morgan R. and Reiner R. (eds), *The Oxford Handbook of Criminology*, Oxford: Oxford University Press.

Newburn T. (2007) *Criminology*, Cullompton, UK: Willan Publishing.

Newburn T. (2013) *Criminology*, 2nd edn, London: Routledge.

Nisbet R. (1970) *The Sociological Tradition*, London: Heinemann.

Orwell G. (1989[1949]) *1984*, Harmondsworth, UK: Penguin.

Parker D. (1998) *Fighting Computer Crime*, New York: Wiley Publishing.

Pavlac B. A. (2006) 'Ten General Historical Theories about the Origins and Causes of the Witch Hunts', *Prof Pavlac's Women's Historical Resource Site* (http://departments.kings.edu/womens_history).

Peak S. (ed.) (2003) *The Media Guide*, London: Guardian Books.

Pearson G. (1983) *Hooligan: A History of Respectable Fears*, London: MacMillan.

Peelo M., Francis P., Soothill K., Pearson J. and Ackerley E. (2004) 'Newspaper Reporting and the Public Construction of Homicide', *British Journal of Criminology*, 44(2):256–275.

Povery D., Coleman C., Kaiza P., Hoare J. and Jansson K. (2008) 'Homicide, Firearm Offences and Intimate Violence', *Home Office Statistical Bulletin*, London: HMSO.

Prison Reform Trust (2008) *Doing Time: The Experiences and Needs of Older People in Prison*, London: Prison Reform Trust briefing.

Quinney R. (1971) 'Who is the Victim?', *Criminology*, November.

Reiner R. (1994) 'The Dialectics of Dixon', in Stephens M. and Becker S. (eds), *Police Force, Police Service*, London: MacMillan.

Reiner R. (2007) 'Media-Made Criminality: The Representation of Crime in the Mass Media', in Maguire M., Morgan R. and Reiner R. (eds), *The Oxford Handbook of Criminology*, 4th edn, Oxford: Oxford University Press.

Reiner R., Livingstone S. and Allen J. (2003) 'From Law and Order to Lynch Mobs: Crime News since the Second World War', in Mason P. (ed.), *Criminal Visions: Media Representations of Crime and Justice*, Cullompton, UK: Willan Publishing.

Reyns B., Henson B. and Fisher B. S. (2011) 'Being Pursued Online: Applying Cyberlifestyle–Routine Activities Theory to Cyberstalking Victimization', *Criminal Justice and Behavior*, 38(11):1149–1169.

Roberts J. V. and Hough M. (2005) *Understanding Public Attitudes to Criminal Justice*, Milton Keynes: Open University Press.

Robins J. (2010) *The Magnificent Spilsbury and the Case of the Brides in the Bath*, London: John Murray.

Runnymede Trust (2008) 'A Tale of Two Englands: "Race" and Violent Crime in the Press', Runnymede Trust, 29 April.

Sampson R. (2007) 'Old Inside', Prison Reform Trust (www.prisonreformtrust.org.uk).

Schlesinger P. and Tumber H. (1992) 'Crime and Criminal Justice in the Media', in Downes D. (ed.), *Unravelling Criminal Justice*, London: MacMillan.

Schmid D. (2005) *Natural Born Celebrities*, Chicago: University of Chicago Press.

Schwartz T. (1999) *Millennium Bomb*, New Brunswick, Canada: Global Communications.

Seaton J. (1981) 'Broadcasting History', in Curran J. and Seaton J. (eds), *Power without Responsibility: The Press and Broadcasting in Britain*, London: Fontana.

Sharpe J. A. (1999) *Crime in Early Modern England 1550–1750*, 2nd edn, Harlow: Longman.

Shaw C. S. and McKay H. D. (1942) *Juvenile Delinquency and Urban Areas*, Chicago: University of Chicago Press.

Social Trends (2009) *Social Trends 39*, London: Office for National Statistics.

Social Trends (2011) *Social Trends 41*, London: Office for National Statistics.

Solomon E. (2005) 'Is the Press the Real Power Behind Punitivism?' *Criminal Justice Matters*, 59: 34–35.

Sparks R. (2001) 'The Media, Populism, Public Opinion and Crime', *Criminal Justice Matters*, 43:6–7.

Stepniak D. (2003) 'British Justice: Not Suitable for Public Viewing', in Mason P. (ed.), *Criminal Visions: Media Representations of Crime and Justice*, Cullompton, UK: Willan Publishing.

Strinati D. (1992) 'Postmodernism and Popular Culture', *Sociology Review*, April.

Surette R. (2002) 'Self-Reported Copycat Crime among a Population of Serious and Violent Juvenile Offenders', *Crime and Delinquency*, 48:46–65.

Sutherland E. H. (1960) *White Collar Crime*, New York: Holt, Rinehart and Winston.

Sutton M. and Wright C. (2009) 'Finding the Far Right Online: An Exploratory Study of White Supremacist Websites', *Internet Journal of Criminology*.

Taylor P. (1999) *Hackers: Crime and the Digital Sublime*, London: Routledge.

Tocqueville de A. (2000[1835]). *Democracy in America*, Chicago: University of Chicago Press.

Tombs S. and Whyte D. (2001) 'Media Reporting of Crime: Defining Corporate Crime Out of Existence?' *Criminal Justice Matters*, 43:22–23.

Tönnies F. (1957) *Community and Society*, New York: Harper & Row.

Trevor-Roper H. (1967) *The European Witch Craze of the 16th and 17th Centuries*, Harmondsworth, UK: Penguin.

Tuchman G. (1978) 'The Symbolic Annihilation of Women by the Mass Media', in Tuchman G., Daniels A. K. and Benét J. (eds), *Hearth and Home*, Oxford: Oxford University Press.

Von Hentig H. (1948) *The Criminal and His Victim*, New Haven: Yale University Press.

Wainwright M. (2008) 'The Real Moorside Story', *The Guardian*, 11 April.

Walklate S. (1989) *Victimology: The Victim and the Criminal Justice Process*, London: Unwin Hyman.

Walklate S. (1990) 'Researching Victims of Crime: Critical Victimology', *Social Justice*, 17:2.

Wall D. S. (1998) 'Policing and the Regulation of Cyberspace', *Criminal Law Review*, December, 79–91.

Wall D. S. (1999) 'Cybercrimes: New Wine, No Bottle?' in Davies P., Francis P. and Jupp V. (eds), *Invisible Crimes: Their Victims and their Regulation*, London: MacMillan.

Wall D. S. (ed.) (2001) *Crime and the Internet*, London: Routledge.

Wall D. S. (2005) 'The Internet as a Conduit for Criminal Activity', in Pattavina A. (ed.), *Information Technology and the Criminal Justice System*, London: Sage.

Wall D. S. (2007) *Cybercrime*, Cambridge: Polity Press.

Walliss J. (2013) 'Representations of Justice Executed at Norwich Castle: A Comparative Analysis of Execution Reports in *The Norfolk Chronicle* and *Bury and Norwich Post*, 1805–1867', *Law, Crime and History*, 3(2):30–51.

Wardle C. (2007) 'Monsters and Angels: Visual Press Coverage of Child Murders in the USA and UK, 1930–2000', *Journalism*, 8:263–284.

Watson J. B. (1925) *Behaviorism*, New York: Norton.

Webster D. (1989) ' "Whodunnit? America Did": *Rambo* and post-Hungerford Rhetoric', *Cultural Studies*, 3(2):173–193.

Weimann G. (2006) *Terror on the Internet*, Washington, DC: US Institute of Peace Press.

Wertham F. (1949) *The Show of Violence*, New York: Doubleday.

Whine M. (2006) 'Common Motifs on Jihadi and Far Right Websites', NATO Advanced Research Workshop on Hypermedia Seduction for Terrorist Recruiting.

Williams A. and Thompson W. (2004) 'Vigilance or Vigilantes: The Paulsgrove Riots and Policing Paedophiles in the Community', *Police Journal*, 1 June.

Williams K. S. (2004) *Criminology*, 5th edn, Oxford: Oxford University Press.

Williams M. (2005) 'Cybercrime', in Miller J. M. (ed.), *Encyclopaedia of Criminology*, London: Routledge.

Williams M. (2006) *Virtually Criminal: Crime, Deviance and Regulation Online*, London: Routledge.

Wilson D. and O'Sullivan S. (2004) *Representations of Prison in Film and Television Drama*, Winchester: Waterside Press.

Wolak J., Finkelhor D. and Mitchell K. (2005) *Child Pornography Possessors Arrested in Internet-Related Crime: A National Study*, Alexandria, VA: National Centre for Missing and Exploited Children.

Wykes M. and Gunter B. (2004) *Media and Body Image: If Looks Could Kill*, London: Sage.

Yates N. (2003) *Beyond Evil*, London: Blake Publishing.

Young J. (1971) 'The Role of the Police as Amplifiers of Deviancy', in Cohen S. (ed.), *Images of Deviance*, Harmondsworth, UK: Penguin.

INDEX

Page numbers in **bold** refer to figures, page numbers in *italic* refer to tables.